instant
JAVA™

SECOND EDITION

THE SUNSOFT PRESS
JAVA SERIES

instant
JAVA™

SECOND EDITION

JOHN A. PEW

SunSoft Press
A Prentice Hall Title

The publisher offers discounts on this book when ordered in bulk quantities.
For more information, contact Corporate Sales Department, Prentice Hall PTR ,
One Lake Street, Upper Saddle River, NJ 07458. Phone: 800-382-3419; FAX: 201- 236-7141.
E-mail: corpsales@prenhall.com.

Editorial/production supervision: *Eileen Clark*
Cover design director: *Jerry Votta*
Cover designer: *Anthony Gemmellaro*
Cover illustration: *Karen Strelecki*
Manufacturing manager: *Alexis R. Heydt*
Marketing manager: *Stephen Solomon*
Acquisitions editor: *Gregory G. Doench*
SunSoft Press publisher: *Rachel Borden*

10 9 8 7 6 5 4 3 2 1

ISBN 0-13-272287-9

SunSoft Press
A Prentice Hall Title

Contents

Chapter 7
Bonus Animation Examples, 263

Appendix A
Supported Applet Colors, 397

Preface

The second edition of *Instant Java* includes all the applets from the first edition. In addition there are new applets, parameters, examples, and other features that will make using these applets easier and more flexible.

Why I Wrote Instant Java

The first time I saw a Java applet running on a Web page I said to myself: "I've got to do that!" I started looking at some Java code and reading up on how to program in Java. I began to realize that there were many things that Java could do, but the first thing I wanted to try was some simple animation.

As I began to understand the requirements of the Java code, I began to consider what it was that I was going to animate. This turned out to be a challenging task. I'm not an artist, and even though I own both Adobe Illustrator and Adobe Photoshop I'm an expert in neither. What was I to use for images to animate? I had access to a fair number of digital images such as photos of my children, my company logo, and plenty of other stuff that I had gathered from the net, but animation requires a series of images that, when shown in rapid succession, give the appearance of an animate object. These, I did not have!

Who Should Use Instant Java

As I began organizing and designing this book, I wondered how many other people were like me: wanting to create animation with Java, but unable to do so because they lack the necessary resources. I also wondered how many would want to use animation on their Web pages but not have the programming skills required to write the necessary Java code. If you fit into either or both of these categories, this book is for you!

Instant Java is written primarily for HTML authors who want to include Java applets on their Web pages. I have tried to create useful, general-purpose applets that will appeal to the majority of Web authors. Since most Web pages are composed of text and images, I have concentrated on developing applets that display these in interesting ways.

Instant Java is also for people who don't have access to the tools that can create animation, or who don't have the skills needed to create images for an animation sequence. While I am not an artist and would be hard-pressed to create images that would look good in animation, I have discovered that there are many interesting things that can be done using just text or a single image. Many people have access to a single digital image, such as a company logo or scanned photograph. Using the applets in this book, you will be able to easily create your own interesting and provocative animation sequences.

Java Programming

One of the reasons the Web has been so successful is the ease with which programmers and non-programmers have been able to create and maintain Web pages. HTML is a truly simple language and almost anyone can learn the basics in a couple of hours.

While Java is often described as "simple," this is really true only from the point of view of a C or C++ programmer. If you are not a programmer, you'll find Java to be orders of magnitude more complex than HTML. It is a full-blown high level programming language that requires considerable programming experience.

If you are already a programmer, you may want to become familiar with Java programming so that you can develop your own customized applets. Though *Instant Java* does not actually teach Java programming, you may find it useful to study the source code in the appendix and on the CD. Furthermore, you can extend the existing Java code by writing your own text generating or image processing filters, as described in the Tips For Programmers sections that end Chapters 3 and 4.

Instant Java Updates

Java is still evolving and there are certain to be changes as well as bug fixes. Sun Microsystems already posts a list of known Java bugs on their Java Web site (http://java.sun.com). I have also come across a number of bugs in the course of development for this book. I am confident that these problems will be worked out in future versions of Java.

Though I'd like to think that my code is bug free, I'm sure it is not perfect. If you have a problem with an applet in this book, you should first try to isolate it by replacing an image or an audio file or some parameter in the HTML file. You will also want to check the Instant Java Web site at:

```
http://www.vivids.com
```

I will post known problems, bug fixes, and new versions at this site that you may freely download. If you cannot find an answer there and are convinced that you have discovered a bug, send a complete description (including the HTML code) to:

```
support@vivids.com
```

Bug fixes and code updates will be posted to the Web site on an ongoing basis.

You may also want to check the Web site to find additional Instant Java applet samples, tips on creating audio files, and other useful information.

Second Edition Changes

The second edition of *Instant Java* has several significant changes:

- 14 new applets
- 60 new animation examples
- Browsable applets on the CD
- Improved applet installation method
- New parameters for existing applets
- Performance improvements
- Easily browsable source code

New Applets

Instant Java contains 14 new applets since the first edition. Here is a brief description of each of the new applets:

MultiColorShadow (page 89)	Draws a string of characters using different colors and a shadow
ImageShadow (page 110)	Display an image with a shadow
SqueezeRight (page 120)	Squeeze the right side of an image
SqueezeLeft (page 122)	Squeeze the left side of an image
SqueezeUp (page 124)	Squeeze the top side of an image
SqueezeDown (page 126)	Squeeze the bottom side of an image

ReplaceColor (page 140) Displays an image with colors replaced

BlackAndWhite (page 142) Displays an image with a degree of black and white

AnimateOnPressRelease (page 206) Forward animation activated by button press Backward animation activated by button release

InOrder (page 225) Displays each character in a string from left to right

CoalesceContinuous (page 231) Displays characters from a string at random positions The string coalesces and returns to random positions continuously

CenterExpand (page 239) Displays a string of characters that expand from the center to their final positions

EveryOther (page 242) Alternate characters in a string move into position from opposite sides of the applet

VerticalTicker (page 246) Displays a scrolling string characters

New Animation Examples

I had hoped that readers of *Instant Java* would understand that the animation applets, combined with the text and image applets, could be used like a toolkit. Users can invent their own combinations to create unique animations that are activated by different user input. What I've found is that few users fully grasp the power and functionality of the applets in this book. In order to demonstrate the versatility of these applets I have created Chapter 7, **Bonus Animation Examples** (page 263), to demonstrate different ways that the existing applets can be used. I hope that these 60 examples will spur your imagination so that you create your own unique animation sequences.

Browsable applets on the CD

The CD that comes with this book contains all the applets and examples from the book. The CD is configured so that it can be browsed, using your favorite browser, without having to install anything to your hard drive. This means that you can run any of the applets from the book before installing anything on your hard drive.

Improved Applet Installation Method

The most common problem that readers of the first edition had was that when they went to use an applet from the book, they couldn't make it work properly because they did not include all the necessary files. To run most of the applets in the first edition of *Instant Java* you had to install multiple class files. Understanding this fact and determining which class files to include became a major problem for some users.

To solve this problem I have created a new format for all the applets in the book. First, the CD included with this edition of *Instant Java* contains all the applets from the book in a browsable format. Each Web page on the CD contains one applet example. Each page also includes a **Download** button. When you press the Download button you download all the necessary files (class files, audio and image files) that are required to make that applet run— no more, no less. This new feature eliminates any confusion about which files are necessary. For additional details, see Chapter 1 (page 9).

New parameters for existing applets

Many of the existing applets have been enhanced with new parameters. Though I can't list all of the new parameters, here is a list of some of the new features:

- The animation applets now have parameters to change the text, font, style, pointsize, and color of the text per frame of animation
- Each of the SlideShow applets now has a **BGSound** parameter for playing a background audio track in addition to the **SoundN** parameter for playing an audio file per slide.
- The ImageMap applet now supports an audio clip for each map. Each applet that supports image maps, includes this feature.
- The animation applets contain a new parameter, **WaitForEverything**, which, when set to true, delays the displays of any image or text until everything is loaded and ready to display.
- The animation applets now support a simple way to move an image or text without specifying all the positions. This is done by using the **TxAutoMove** and **ImgAutoMove** parameters.

Performance improvements

In my attempt to write good object-oriented code for the first edition of *Instant Java*, I created many small, or relatively small, class files. This helped reusability, but meant that some applets required many class files to run. Some of the animation applets from the first edition required over 15 separate class files. The problem with this is that it takes longer to load many small files than it does to load one big file that is the sum of all the small files.

In order to speed up load time, I reorganized much of the source code to consolidate the applets into as few class files as reasonably possible. Many of the applets in the book now require a single class file. After I had completed the consolidation of the applets, Netscape announced support of the new **archive** parameter (see pages 10–12), which somewhat obviated the consolidation work I had done. However, the consolidation work is still of value for browsers that don't support the **archive** parameter, and you may not always want to use the **archive** parameter, depending on the nature of your Web site.

The single greatest performance improvement is the advent of the Just-In-Time (JIT) compiler that is now included in Netscape Navigator 3.0 for Windows 95 and Microsoft Internet Explorer 3.0. Because the applets in this book tend to be compute intensive, they are greatly accelerated by having the JIT compiler. I only hope that JIT compilers are forthcoming for other platforms.

Easily browsable source code

The first edition of *Instant Java* contained all the source code on the CD and about 100 pages of source code printed in Appendix A. This edition does not contain any printed Java source code, though the complete source code is still on the CD. The source code is now much easier to peruse. Each applet page on the CD (and the Web site) includes a **View Java Source** button. By pressing this button you can view the source code in your browser.

A Note About Performance

In building these Java applets I have tried to be as creative and far-ranging as possible. But it is worth bearing in mind that the more complex an applet is, the longer it takes to execute. When deciding which applets to install on your Web pages, you should always consider this tradeoff between complexity and performance.

Remember also that on any given visitor's machine, an applet might run more slowly than it does on yours; even if you find its performance acceptable it may not be so on your visitor's. This depends in large part, of course, on the speed and power of the system on which you construct and test your applets.

Images in particular present performance concerns. The larger the image file, the greater the processing time required. Often you can speed execution considerably by choosing smaller images for your applets.

Known Problems

I have received many e-mail messages from users around the world about problems they have encountered. I have genuinely tried to address these problems in this second edition. Most of the reported problems have been addressed, however, a solution to some of the problems are still pending.

The most serious bug that still exists is exhibited on the Macintosh platform. Most of the applets in the book that display text do not work correctly on the Macintosh. The applets in Chapter 2 and Chapter 6 should work correctly on all platforms, but the applets in Chapter 3 (Text Applets) and any animation applets that display text will not work. I have identified the problem and reported it to Netscape. The problem does not appear when running the applets on the Macintosh in the Appletviewer.

I am confident that this bug will soon be fixed and that the applets will then work without alteration. Perhaps by the time you read this book or try these applets, the problem will have been resolved. I will continue to work with Netscape and post any changes or bug fixes to the Instant Java Web site.

There are some other less obtrusive bugs that exist on each platform. In particular, there are a variety of font problems in Netscape for Solaris and Macintosh. Fonts do not always appear at the correct point size. These and other bugs are well known by Netscape, and should be fixed in the near future.

Using
the Instant Java
CD-ROM

About the CD-ROM

Welcome to the Instant Java CD-ROM – a disc packed with all the Java tools and source code discussed in the book.

Since this CD-ROM has been designed for use by Windows 95, Windows NT, Macintosh and Unix users, you'll notice a directory for each of these operating systems.

NOTE: 1) Windows 95 and NT 4.0 files are located inside the "Windows" directory. The "Nt35" directory contains a version of the Road Map file described below that you should use if you are running Windows NT 3.5. 2) Because this is a cross-platform CD-ROM, Solaris users may encounter error messages when loading the CD indicating the presence of files that do not conform to the ISO-9660 specification. These error messages should be ignored. Follow the instructions below for touring the CD with your Web browser.

Road Map

In addition to the various operating systems directories, the top level of this CD-ROM also contains a file named RoadMap.html. RoadMap.html is actually a Web page designed to help make sense of the contents of this disc and is a convenient way to find and preview the Java applets on the disc.

To begin your tour of the disc, open RoadMap.html with your Web browser. If you are running Windows NT 3.5, first open the "Nt35" folder and use the Roadmap.html file in that directory.

You'll notice three distinct buttons: Applets, Goodies and JDK. These buttons correspond to the main parts of this CD-ROM. Let's begin by taking a peek behind the first button on the Road-Map, "Applets."

Applets

Clicking on the "Applets" button on the RoadMap will load an applets page. This page contains links to the various applets discussed in the book, and provides you with the option of installing each on your computer systems. In this way, you can see each of the applets in action, view the associated Java source code, and actually place the applet and all related files on your computer's hard drive.

But what if you want them all? Does this mean you have to install each applet, one at a time? Absolutely not. If you want to install the entire set of applets and their associated Java source code files directly onto your own computer, open the "Code" subdirectory located inside the directory for your operating system.

Apple Macintosh users will find a file named "ij2.sea" located in their "Code" directory. This file is a self-extracting archive, as indicated by the ".sea" extension. To begin the installation, simply double-click on this file and choose the location on your Macintosh that you want the applets and source code to be installed.

Windows 95 and NT users will find a file named "ij2.zip" located in their "Code" directory. This file is a ZIP archive, as indicated by the ".zip" extension. To open this archive, you must use a "ZIP" utility that understands how to deal with long file names. If you don't already have such a utility, first install the "WinZip" utility that is provided on this CD-ROM – see "Goodies" below for details.

To begin the installation, simply open the "ij2.zip" archive with the ZIP utility and specify the location on your Windows system where you want the applets and source code to be installed.

NOTE: Be sure to use a ZIP utility that understands long file names, since a number of files in this archive have long file names!

UNIX users will find a file named "ij2.tar.Z" located in their "Code" directory. This file is a compressed TAR archive. To open this archive, you must decompress and untar it using the *uncompress* and *tar* commands.

Goodies

Clicking on the "Goodies" button on the RoadMap page will load the page that describes the four utilities provided on the disc, and explains how to install them on your own computer. Let's take a look at each, beginning with the Java Workshop.

NOTE: The "Goodies" provided on this disc are not available for Macintosh users. Java Workshop is available only for Windows and UNIX users.

Java Workshop

The Java WorkShop is an integrated Java development environment that helps you develop projects, manage those projects, and incorporate them into Web pages. A brief interactive tour is available as well as a 30-day trial version...

How do I install it?

See the instructions below for Windows and UNIX systems.

Windows NT & 95

1. Insert the Instant Java CD into your CD-ROM drive.
2. Run the "Setupws.exe" installer -- it will uncompress and copy all the necessary files to your hard drive (default directory is C:\Java-Workshop)
3. Follow the installation instructions, by clicking the appropriate buttons and entering the installation directory when, and if, needed.
4. After the installation is complete, double-click on the Java WorkShop icon to start the workshop (A program group containing all the icons will be created)
5. When Java WorkShop loads for the first time, you will be prompted to enter a serial number. Click on the "30-day trial" button and a serial number will be entered automatically.
6. To uninstall Java Workshop, double-click the uninstall icon in the Java WorkShop Program Group.

Solaris 2.x

1. Insert the Instant Java CD into your CD-ROM drive.
2. If Volume Manager is running on your machine, the CD-ROM is automatically mounted to the /cdrom/instantjava directory. Skip to step 3.

   If the Volume Manager is NOT running on your machine, create a directory called /cdrom/instantjava and mount the CD-ROM manually by becoming root and typing:

   ```
   # mkdir -p /cdrom/instantjava
   # mount -rF hsfs /dev/dsk/c0t6d0s0 /cdrom/instantjava
   ```
3. Go to the directory where intend to install the Java WorkShop files:

   ```
   % cd /<destination_directory>
   ```
4. Extract the Java WorkShop files by typing:

   ```
   % tar -xvf /cdrom/instantjava/unix/workshop/jw_<platform>.tar
   ```

   Where <platform> is either "sparc" or "intel" depending on whether you use a SPARC or Intel system.
5. If you mounted the CD-ROM manually, unmount the drive becoming root and typing:

   ```
   # cd /
   # umount /dev/dsk/c0t6d0s0
   ```

   Otherwise, go to Step 6.
6. Eject the CD by typing:

   ```
   % cd /
   % eject
   ```

   You can now use Java WorkShop.
7. Start Java WorkShop by typing:

   ```
   % /<destination_directory>/JWS/<platform>-S2/bin/jws &
   ```

Café Lite

Café Lite is a version of Symantec's integrated Java development environment for Windows 95 and Windows NT that allows you to edit, build, and execute Java programs from the Windows desktop.

How do I install it (Windows 95 & NT only)?

Locate the "Cafelite" installer inside the "Goodies" folder in the Windows directory.

Double-click the Cafelite installer program. This will begin the installation process.

WinEdit

WinEdit is the Windows Editor that you can use to edit virtually any text file. It is specifically designed to be a programmer's editor and can execute compilers and check for error messages.

How do I install it?

This package contains all the pieces to install WinEdit for Windows NT and Windows 95

1. Locate the "WinEdit" installer inside the "Goodies" folder in the Windows Directory.
2. Double-click the WinEdit installer program. This will begin the installation process.

The installation program adds the directory you specified for installing WinEdit to the PATH statement in your AUTOEXEC.BAT file.

WinZip

WinZip brings the convenience of Windows to the use of ZIP files. It features an intuitive point-and-click drag-and-drop interface for viewing, running, extracting, adding, deleting, and testing files in archives.

How do I install it?

1. Locate the "WinZip95" installer inside the "Goodies" folder in the Windows Directory.
2. Double-click the WinZip95 installer program. This will begin the installation process.
3. The setup program will display a dialog box first prompting you to proceed with set up and then asking you where to install WinZip95.
4. Follow the on-screen installation instructions.

JDK

How do I install it?

To install the JDK, follow the instructions below for your particular operating system.

Windows NT & 95

1. Create a directory named "java" on the top level of your hard drive (usually the C drive). Copy the "Jdk_x86" ZIP archive file from the CD into the "java" directory you've just created. You can either drag and drop the file using your mouse, or issue the following command from the DOS prompt (where "d" is the drive containing the CD):

    ```
    copy d:\windows\Jdk\Jdk_x86.zip c:\java
    ```

NOTE: The installation takes up about 5.5Mbytes. Be SURE to remove any previous version of the JDK that may already exist on your computer.

2. Open the "Jdk_x86" archive with a ZIP utility that supports long file names (such as Win-Zip, a popular ZIP program supplied on this CD-ROM) and unpack the files it contains into the "java" directory created in step 1.

   NOTE: This step will fill the "java" directory with the various files and subdirectories that make up the JDK. In the resulting "lab" directory you'll find a another ZIP archive named "classes.zip" -- this archive should not be further unpacked, as the compiler needs to see it in this form. You can, however, unpack the "src.zip" archive to review the source for the runtime library. It's essential to use a ZIP utility that preserves long file names.

3. Once the JDK files have been unpacked onto your hard drive, you'll need to add (or modify) 2 variables in your autoexec.bat. To do this, open your autoexec.bat file with a text editor.

   First, add the "java\bin" directory to your path:

   ```
   SET PATH=c:\java\bin; (... the rest of your path follows...)
   ```

   Next, set the CLASSPATH variable to point to the current directory and the Java runtime library (the classes.zip archive):

   ```
   SET CLASSPATH=.;c:\java\lib\classes.zip
   ```

4. Save these changes to your autoexec.bat, and restart your computer so the new variables take effect.

NOTE: Once installed, you can delete the installer archive (JDK_x86.zip) from your hard drive.

Macintosh

Macintosh System Requirements: A Macintosh with at least a 68030/25MHz or better CPU or a Power Mac. System 7.5.3. revision 2 is recommended. Approximately 7MB of free disk space is also required.

1. Copy the "JDK-1_0_2-MacOS.sea" installer file found in the JDK folder onto your hard disk.

2. Double-click on the "JDK-1_0_2-MacOS.sea" installer icon, and follow the instructions that appear.

NOTE: Quicktime 2.0 or later is needed for the installation to work properly. Some people have reported problems due to old Mac software installing a down-rev version of the Quicktime extension. If you run into a problem, reinstall Quicktime 2.x and try again.

Solaris 2.x

Installation instructions are the same for Solaris 2.x for SPARC and Solaris 2.x for x86. On Intel systems, use "x86" instead of "sparc" in the filenames below. Make sure you are running an up-to-date version of Solaris 2.x, preferably Solaris 2.5.1.

1. Change directory to the location where you want to install the JDK. Let's assume you're installing it in /home/jones:

   ```
   cd /home/jones
   ```

2. Untar the file:

   ```
   tar -xvf /cdrom/instantjava/unix/jdk/sparc.tar
   ```

This is a 4.7Mbyte file, so it will take a few seconds to pull off the CD.

You should see dozens of lines indicating the files being untar'd.

3. Add the JAVA_HOME environment variable to your .cshrc (or whatever initialization for the shell you use). For the cshell, add the following line:

```
setenv JAVA_HOME /home/jones/java
```

Also add $JAVA_HOME/bin to your existing search path:

```
set path=($JAVA_HOME/bin ... rest of path ...)
```

4. Logout and login again so the new variables take effect.

Acknowledgments

First and foremost, my deepest gratitude for the support of my wife, Renée, and to each of our children: Douglas, Brian, Jeffrey, Bradley, and Mary. They quietly sustained and encouraged me throughout the first and second editions of this book. Though none of them contributed to the book directly, their support was crucial. I couldn't have done it without them. Thank you family!

A very big thanks to Bob Binstock, the developmental editor for this book. Bob's editorial suggestions and comments greatly influenced my writing style and the content and tone of the book. I also thank Jim Markham who contributed substantially to the second edition of this book. I appreciate the contributions and professionalism of the Prentice Hall staff, especially Greg Doench, Eileen Clark, and Joanne Anzalone.

I want to thank my brother Steve for his involvement in testing the applets and reading the manuscript. He helped me find and solve some bugs in my code; his PC experience was extremely helpful to me at a critical time during development.

Thanks to Eric Smith, my business associate, for relieving me of some business commitments. Eric filled in for me on more than one occasion, freeing me to work on the book.

Chris Scott developed much of the artwork in the book. His expertise in Adobe Illustrator and Photoshop, and his creative design work contributed substantially to the book. Thanks, Chris.

Thanks to Don Hackler of Netscape Communications. Don helped identify and track down some bugs that exhibited themselves in Netscape. He submitted several bugs and worked with developers at Netscape to solve several important problems.

I also want to thank Kimball Ungerman and Mike Macias for filling in for me in some of my non-professional commitments. These friends relieved me of some responsibilities that allowed me to meet some critical deadlines.

Rachel Borden, the SunSoft Press Publisher, and Karin Ellison, her predecessor, deserve most of the credit for the idea behind this book. Despite my insistence that I didn't want to write another book, they persisted and convinced me to do it. Thanks for believing in me.

CHAPTER
1

Introducing Java Applets

Java and the Web

The World Wide Web is rapidly gaining popularity as a way of sharing information. Its appeal is due largely to the ease with which that information, usually in the form of text and graphics, can be retrieved by any user from anywhere in the world. As exciting as the Web is, however, it has always been limited by the one-way nature of Web pages, which have provided only unchanging words and images.

Java™ is an indispensable tool for creating dynamic Web pages. *Instant Java* helps you create dynamic Web pages as quickly and easily as possible.

With Java you can bring life to otherwise static Web pages. As a programming language specifically designed to work with HTML and the Web, Java allows you to insert programs in a Web page that are automatically executed on the machine of any user who visits the page. Through this feature you can animate your Web pages and even make them interactive.

When you load a Web page that contains a Java reference, you are downloading a small program, called a Java applet, that is then executed within your browser. The ability to provide "executable content" is one of Java's most exciting features.

Using Java Applets

Java applets can do all sorts of things. Rather than simply displaying a still image, for example, you can use Java to display consecutive images, producing live animation. Java applets can also be fully interactive; a Java calculator applet might perform mathematical calculations and graphs the results.

Java's capabilities are very broad, but this book concentrates on the fundamental tasks of every Web page: displaying text and graphics, loading Uniform Resource Locators (URLs), and playing audio files in interesting, animated, interactive ways.

Instant Java

This book provides and describes a collection of general purpose applets that anyone can use. These applet are ready as is; they are off-the-shelf programs that you can use in your Web pages right away. Just specify the text or image you want to display and customize the settings, if you wish, and the applet does the rest.

The applets in this book are designed to be as flexible as possible. You can customize as few or as many settings as you like. Just flip through the book to find the applet that does what you want, insert it into your Web page, set the parameters, and begin using it. With very little effort you can create applets that are both personal and unique.

For example, perhaps you'd like to animate your company logo where it appears in the corner of your home page. Or maybe you want an eye-catching title that flashes or changes colors. These types of tasks, and many more, are easily accomplished with these applets.

Java and HTML

It will help if you are already familiar with basic HTML, but you don't need to be an expert to use these applets. Each applet's description provides HTML code samples which show you exactly how to use it.

Which Browser?

In order to run a Java applet, you (or any Web user) must have a Java-enabled browser. As of this writing (September, 1996) Netscape Navigator™ 3.0 from Netscape Communications Corporation™ and Microsoftl Internet Explorer 3.0 both support Java. Netscape Navigator 2.0 also supports Java for some platforms, including Windows 95 and Solaris, but not Macintosh nor Windows 3.1.

Alert: If you are using Netscape Navigator 2.0, it is strongly recommended that you upgrade to Netscape Navigator 3.0 or Microsoft Internet Explorer 3.0. Bugs in Navigator 2.0 will cause it to crash under certain circumstances when running some of these applets.

The Instant Java CD

The CD that came with this book includes all source and compiled code for the applets described. You can install the contents of the CD on you hard drive or you can view the applets from the CD. The CD contains all the applets from the book in a navigatable Web site format. As you view an applet from the CD you can easily install that applet with all the associated files (images, audio, class, and html) for it to run on your system.

The CD also contains the Java Development Kit (JDK 1.0.2), Java WorkShop from SunSoft, and Café Lite from Symantec Corporation. The JDK contains the Java run-time environment, the appletviewer, and some popular Java demo applets. Java WorkShop is an integrated Java development environment for programmers. Café Lite is a Java development tools for Windows 95.

Using This Book

Chapters 2 through 6 contain applet descriptions. Each of these chapters cover a set of related applets. As an added benefit, Chapter 7 contains 60 new Bonus Animation examples. These are not new applets, but are new examples of using other applets from Chapters 3, 4, and 5.

You do *not* need to read the book sequentially. You might want to begin by looking through the chapters to get a feeling for the kinds of things the applets can do.

Each applet description contains the following:

- One or more pictures of what the applet looks like

- A description of what the applet does

- Sample HTML code that you can use as a model for your own HTML code

- A description of the applet's customization settings, or parameters

Most of the descriptions are self-contained. However, the applets have been written in such a way that they can be used together. For example, you can use the features of several different applets to display text that has been rotated, slanted, embossed, and made transparent. To learn how this is done you may want to read the beginning of Chapter 4.

You might also want to read the beginning of Chapter 5 to learn how to do animation. Because animation applets are the most advanced, I've provided some more narrative detail before delving into my customary chapter set up. You can create animation by supplying a series of images that are shown in rapid succession. One way to create such a series is to begin with a single image and manipulate it—move it, rotate it, change its color—many times. In fact, you can even use this technique to animate text!

Java Programming

If you're already a Java programmer, or want to learn to program in Java, you can refer to the Java source code on the CD. This book was not designed to be a programmer's guide, but looking at working code can be very instructive.

Chapters 3 and 4 each include a **Tips for Programmers** section. Read these sections if you are a Java programmer and want to write Java code that will extend the functionality of applets described in these two chapters.

What's Next?

The rest of this chapter describes how to get started using the applets in this book. You can skip these instructions for now if you want; you can always come back to them later, when you are ready to use an applet in a Web page.

The Instant Java Tutorial

If you already have Netscape Navigator 3.0 or Microsoft Internet Explorer 3.0 installed on your system then you are ready to begin. Just insert the Instant Java CD into you CD drive, start your browser, and load the **roadmap.html** file located in the top-level directory of the CD. The entire Instant Java Web site is included on the CD. Once there, you are presented with the roadmap page as shown in Figure 1–1.

Figure 1-1 The Roadmap Page

The Roadmap page provides three selections:

- **Applets**
  Navigate through the Instant Java applets

- **Goodies**
  Load optional software (WinZip, Café Lite, WinEdit, and Java WorkShop)

- **JDK**
  Load the Java Developer's Kit version 1.0.2

If you prefer, you may load the entire CD Web Site onto your hard drive.

Running Applets from the CD

The applet pages have been designed to run the applets described in the book (and a few not described in the book) to demonstrate their use. When you select Applets from the Roadmap page, you will see the Instant Java home page as shown in Figure 1–2.

Figure 1–2 The Instant Java Home Page

The applets are organized according to chapter (beginning with Chapter 2). Click on the chapter title to display the Chapter page that contains a list of the applets from that chapter. Figure 1–3 shows the Fundamental Applets page.

Fundamental Applets

Back	Back to Instant Java Home Page
BasicText	Displays a string of characters
BasicImage	Displays an image and a string of characters
Audio	Plays an audio file when the page is visited
AudioButton	Plays an audio file when the button is pressed
AudioText	Plays an audio file when the pointer enters the image or text
AudioImageText	Loads the specified URL when the button is pressed
URLButton	Loads a URL, plays an audio file in image or text
URLAudImgTxt	Loads a URL, plays an audio file in text with background image
URLAudImgTxtBG	Loads a URL, plays an audio file in text with background image and image maps
ImageMap	Displays a string of characters

Figure 1–3 Fundamental Applets Page

From the chapter page you select the applet you want to run and click on the name. This brings you to the page for that applet. For example, Figure 1–4 shows the BasicText applet page.

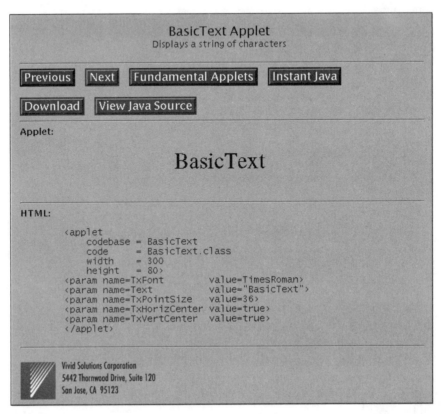

Figure 1–4 The Basic Text Applet Page

Each applet page is laid out with the same format. It includes the name and description of the applet, six navigation buttons, the applet itself, and the sample HTML code. The six navigation buttons are used as follows:

- **Previous**
  Loads the previous applet page

- **Next**
  Loads the next applet page

- **Fundamental Applets**
  Loads the current Chapter page

- **Instant Java**
  Loads the Instant Java home page

- **Download**
  Loads the download page for this applet

- **View Java Source**
  Loads the page containing the Java source code for this applet

By using the **Next** and **Previous** buttons you can navigate through all the applets in a chapter without having to go back to the Chapter page.

Downloading an Applet

Pressing the **Download** button brings you to the Download page for that applet, from which you can easily download the entire applet to the hard drive of your system. All the necessary files are included in the file you download. Figure 1–5 shows the Download page for the BasicText applet.

> ### Download BasicText Applet
>
> - Download zip format. (9101 bytes)
> - Download tar format. (20480 bytes)
>
> Back to BasicText

Figure 1–5 The BasicText Download Page

You may choose to download either the zip file or the tar file. Each file contains an archive including the HTML file, all necessary class files, and any audio or image files that may be included in this applet example.

The zip file is a compressed archive, while a tar file is not compressed so it will be a larger file in all cases. If you have an unzip utility (such as unzip, or WinZip) it will be faster to download the zip file. If you do not have an unzip utility but have the tar command (available on most UNIX systems), you can download the tar file. The end result will be the same because the contents of the two archives are identical. Netscape Navigator 3.0 for the Macintosh has unzip capability built in so you should download the zip file.

Using the Downloaded Applet

After you have downloaded the zip or tar file, you must, of course, either unzip or extract the file. After you have unzipped or extracted, you will find an HTML file and a directory. The name of the directory will be identical to the name of the applet. The name of the HTML file will also be identical to the name of the applet with a .html suffix. For example, if you were downloading the BasicText applet, you would have a file named **BasicText.html** and a directory named **BasicText**. The directory contains the class file or files necessary to run the applet, along with any image or audio files required for the applet.

You may run the applet by loading the html file in your browser. To customize the applet you must edit the HTML file. If you make reference to your own image or audio files, you must edit the HTML file and put the image or audio files into place.

Image files may reside in a directory of your choosing, they don't have to reside in the applet directory. Audio files, however, must reside in the applet directory or subdirectory.

Adding an Applet to an HTML file

Adding an applet to a Web page is very simple. The HTML applet start tag is **<applet>**; the end tag is **</applet>**. Between these two tags you must specify the name of the applet and its dimensions, as in this basic example:

```
<applet code=BasicText.class width=200 height=200>
</applet>
```

In addition to the start and end tags, three parameters (another word for settings) are required when specifying an applet in an HTML file.

- **code=<appletname>.class**
  The **code** parameter specifies the name of the applet. Compiled applet program names usually end with **.class**.

- **width=<size in pixels>**
  The **width** parameter specifies the width of the applet.

- **height=<size in pixels>**
  The **height** parameter specifies the height of the applet.

Note that while the **code** parameter specifies the primary applet file, many applets require other **.class** files in the same directory.

In addition to these required parameters, there is an optional parameter called **codebase**. The **codebase** parameter specifies a directory in which to find the applet program files, or **.class** files. By default, the **.class** file specified by the **code** parameter is assumed to be in the same directory as the HTML file. You can choose to put the **.class** file in another directory by using the **codebase** parameter. If you wanted to keep your Java **.class** file in a subdirectory named **javadir**, for example, you would use the following code:

```
<applet codebase=javadir code=BasicText.class width=200 height=200>
</applet>
```

All of the applets in this book use the **codebase** parameter. The directory containing the class files is specified as the **codebase**. To make it easier to read, the applet tag in the HTML files throughout this book are formatted as shown here:

```
<applet
    codebase = BasicText
    code     = BasicText.class
    width    = 300
    height   = 80>
<param name=Text value=Hello>
</applet>
```

Many of the applets in the book contain another applet parameter called **archive**. The **archive** parameter is a new parameter supported by Netscape Navigator 3.0 only (as of September 1996). The **archive** parameter specifies a zip file that contains all the class files that the applet requires. This features can make an applet load faster. If an applet requires multiple class files, it usually has to request each one individually, requiring a new network connection for each file.

The archive feature makes it possible to consolidate all the class files into a single zip file which Netscape Navigator 3.0 is able to unzip and use. All the of applets in this book that require multiple class files, use the **archive** parameter. Here's an example of an applet that uses the **archive** parameter:

```
<applet
    archive  = Img.zip
    codebase = Img
    code     = Img.class
    width    = 144
    height   = 204>
<param name=Image value=Img/brad.jpg>
</applet>
```

You can put more than one applet in an HTML document. In fact, there is no limit to the number of applets that can reside on one Web page. Java applets are positioned in the same manner as any other component of a page.

Customizing Applet Settings

In order to customize an applet you must provide it with operating information. This is done by setting parameters with the optional **<param>** tag, the only HTML tag that Java recognizes.

To use the **<param>** tag, just specify a parameter name and value. To specify a value of 10 for the **XOffset** parameter of the **BasicText** applet, for example, you would use the following lines:

```
<applet
    codebase = BasicText
    code     = BasicText.class
    width    = 200
    height   = 200>
<param name=XOffset value=10>
</applet>
```

To specify several parameters, include a **<param>** tag for each. To set both the **XOffset** and the **YOffset** parameters, for example, you would use the following lines:

```
<applet
    codebase = BasicText
    code     = BasicText.class
    width    = 200
    height   = 200>
<param name=XOffset value=10>
<param name=YOffset value=25>
</applet>
```

Some parameter values contain more than one word. When a value contains one or more spaces, you must enclose the value in double quotes. To set the **Text** parameter to **Hello Web!**, for example, you would enclose **Hello Web!** in double quotes, as shown in the following lines:

```
<applet
    codebase = BasicText
    code     = BasicText.class
    width    = 200
    height   = 200>
<param name=Text value="Hello Web!">
<param name=XOffset value=10>
<param name=YOffset value=25>
</applet>
```

You may include a comment line in the parameter list by using the standard comment tag, **<!>**.

```
<applet
    codebase = BasicText
    code     = BasicText.class
    width    = 200
    height   = 200>
<param name=Text value="Hello Web!">
<! These next two parameters set the X and Y offsets>
<param name=XOffset value=10>
<param name=YOffset value=25>
</applet>
```

Don't forget to include the closing angle bracket on a parameter; if you leave it out, or forget the closing double quote, your results will be unpredictable and your applet probably won't run.

Running Applets in Netscape (Windows 95)

Running an applet in Netscape Navigator 3.0 is very simple. Just select **Open File...** from the **File** menu. Figure 1–6 shows the Netscape Navigator Open dialog box.

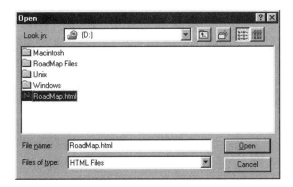

Figure 1–6 The Netscape Navigator 3.0 Open Dialog Box for Windows 95

Locate the HTML file on the CD or hard drive and press the **Open** button.

You can also use drag and drop to drag the HTML file containing an applet from Windows Explorer and drop it on Netscape Navigator, as follows:

1. Bring up Windows Explorer
2. Bring up Netscape Navigator

3. Use Windows Explorer to find the HTML file to load

4. Drag the HTML file from Windows Explorer and drop it on Navigator

Another method is to enter the complete path of the HTML file in the **Location** field of Netscape Navigator.

Running Applets in Microsoft Internet Explorer

Running an applet in Microsoft Internet Explorer is also very simple. Select **Open** from the **File** menu to display the Open dialog box as shown in Figure 1–7.

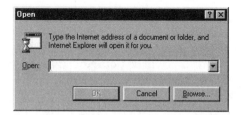

Figure 1–7 The Microsoft Internet Explorer Open Dialog Box

Then press the **Browse** button to display the Browse dialog box as shown in Figure 1–8.

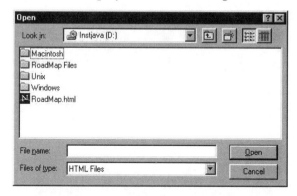

Figure 1–8 The Microsoft Internet Explorer Browse Dialog Box

From the Browse dialog box, locate the HTML file you want to load then press the **Open** button.

You can also use drag and drop to drag the HTML file containing an applet from Windows Explorer and drop it on Internet Explorer, as follows:

1. Bring up Windows Explorer

2. Bring up Internet Explorer

3. Use Windows Explorer to find the HTML file to load

4. Drag the HTML file from Windows Explorer and drop it on Internet Explorer

Another method is to enter the complete path of the HTML file in the **Address** field of Internet Explorer.

Running Applets in Netscape (Solaris)

Running an applet in Netscape Navigator on Solaris requires you to display the **File Open** dialog by selecting **Open File** from the **File** menu. Figure 1–9 displays the File Open dialog box.

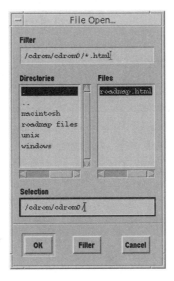

Figure 1–9 The File Open Dialog Box for Solaris

Enter the directory that contains the HTML file to load in the **Filter** field. Remember to include a /* at the end of the line and press **Return** or press the **Filter** button. You can then select the HTML file from the Files list and press the **OK** button.

Under Solaris, there is no way to drag HTML files to Netscape Navigator, but you can enter the path of the HTML file in the **Location** field of Navigator. For example, if your CD is mounted in the default location by the volume manager you could load the Roadmap.html file by entering the following path name:

```
file:/cdrom/cdrom0/roadmap.html
```

Running Applets in Netscape (Macintosh)

To run an applet in Netscape Navigator on Macintosh, select **Open File** from the **File** menu. Figure 1–10 displays the File Open dialog box.

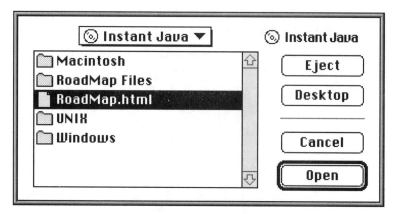

Figure 1–10 The Open File Dialog Box for Macintosh

Select the HTML file to load and press the **Open** button.

You can also use drag and drop to drag the HTML file containing an applet from the hard drive or CD and drop it on Netscape Navigator. Or you can enter the complete path of the HTML file in the **Location** field of Netscape Navigator.

Planning for Users Without Java-enabled Browsers

It's important to remember that not everyone on the Web has a browser that supports Java. As noted earlier, Netscape Navigator 3.0 and Microsoft Internet Explorer 3.0 are the most up to date browsers and will support Solaris, Windows 95, and Macintosh platforms. Both of these can be downloaded if you have Internet access.

In order to make your Web pages work reasonably well on browsers that do not support Java, you must include standard HTML commands between the applet start and applet end tags. Since Java recognizes only the **<param>** tags, it will ignore these HTML commands. And since most browsers ignore HTML tags they don't understand, non Java-enabled browsers will ignore the **<param>** tags and execute the standard HTML commands, while Java-enabled browsers will recognize the **<param>** tags and execute the Java applet.

Here's an example:

```
<html>
<head>
<title>Vivid Solutions Home Page</title>
</head>
<body bgcolor=#cecece>

<center>
<! Here's the Java applet that displays an image>
<applet
     codebase=classes
     code=BasicImage.class
     width=187
     height=288>
<param name=Image value=vivid9.gif>

<! Here's the HTML code for non-Java-enabled browsers>
<! Java applets will ignore the <img src=..> line>
<! Browsers that don't support Java will use the <img src=..> line>
<ung src="vivid9.gif" alt="Vivid Solutions Corporation">
<p>
You are running a <i>Java-challenged</i> browser.
<br>
<a hreh="http://home.netscape.com/comprod/mirror/index.html">
Download</a>
Netscape Navigator Now!
<br>
<br>
<a href="http://home.netscape.com/comprod/mirror/index.html">
<img src="http://home.netscape.com/comprod/mirror/images/now8.gif"
align=center>
</a>
</applet>
<br>
<applet codebase=classes code=Text.class width=300 height=150>
<param name=AppBGColor value=#cecece>
<param name=Text value="Java-enabled!">
<param name=TxPointSize value=36>
<param name=TxFilter value="depthshade 25 -25 yellow|waveimage 30 30">
</applet>
</center>
</body>
</html>
```

Note that between the applet start and end tags are commands to display some text, an image, and a hyperlink. The Java applet may produce some animation that would be visible only to a Java-enabled browser. The non-Java-enabled browser would see a single non-animated image with the text about downloading Netscape Navigator. Figure 1–11 shows what the page would look like in the two different browsers:

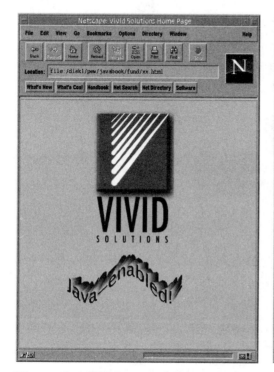
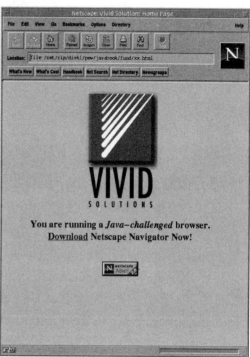

Figure 1–11 Web page displayed with and without Java-enabled browser

Now that we've covered the basics, we're ready to begin looking at Java applets that you can customized and use on your own Web pages. Chapters 2 through 6 document 79 applets that you can use to display text, images, and animation. Chapter 7 demonstrates the use of animation with 60 additional animation examples. Enjoy!

CHAPTER 2

Fundamental Applets

This chapter introduces some fundamental applets. Each performs a basic function such as displaying text, displaying an image, playing an audio file, or loading a Uniform Resource Locator (URL). These functions are also combined in applets that perform complex actions such as displaying an image, playing an audio file when the pointer enters the image, and loading a URL when any mouse button is pressed.

Much of what these applets do is not unique to Java. You could easily write HTML code to do similar things. Subsequent chapters build on these applets to perform more interesting tasks that *only* Java can accomplish.

BasicText

Displays a string of characters

Description

The **BasicText** applet is the most fundamental applet in this book. It simply displays a string of characters. This may be centered, colored, used as a heading, title, or wherever text is used on a Web page.

There are a few advantages to using **BasicText** over the standard text that can be created with HTML. One is that it allows the explicit selection of the font, style, size, and color of the text. This ensures that the text will appear on the visitor's screen exactly as it appears on yours. HTML text, on the other hand, may be set to various fonts or sizes based on preferences selected for the user's particular browser. Another advantage of **BasicText** is that a border and frame can be drawn around the text.

Using **BasicText** in HTML Code

The following HTML code uses the **BasicText** applet to display the string *Welcome!* enclosed in a **ShadowEtchedOut** frame:

```
<applet
    codebase = BasicText2
    code     = BasicText.class
    width    = 300
    height   = 80>
<param name=Text              value=Welcome!>
<param name=TxFont            value=Helvetica>
<param name=TxPointSize       value=40>
<param name=TxHorizCenter     value=true>
<param name=TxVertCenter      value=true>
<param name=TxFrameThickness  value=2>
<param name=TxFrameType       value=ShadowEtchedOut>
<param name=TxFrameMargin     value=5>
</applet>
```

Settings

Use the parameters in Table 2–1 to set the color of the text and the background, the position of the text including centering, the font, an optional border or frame, and of course the text itself. You can also create a border or frame around the entire applet.

Note that colors can be set in one of two ways: by the color name or by a hexadecimal value. The color names are limited to those that are listed in Appendix A on page 397. This includes over 130 color names.

Specifying a color by a hexadecimal value is done by using a pound sign (#) followed by six hexadecimal digits as shown here:

```
#FA8072
```

The first two digits (FA) represent the red content, the next two digits (80) represent the green content, and the final two digits (72) represent the blue content. Each pair of digits must be a value between 0 and 255 (FF).

Throughout this book parameters that apply to an entire applet begin with **App**, parameters that apply to text begin with **Tx**, and parameters that apply to images begin with **Img**.

Table 2–1 BasicText Applet Settings

Name	Description	Default
Text	The string of characters to display	(none)
TxColor	The text color	Set by browser
TxYOffset	The vertical distance (in pixels) from the top of the applet to the lower left corner of the text	The height of the text
TxXOffset	The horizontal distance (in pixels) from the left side of the applet to the text	0
TxHorizCenter	If true, the text is horizontally centered	false
TxVertCenter	If true, the text is vertically centered	false
TxFont	The font of the text: **TimesRoman, Helvetica, Courier, Dialog, DialogInput,** or **ZapfDingbats**	**Dialog**
TxStyle	The style of the font: **Plain, Bold, Italic,** or **BoldItalic**	**Plain**
TxPointSize	The size of the font in points	10
TxUnderLine	If true, the text is underlined	false
TxBorderWidth	The width of the text border (must be greater than 0 in order for a border to be drawn)	0
TxBorderColor	The color of the text border	black
TxBorderMargin	The distance (in pixels) from the text border to the text on all sides	0

Table 2–1 BasicText Applet Settings

Name	Description	Default
TxFrameThickness	The thickness of the text frame (must be greater than 0 in order for a frame to be drawn)	0
TxFrameType	The type of text frame: **ShadowIn, ShadowOut, ShadowEtchedIn**, or **ShadowEtchedOut**	**ShadowIn**
TxFrameMargin	The distance (in pixels) from the text frame to the text	0
AppBGColor	The background color of the applet	Set by browser
AppBorderWidth	The width of the applet border (must be greater than 0 in order for a border to be drawn)	0
AppBorderColor	The color of the applet border	black
AppFrameThickness	The thickness of the applet frame (must be greater than 0 in order for a frame to be drawn)	0
AppFrameType	The type of applet frame: **ShadowIn, ShadowOut, ShadowEtchedIn**, or **ShadowEtchedOut**	**ShadowIn**

Using the **AppBGColor** parameter to set the background color of the applet can be particularly useful if you use the HTML **<BODY BGCOLOR=*color*>** tag in a Web page to force a background color. By using the same color for **AppBGColor** and **<BODY BGCOLOR>**, you can ensure that the entire page has the same background color. If you want a Web page that contains the **BasicText** applet to have its entire background color set to #FA8072 (salmon), for example, you would use the following code:

```
<Title>Text Applet<Title>
<BODY BGCOLOR=#FA8072>
<applet
    code   = BasicText.class
    width  = 300
    height = 80>
<param name=Text       value=Welcome!>
<param name=AppBGColor value=#FA8072>
</applet>
```

The frame and border parameters allow you to draw a frame or border around the text and the entire applet. Since these parameters are available for almost every applet in this book, let's take a closer look at them.

Frames come in four types: **ShadowIn, ShadowOut, ShadowEtchedIn,** and **ShadowEtchedOut**. Each of these is shown in the following figures:

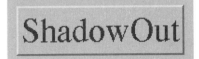
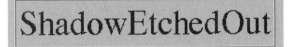

Setting the **TxFrameType** to one of these four values, and setting the **TxFrameThickness** parameter to some value other than the default, 0, draws a frame of the specified type directly around the text, regardless of the size of the applet. The **TxFrameThickness** parameter changes the thickness of the frame, while the **TxFrameMargin** parameter sets the distance from the text at which the frame is drawn. The following figure shows a **ShadowEtchedOut** frame with a **TxFrameThickness** of 4 and a **TxFrameMargin** of 5:

Borders work in much the same way. Specify a **TxBorderWidth** greater than 0 and a border is drawn around the text. You can also specify a color for the border. The following figure shows a border drawn around text with a **TxBorderWidth** of 1.

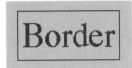

In addition to borders and frames around text, you can also draw a border or frame around the entire applet. The following figure displays a **ShadowIn** frame around the text, and a **ShadowEtchedOut** frame around the applet:

You can combine frames and borders in anyway you like. The following figure displays text drawn with a **ShadowEtchedIn** frame with thickness 4, within an applet that has a **App-BorderWidth** of 2:

The **TxHorizCenter** and **TxVertCenter** parameters take precedence over the **TxXOffset** and **TxYOffset** parameters. The **TxBorderColor** and **TxBorderMargin** parameters have no effect unless a **TxBorderWidth** is set. Likewise, the **TxFrameType** and **TxFrameMargin** have no effect unless a **TxFrameThickness** is set. The same is true for the applet border and frame settings.

See Also

URL for **BasicText**:   http://www.vivids.com/ij2/fund/BasicText.html

BasicImage

Displays an image and a string of characters

Description

The **BasicImage** applet displays a single static image. The image source must be in either GIF or JPEG format.

Setting the **Text** parameter allows you to include text with your image. You specify the text's position, color, font, and so forth, exactly as you would for the **BasicText** applet.

You must leave enough space for the text and the image to be displayed. If you position the text or the image partially or completely outside the applet, you'll be able to see only the portion that is within the boundaries of the applet.

Using **BasicImage** in HTML Code

The following HTML code uses the **BasicImage** applet to display the Doutone image enclosed in a border with a margin of 34. Notice that the text positioning is identical to that in the **BasicText** example.

```
<applet
    codebase = BasicImage2
    code     = BasicImage.class
    width    = 550
    height   = 160>
<param name=Image            value=BasicImage2/duotone.gif>
<param name=Text             value="Doutone">
<param name=TxHorizCenter    value=true>
<param name=TxYOffset        value=142>
<param name=TxFont           value=Dialog>
<param name=TxPointSize      value=22>
<param name=ImgVertCenter    value=true>
<param name=ImgHorizCenter   value=true>
<param name=ImgBorderMargin value=34>
<param name=ImgBorderWidth   value=2>
</applet>
```

Settings

The parameters in Table 2–2 relate to both the image and the text. You must specify the image that is to be displayed, its location, and whether you want to display the image as it is loaded or wait until the entire image is available before displaying it.

Table 2–2 BasicImage Applet Settings

Name	Description	Default
Image	The image to display	(none)
ImgLoadWait	If true, the image is not displayed until it is completely loaded	false
ImgXOffset	The horizontal distance (in pixels) from the left side of the applet to the image	0
ImgYOffset	The vertical distance (in pixels) from the top of the applet to the image	0
ImgHorizCenter	If true, the image is horizontally centered	false
ImgVertCenter	If true, the image is vertically centered	false
ImgBorderWidth	The width of the image border (must be greater than 0 in order for a border to be drawn)	0
ImgBorderColor	The color of the image border	Set by browser
ImgBorderMargin	The distance (in pixels) from the image border to the image on all sides	0
ImgFrameThickness	The thickness of the image frame (must be greater than 0 in order for a frame to be drawn)	0
ImgFrameType	The type of image frame: **ShadowIn**, **ShadowOut**, **ShadowEtchedIn**, or **ShadowEtchedOut**	**ShadowIn**
ImgFrameMargin	The distance (in pixels) from the image frame to the image	0
Text	The string of characters to display	(none)
TxColor	The text color	Set by browser

Table 2–2 BasicImage Applet Settings (Continued)

Name	Description	Default
TxYOffset	The vertical distance (in pixels) from the top of the applet to the lower left corner of the text	The height of the text
TxXOffset	The horizontal distance (in pixels) from the left side of the applet to the text	0
TxHorizCenter	If true, the text is horizontally centered	false
TxVertCenter	If true, the text is vertically centered	false
TxFont	The font of the text: **TimesRoman, Helvetica, Courier, Dialog, DialogInput,** or **ZapfDingbats**	**Dialog**
TxStyle	The style of the font: **Plain, Bold, Italic,** or **BoldItalic**	**Plain**
TxPointSize	The size of the font in points	10
TxUnderLine	If true, the text is underlined	false
TxBorderWidth	The width of the text border (must be greater than 0 in order for a border to be drawn)	0
TxBorderColor	The color of the text border	black
TxBorderMargin	The distance (in pixels) from the text border to the text on all sides	0
TxFrameThickness	The thickness of the text frame (must be greater than 0 in order for a frame to be drawn)	0
TxFrameType	The type of text frame: **ShadowIn, ShadowOut, ShadowEtchedIn,** or **ShadowEtchedOut**	**ShadowIn**
TxFrameMargin	The distance (in pixels) from the text frame to the text	0
AppBGColor	The background color of the applet	Set by browser
AppBorderWidth	The width of the applet border (must be greater than 0 in order for a border to be drawn)	0
AppBorderColor	The color of the applet border	black
AppFrameThickness	The thickness of the applet frame (must be greater than 0 in order for a frame to be drawn)	0
AppFrameType	The type of applet frame: **ShadowIn, ShadowOut, ShadowEtchedIn,** or **ShadowEtchedOut**	**ShadowIn**

See Also

Related applets: **BasicText** on page 22

URL for **BasicImage**: `http://www.vivids.com/ij2/fund/BasicImage.html`

Audio

Plays an audio file when the page is visited

Description

The **Audio** applet plays an audio file when the page containing it is visited. There is no associated text or image. The audio source must be in **au** format.

This applet is useful if you want a particular audio file played every time a page is visited. For example, you may want to play a greeting when your home page is loaded.

You can specify that the file is to be played repeatedly; you can even play your file in a loop, in which case it will repeat indefinitely. You should be cautious, however, about using lengthy or repetitive audio, so as not to annoy your visitor.

A loop can include a fixed delay between repetitions, which is suitable for a greeting message that would repeat once in a while–say every 60 seconds or so. That way, the visitor is not deluged with audio information, but only occasionally reminded of the page's purpose or other information.

To ensure that this applet does not use any display space on the page, specify 0 for the **width** and **height**.

Using Audio in HTML Code

The following HTML code uses the **Audio** applet to play the **welcome.au** audio file.

```
<applet
    codebase = Audio
    code     = Audio.class
    width    = 2
    height   = 2>
<param name=audio     value=Audio/welcome.au>
<param name=PlayDelay value=8>
<param name=Loop      value=true>
</applet>
```

Settings

The **Audio** applet has just three parameters shown in Table 2–3. The **Audio** parameter specifies the audio source file. If you want the audio to play in a continuous loop, set the **Loop** parameter, and use the **PlayDelay** parameter to specify the delay between repetitions.

Table 2–3 Audio Applet Settings

Name	Description	Default
Audio	The audio file to play	(none)
PlayDelay	The delay in seconds between repetitions (valid if **Loop** is true)	0
Loop	If true, the audio file is played continuously (repetitions are separated by **PlayDelay** seconds)	false

Since the only purpose of the **Audio** applet is to play an audio file, failing to specify the **Audio** parameter results in an error.

At the time of publication the only audio format supported by Java is 8-bit u-law 8kHz mono channel audio. This is the format commonly used on Sun workstations. Files containing audio data in this format generally have the **.au** suffix.

See Also

URL for **Audio**:   `http://www.vivids.com/ij2/fund/Audio.html`

AudioButton

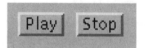

Plays an audio file when the Play button is pressed
Stops playing when the Stop button is pressed

Description

The **AudioButton** applet provides two buttons and a label. One button plays the audio file and the other stops it. The buttons are labeled *Play* and *Stop* by default, but you can rename them with parameters.

Pressing *Play* starts the audio at the beginning; pressing *Stop* halts it. The audio always starts at the beginning, even if *Play* is pressed while it is already playing.

If you set a button label to a value other than the default, the size of the button changes to accommodate the size of the label.

Using AudioButton in HTML Code

The following HTML code uses the **AudioButton** applet to label the two buttons *Play it!* and *Halt*. The label is specified as *Press for Audio*.

```
<applet
    codebase = AudioButton2
    code     = AudioButton.class
    width    = 200
    height   = 80>
<param name=audio
value=AudioButton2/whistle.au>
<param name=label           value="Press for Audio">
<param name=PlayLabel       value="Play it!">
<param name=StopLabel       value=Halt>
<param name=Font            value=Helvetica>
<param name=PointSize       value=24>
<param name=ButtonFont      value=TimesRoman>
<param name=ButtonStyle     value=Italic>
<param name=ButtonPointSize value=16>
</applet>
```

Settings

Use the parameters in Table 2–4 to specify the audio file to play, and the text and display information for the buttons and label.

Table 2–4 AudioButton Applet Settings

Name	Description	Default
Audio	The audio file to play	(none)
BGColor	The background color	Set by browser
FGColor	The foreground color	Set by browser
PlayLabel	The Play button label	Play
StopLabel	The Stop button label	Stop
Label	The label displayed beneath the buttons	(none)
Font	The font for the main label	**Dialog**
Style	The style of the main label font: **Plain**, **Bold**, **Italic**, or **BoldItalic**	**Plain**
PointSize	The size of the main label font in points	10
ButtonFont	The font for the button labels	**Dialog**
ButtonStyle	The style of the button label font: **Plain**, **Bold**, **Italic**, or **BoldItalic**	**Plain**
ButtonPointSize	The size of the button label font in points	10

See Also

Related applets: **Audio** on page 30

URL for **AudioButton**:   `http://www.vivids.com/ij2/fund/AudioButton.html`

AudioText

Displays a string of characters
Plays an audio file when the pointer enters the text

Description

The **AudioText** applet displays text and plays an audio file when the pointer enters the text. The text region is defined by a rectangle that encloses the string. You can make this region visible by specifying a one pixel border with a **TxBorderMargin** of 1.

When the pointer enters the text area the audio plays to completion, unless the pointer leaves the text, at which point the audio stops. If the pointer re-enters the text, the audio plays again from the beginning.

Using **AudioText** in HTML Code

The following HTML code uses the **AudioText** applet to display the string *Move pointer here for sound!* When the pointer enters the text region, the **wind.au** audio file is played.

```
<applet
    codebase = AudioText2
    code     = AudioText.class
    width    = 400
    height   = 100>
<param name=TxAudio          value=AudioText2/wind.au>
<param name=Text             value="Move pointer here for sound!">
<param name=TxFont           value=Helvetica>
<param name=TxStyle          value=BoldItalic>
<param name=AppBGColor       value=black>
<param name=TxColor          value=white>
<param name=TxPointSize      value=22>
<param name=TxXOffset        value=35>
<param name=TxYOffset        value=35>
<param name=TxBorderWidth    value=1>
<param name=TxBorderColor    value=white>
<param name=TxBorderMargin   value=2>
</applet>
```

Move pointer here for sound!

Settings

The **AudioText** parameters in Table 2–5 are identical to the **BasicText** parameters with the addition of the **TxAudio** parameter, which specifies the audio file to play.

Table 2–5 AudioText Applet Settings

Name	Description	Default
TxAudio	The audio file to play	(none)
Text	The string of characters to display	(none)
TxColor	The text color	Set by browser
TxYOffset	The vertical distance (in pixels) from the top of the applet to the lower left corner of the text	The height of the text
TxXOffset	The horizontal distance (in pixels) from the left side of the applet to the text	0
TxHorizCenter	If true, the text is horizontally centered	false
TxVertCenter	If true, the text is vertically centered	false
TxFont	The font of the text: **TimesRoman, Helvetica, Courier, Dialog, DialogInput,** or **ZapfDingbats**	**Dialog**
TxStyle	The style of the font: **Plain, Bold, Italic,** or **BoldItalic**	**Plain**
TxPointSize	The size of the font in points	10
TxUnderLine	If true, the text is underlined	false
TxBorderWidth	The width of the text border (must be greater than 0 in order for a border to be drawn)	0
TxBorderColor	The color of the text border	black
TxBorderMargin	The distance (in pixels) from the text border to the text on all sides	0
TxFrameThickness	The thickness of the text frame (must be greater than 0 in order for a frame to be drawn)	0
TxFrameType	The type of text frame: **ShadowIn, ShadowOut, ShadowEtchedIn,** or **ShadowEtchedOut**	**ShadowIn**
TxFrameMargin	The distance (in pixels) from the text frame to the text	0
AppBGColor	The background color of the applet	Set by browser
AppBorderWidth	The width of the applet border (must be greater than 0 in order for a border to be drawn)	0

Table 2–5 AudioText Applet Settings

Name	Description	Default
AppBorderColor	The color of the applet border	black
AppFrameThickness	The thickness of the applet frame (must be greater than 0 in order for a frame to be drawn)	0
AppFrameType	The type of applet frame: **ShadowIn**, **ShadowOut**, **ShadowEtchedIn**, or **ShadowEtchedOut**	**ShadowIn**

See Also

Related applets: **BasicText** on page 22
                        Audio on page 30

URL for **AudioText**:   `http://www.vivids.com/ij2/fund/AudioText.html`

AudioImageText

Displays an image
Displays a string of characters
Plays an audio file when the pointer enters the text
Plays an audio file when the pointer enters the image

Description

The **AudioImageText** applet displays an image and text, and plays one audio file when the pointer enters the image and another when it enters the text. You can, of course, specify the same audio file for the image and the text.

The audio plays to completion unless the pointer leaves the image or text, at which point the audio stops. If the pointer reenters the image or text, the audio plays again from the beginning.

Using **AudioImageText** in HTML Code

The following HTML code uses the **AudioImageText** applet to display an image and text. Separate audio files are specified for the image and the text. Because the image and text overlap, positioning the pointer over the area that contains both text and image results in both audio files playing simultaneously.

```
<applet
    codebase = AudioImageText2
    code     = AudioImageText.class
    width    = 290
    height   = 220>
<param name=AppBGColor      value=white>
<! Text parameters>
<param name=Text            value="Check
This Out!">
<param name=TxAudio
value=AudioImageText2/rooster.au>
<param name=TxPointSize     value=18>
<param name=TxXOffset       value=134>
<param name=TxYOffset       value=150>
<param name=TxBorderWidth   value=1>
<param name=TxBorderMargin  value=3>
<! Image parameters>
<param name=ImgAudio        value=AudioImageText2/welcome.au>
<param name=Image           value=AudioImageText2/vivid.gif>
<param name=ImgHorizCenter  value=true>
<param name=ImgYOffset      value=20>
```

```
<param name=ImgBorderWidth value=1>
</applet>
```

Settings

The **AudioImageText** parameters in Table 2–6 are identical to the **BasicImage** parameters with the addition of the **TxAudio** and **ImgAudio** parameters, which specify the audio files to play.

Table 2–6 AudioImageText Applet Settings

Name	Description	Default
TxAudio	The audio file to play when the pointer enters the text	(none)
ImgAudio	The audio file to play when the pointer enters the image	(none)
Image	The image to display	(none)
ImgLoadWait	If true, the image is not displayed until it is completely loaded	false
ImgXOffset	The horizontal distance (in pixels) from the left side of the applet to the image	0
ImgYOffset	The vertical distance (in pixels) from the top of the applet to the image	0
ImgHorizCenter	If true, the image is horizontally centered	false
ImgVertCenter	If true, the image is vertically centered	false
ImgBorderWidth	The width of the image border (must be greater than 0 in order for a border to be drawn)	0
ImgBorderColor	The color of the image border	Set by browser
ImgBorderMargin	The distance (in pixels) from the image border to the image on all sides	0
ImgFrameThickness	The thickness of the image frame (must be greater than 0 in order for a frame to be drawn)	0
ImgFrameType	The type of image frame: **ShadowIn, ShadowOut, ShadowEtchedIn,** or **ShadowEtchedOut**	**ShadowIn**
ImgFrameMargin	The distance (in pixels) from the image frame to the image	0
Text	The string of characters to display	(none)
TxColor	The text color	Set by browser
TxYOffset	The vertical distance (in pixels) from the top of the applet to the lower left corner of the text	The height of the text
TxXOffset	The horizontal distance (in pixels) from the left side of the applet to the text	0
TxHorizCenter	If true, the text is horizontally centered	false

Table 2–6 AudioImageText Applet Settings (Continued)

Name	Description	Default
TxVertCenter	If true, the text is vertically centered	false
TxFont	The font of the text: **TimesRoman, Helvetica, Courier, Dialog, DialogInput,** or **ZapfDingbats**	**Dialog**
TxStyle	The style of the font: **Plain, Bold, Italic,** or **BoldItalic**	**Plain**
TxPointSize	The size of the font in points	10
TxUnderLine	If true, the text is underlined	false
TxBorderWidth	The width of the text border (must be greater than 0 in order for a border to be drawn)	0
TxBorderColor	The color of the text border	black
TxBorderMargin	The distance (in pixels) from the text border to the text on all sides	0
TxFrameThickness	The thickness of the text frame (must be greater than 0 in order for a frame to be drawn)	0
TxFrameType	The type of text frame: **ShadowIn, ShadowOut, ShadowEtchedIn,** or **ShadowEtchedOut**	**ShadowIn**
TxFrameMargin	The distance (in pixels) from the text frame to the text	0
AppBGColor	The background color of the applet	Set by browser
AppBorderWidth	The width of the applet border (must be greater than 0 in order for a border to be drawn)	0
AppBorderColor	The color of the applet border	black
AppFrameThickness	The thickness of the applet frame (must be greater than 0 in order for a frame to be drawn)	0
AppFrameType	The type of applet frame: **ShadowIn, ShadowOut, ShadowEtchedIn,** or **ShadowEtchedOut**	**ShadowIn**

If the text and image overlap, you will hear both audio files play when the pointer is within the overlapped region.

See Also

Related applets: **BasicImage** on page 27
                         BasicText on page 22

URL for **AudioImageText**:   `http://www.vivids.com/ij2/fund/AudioImageText.html`

URLButton

`http://java.sun.com`

Loads the specified URL when the button is pressed

Description

The **URLButton** applet displays a button with a label that you specify. When the button is pressed, the specified URL is loaded into the visitor's browser.

Using **URLButton** in HTML Code

The **URLButton** applet might be used to let the visitor load the next page in a sequence of pages. When the visitor presses the button, the specified URL is loaded.

```
<applet
    codebase = URLButton2
    code     = URLButton.class
    width    = 200
    height   = 60>
<param name=URL               value=http://java.sun.com>
<param name=ButtonFont        value=TimesRoman>
<param name=ButtonPointSize value=36>
<param name=Label             value="Next ->">
</applet>
```

Next ->

`http://...`

Settings

Specify the URL to load with the **URL** parameter shown in Table 2–7. Other parameters set the button label text, font, and color.

Table 2–7 URLButton Applet Settings

Name	Description	Default
URL	The URL to load when the button is pressed	(none)
BGColor	The background color	From browser
FGColor	The foreground color of the text	From browser
Label	The button labe	(none)
ButtonFont	The font of the button label	**Dialog**
ButtonStyle	The style of the button label font, e.g. **Plain, Bold, Italic, BoldItalic**	**Plain**
ButtonPointSize	The size of the button font in points	10

See Also

URL for **URLButton**:   http://www.vivids.com/ij2/fund/URLButton.html

URLAudImgTxt

Displays an image
Displays a string of characters
Plays an audio file when the pointer enters the text
Plays an audio file when the pointer enters the image
Loads the specified URL when any mouse button is pressed

Description

The **URLAudImgTxt** applet has the same characteristics as **AudioImageText**, with the additional feature that if the user presses any mouse button while the pointer is within the image or text, the specified URL is loaded into the browser.

You can specify separate URLs for the text and the image. If the image and text overlap, the URL specified for the text takes precedence in the overlapping region.

When the pointer is within the text region or image region, the specified URL (if any) is displayed in the browser's status line.

Using **URLAudImgTxt** in HTML Code

The following HTML code uses the **URLAudImgTxt** applet to display an image and text. When the pointer moves within the image, the specified URL (http://www.powertr.com) is displayed in the browser's status line. When the user presses any mouse button, the URL is loaded.

This example specifies only one URL, but you can specify separate URLs for both the text and the image.

```
<applet
    codebase = URLAudImgTxt2
    code     = URLAudImgTxt.class
    width    = 600
    height   = 150>
<param name=Image            value=URLAudImgTxt2/powertr.gif>
<param name=ImgURL           value=http://www.powertr.com>
<param name=ImgAudio         value=URLAudImgTxt2/powertr.au>
<param name=ImgHorizCenter   value=true>
<param name=ImgYOffset       value=10>
<param name=ImgFrameThickness value=4>
<param name=ImgFrameType     value=ShadowEtchedOut>
<param name=ImgFrameMargin   value=4>
<param name=Text             value="Power Trac">
<param name=TxPointSize       value=24>
<param name=TxHorizCenter    value=true>
```

```
<param name=TxYOffset        value=115>
</applet>
```

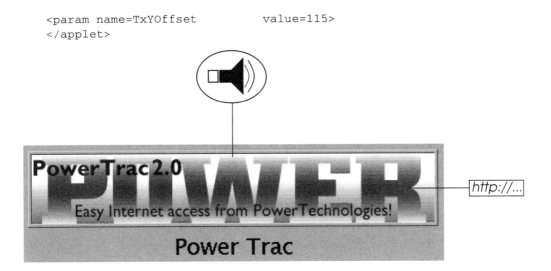

Settings

The parameters in Table 2–8 are identical to those for **AudioImageText** with the addition of the **TxURL** and **ImgURL** parameters, which specify the URLs to load when the user presses any mouse button while the pointer is within the text or image area.

Table 2–8 URLAudImgTxt Applet Settings

Name	Description	Default
TxURL	The URL to load when the pointer is within the text and any mouse button is pressed	(none)
ImgURL	The URL to load when the pointer is within the image and any mouse button is pressed	(none)
TxAudio	The audio file to play when the pointer enters the text	(none)
ImgAudio	The audio file to play when the pointer enters the image	(none)
Image	The image to display	(none)
ImgLoadWait	If true, the image is not displayed until it is completely loaded	false
ImgXOffset	The horizontal distance (in pixels) from the left side of the applet to the image	0
ImgYOffset	The vertical distance (in pixels) from the top of the applet to the image	0
ImgHorizCenter	If true, the image is horizontally centered	false
ImgVertCenter	If true, the image is vertically centered	false

Table 2–8 URLAudImgTxt Applet Settings (Continued)

Name	Description	Default
ImgBorderWidth	The width of the image border (must be greater than 0 in order for a border to be drawn)	0
ImgBorderColor	The color of the image border	Set by browser
ImgBorderMargin	The distance (in pixels) from the image border to the image on all sides	0
ImgFrameThickness	The thickness of the image frame (must be greater than 0 in order for a frame to be drawn)	0
ImgFrameType	The type of image frame: **ShadowIn, ShadowOut, ShadowEtchedIn,** or **ShadowEtchedOut**	**ShadowIn**
ImgFrameMargin	The distance (in pixels) from the image frame to the image	0
Text	The string of characters to display	(none)
TxColor	The text color	Set by browser
TxYOffset	The vertical distance (in pixels) from the top of the applet to the lower left corner of the text	The height of the text
TxXOffset	The horizontal distance (in pixels) from the left side of the applet to the text	0
TxHorizCenter	If true, the text is horizontally centered	false
TxVertCenter	If true, the text is vertically centered	false
TxFont	The font of the text: **TimesRoman, Helvetica, Courier, Dialog, DialogInput,** or **ZapfDingbats**	**Dialog**
TxStyle	The style of the font: **Plain, Bold, Italic,** or **BoldItalic**	**Plain**
TxPointSize	The size of the font in points	10
TxUnderLine	If true, the text is underlined	false
TxBorderWidth	The width of the text border (must be greater than 0 in order for a border to be drawn)	0
TxBorderColor	The color of the text border	black
TxBorderMargin	The distance (in pixels) from the text border to the text on all sides	0
TxFrameThickness	The thickness of the text frame (must be greater than 0 in order for a frame to be drawn)	0
TxFrameType	The type of text frame: **ShadowIn, ShadowOut, ShadowEtchedIn,** or **ShadowEtchedOut**	**ShadowIn**
TxFrameMargin	The distance (in pixels) from the text frame to the text	0
AppBGColor	The background color of the applet	Set by browser

Table 2–8 URLAudImgTxt Applet Settings (Continued)

Name	Description	Default
AppBorderWidth	The width of the applet border (must be greater than 0 in order for a border to be drawn)	0
AppBorderColor	The color of the applet border	black
AppFrameThickness	The thickness of the applet frame (must be greater than 0 in order for a frame to be drawn)	0
AppFrameType	The type of applet frame: **ShadowIn**, **ShadowOut**, **ShadowEtchedIn**, or **ShadowEtchedOut**	**ShadowIn**

See Also

Related applets: **AudioImageText** on page 37
                                       BasicImage on page 27
                                       BasicText on page 22

URL for **URLAudImgTxt**:   `http://www.vivids.com/ij2/fund/URLAudImgTxt.html`

URLAudImgTxtBG

Displays an image
Displays a string of characters
Plays an audio file when the pointer enters the text
Plays an audio file when the pointer enters the image
Loads the specified URL when any mouse button is pressed
Displays a background image which can be tiled

Description

The **URLAudImgTxtBG** applet has all the same characteristics as **URLAudImgTxt**, which means that it can display text and an image, play an audio file, and load URLs.

In addition, you can specify a background image. The text and image overlie the background image. The background image can be *tiled*. This means that it is repeated so that it fills the entire applet area.

Using **URLAudImgTxtBG** in HTML Code

The following HTML code uses the **URLAudImgTxtBG** applet to display an image and text against a tiled background image. When the pointer enters the text area, the `welcome.au` audio file is played. When the pointer moves within the image, the specified URL (`http://www.powertr.com`) is displayed in the browser's status line; when the visitor presses any mouse button, the URL is loaded.

```
<applet
    codebase = URLAudImgTxtBG2
    code     = URLAudImgTxtBG.class
    width    = 300
    height   = 180>
<param name=TxURL               value=http://www.vivids.com>
<param name=Text                value="Welcome!">
<param name=TxAudio             value=URLAudImgTxtBG2/welcome.au>
<param name=TxPointSize         value=36>
<param name=TxFont              value=Helvetica>
<param name=TxStyle             value=BoldItalic>
<param name=TxColor             value=white>
<param name=TxYOffset           value=110>
<param name=TxXOffset           value=120>
<param name=Image               value=URLAudImgTxtBG2/vivid.gif>
<param name=ImgYOffset          value=10>
<param name=ImgXOffset          value=15>
<param name=AppBGImage          value=URLAudImgTxtBG2/plaid.gif>
<param name=AppBGImageXOffset value=2>
```

```
<param name=AppBGImageYOffset value=2>
<param name=AppTile            value=true>
</applet>
```

Settings

The parameters in Table 2–9 are identical to those for **URLAudImgTxt** with the addition of the parameters that specify the background image, the background image offsets, and the tiling. Since the background image applies to the entire applet, the parameters begin with the **App** prefix.

Table 2–9 URLAudImgTxtBG Applet Settings

Name	Description	Default
AppBGImage	The background image	(none)
AppBGImageXOffset	The horizontal offset at which to position the background image	0
AppBGImageYOffset	The vertical offset at which to position the background image	0
AppTile	If true, tile the background image	false
TxURL	The URL to load when the pointer is within the text and any mouse button is pressed	(none)
ImgURL	The URL to load when the pointer is within the image and any mouse button is pressed	(none)
TxAudio	The audio file to play when the pointer enters the text	(none)
ImgAudio	The audio file to play when the pointer enters the image	(none)
Image	The image to display	(none)
ImgLoadWait	If true, the image is not displayed until it is completely loaded	false
ImgXOffset	The horizontal distance (in pixels) from the left side of the applet to the image	0

Table 2–9 URLAudImgTxtBG Applet Settings (Continued)

Name	Description	Default
ImgYOffset	The vertical distance (in pixels) from the top of the applet to the image	0
ImgHorizCenter	If true, the image is horizontally centered	false
ImgVertCenter	If true, the image is vertically centered	false
ImgBorderWidth	The width of the image border (must be greater than 0 in order for a border to be drawn)	0
ImgBorderColor	The color of the image border	Set by browser
ImgBorderMargin	The distance (in pixels) from the image border to the image on all sides	0
ImgFrameThickness	The thickness of the image frame (must be greater than 0 in order for a frame to be drawn)	0
ImgFrameType	The type of image frame: **ShadowIn**, **ShadowOut**, **ShadowEtchedIn**, or **ShadowEtchedOut**	**ShadowIn**
ImgFrameMargin	The distance (in pixels) from the image frame to the image	0
Text	The string of characters to display	(none)
TxColor	The text color	Set by browser
TxYOffset	The vertical distance (in pixels) from the top of the applet to the lower left corner of the text	The height of the text
TxXOffset	The horizontal distance (in pixels) from the left side of the applet to the text	0
TxHorizCenter	If true, the text is horizontally centered	false
TxVertCenter	If true, the text is vertically centered	false
TxFont	The font of the text: **TimesRoman**, **Helvetica**, **Courier**, **Dialog**, **DialogInput**, or **ZapfDingbats**	**Dialog**
TxStyle	The style of the font: **Plain**, **Bold**, **Italic**, or **BoldItalic**	**Plain**
TxPointSize	The size of the font in points	10
TxUnderLine	If true, the text is underlined	false
TxBorderWidth	The width of the text border (must be greater than 0 in order for a border to be drawn)	0
TxBorderColor	The color of the text border	black
TxBorderMargin	The distance (in pixels) from the text border to the text on all sides	0
TxFrameThickness	The thickness of the text frame (must be greater than 0 in order for a frame to be drawn)	0

Table 2–9 URLAudImgTxtBG Applet Settings (Continued)

Name	Description	Default
TxFrameType	The type of text frame: **ShadowIn**, **ShadowOut**, **ShadowEtchedIn**, or **ShadowEtchedOut**	**ShadowIn**
TxFrameMargin	The distance (in pixels) from the text frame to the text	0
AppBGColor	The background color of the applet	Set by browser
AppBorderWidth	The width of the applet border (must be greater than 0 in order for a border to be drawn)	0
AppBorderColor	The color of the applet border	black
AppFrameThickness	The thickness of the applet frame (must be greater than 0 in order for a frame to be drawn)	0
AppFrameType	The type of applet frame: **ShadowIn**, **ShadowOut**, **ShadowEtchedIn**, or **ShadowEtchedOut**	**ShadowIn**

Applets do not use the background image of the Web page; they overwrite the background image with a solid background color. By using the same background color or image for the Web page and the applet, you can create a uniform background. If the applet background and the page background contain a repeating pattern, use the **BGImageXOffset** and **BGImageYOffset** parameters to align the applet background with the page background. This may require some experimentation.

The following illustration shows the sample **URLAudImgTxtBG** applet (page 46) on a Web page with the same tiled background image:

Unfortunately, there is no way to make sure that an applet background image will line up with the page background image in precisely the same way for all browsers on all platforms.

See Also

Related applets:

URLAudImgTxt on page 42
AudioImageText on page 37
BasicImage on page 27
BasicText on page 22

URL for **URLAudImgTxtBG**:

`http://www.vivids.com/ij2/fund/URLAudImgTxtBG.html`

ImageMap

Displays an image
Displays a string of characters
Plays an audio file when the pointer enters the text
Plays an audio file when the pointer enters the image
Loads the specified URL when any mouse button is pressed
Displays a background image which can be tiled
Loads the specified URL based on image maps

Description

The **ImageMap** applet has all the same characteristics as **URLAudImgTxtBG**, with the additional feature that image maps can be specified to associate a URL with a given rectangular region of the applet. URLs specified by image maps take precedence over URLs specified for the image or text. You can also play a unique audio file with each image map.

Image maps are useful when you have a single image with graphics that indicate various URLs. For example, a single image might have the appearance of multiple buttons. You could, in this case, map the area of each button to a particular URL.

Using **ImageMap** in HTML Code

The following HTML code uses the **ImageMap** applet to display an image containing four image maps. The image displays four button on a control strip. A URL is specified for each image map; each image map corresponds to one of the four buttons in the image. An audio file is also associated with each image map. When the pointer enters the image map the corresponding audio file plays.

In the map parameter settings the number immediately following **Map** indicates the image map number. **X** and **Y** indicate horizontal and vertical coordinates, and **1** and **2** specify left and right or top and bottom, respectively. To specify the left horizontal coordinate for image map 2, for example, you use **Map2_X1**. To specify the bottom vertical coordinate for image map 3 you use **Map3_Y2**.

```
<applet
    codebase = ImageMap2
    code     = ImageMap.class
    width    = 561
    height   = 132>
<param name=Map1_URL
value=http://www.vivids.com/java/instant/index.html>
<param name=Map2_URL
value=http://www.vivids.com/java/training/index.html>
```

```
<param name=Map3_URL       value=http://www.vivids.com/fontmaker/index.html>
<param name=Map4_URL       value=http://www.vivids.com/services/index.html>
<! Audio for Maps>
<param name=AudioMap1      value=ImageMap2/InstantJava.au>
<param name=AudioMap2      value=ImageMap2/JavaTraining.au>
<param name=AudioMap3      value=ImageMap2/Products.au>
<param name=AudioMap4      value=ImageMap2/Services.au>
<param name=AudioMapLoop4 value=true>
<! Maps >
<param name=AppNumMaps     value=4>
<param name=Map1_X1        value=66>
<param name=Map1_Y1        value=20>
<param name=Map1_X2        value=152>
<param name=Map1_Y2        value=100>

<param name=Map2_X1        value=192>
<param name=Map2_Y1        value=20>
<param name=Map2_X2        value=275>
<param name=Map2_Y2        value=100>

<param name=Map3_X1        value=314>
<param name=Map3_Y1        value=20>
<param name=Map3_X2        value=397>
<param name=Map3_Y2        value=100>

<param name=Map4_X1        value=432>
<param name=Map4_Y1        value=20>
<param name=Map4_X2        value=507>
<param name=Map4_Y2        value=100>

<param name=Image          value=ImageMap2/stripcmp.gif>
<param name=ImgURL         value="http://java.sun.com">

<param name=ImgXOffset     value=20>
<param name=ImgYOffset     value=20>
</applet>
```

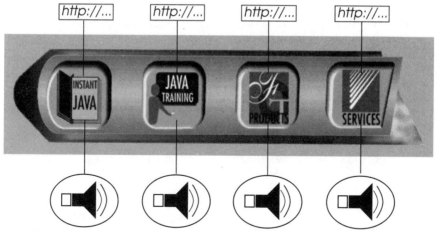

The **AppNumMaps** parameter specifies the number of image maps that the applet contains. The default for **AppNumMaps** is 0, so if you forget to set it none of the image maps you specify will be observed.

The **TestMode** parameter is used to help you determine the horizontal and vertical coordinates of the image map. When you set **TestMode** to **true**, the browser's status line displays the horizontal and vertical coordinates of the pointer as you move it across the applet. This should help you identify the exact coordinates that you want for your image map settings.

Settings

Table 2–10 lists the parameters for **ImageMap**.

Table 2–10 ImageMap Applet Settings

Name	Description	Default
AppNumMaps	The number of image maps (must be set to use image maps)	0
MapN_X1	The left horizontal coordinate for map *N*	0
MapN_Y1	The top vertical coordinate for map *N*	0
MapN_X2	The right horizontal coordinate for map *N*	0
MapN_Y2	The bottom vertical coordinate for map *N*	0
MapN_URL	The URL for map *N*	(none)
TestMode	If true, the pointer position is displayed in the status line	false
AudioMapN	The audio file to play when the pointer enters map *N*	(none)
AudioMapLoopN	If true, play the audio file for map *N* continuously in a loop	false

Table 2–10 ImageMap Applet Settings (Continued)

Name	Description	Default
AppBGImage	The background image	(none)
AppBGImageXOffset	The horizontal offset at which to position the background image	0
AppBGImageYOffset	The vertical offset at which to position the background image	0
AppTile	If true, tile the background image	false
TxURL	The URL to load when the pointer is within the text and any mouse button is pressed	(none)
ImgURL	The URL to load when the pointer is within the image and any mouse button is pressed	(none)
TxAudio	The audio file to play when the pointer enters the text	(none)
ImgAudio	The audio file to play when the pointer enters the image	(none)
Image	The image to display	(none)
ImgLoadWait	If true, the image is not displayed until it is completely loaded	false
ImgXOffset	The horizontal distance (in pixels) from the left side of the applet to the image	0
ImgYOffset	The vertical distance (in pixels) from the top of the applet to the image	0
ImgHorizCenter	If true, the image is horizontally centered	false
ImgVertCenter	If true, the image is vertically centered	false
ImgBorderWidth	The width of the image border (must be greater than 0 in order for a border to be drawn)	0
ImgBorderColor	The color of the image border	Set by browser
ImgBorderMargin	The distance (in pixels) from the image border to the image on all sides	0
ImgFrameThickness	The thickness of the image frame (must be greater than 0 in order for a frame to be drawn)	0
ImgFrameType	The type of image frame: **ShadowIn**, **ShadowOut**, **ShadowEtchedIn**, or **ShadowEtchedOut**	**ShadowIn**
ImgFrameMargin	The distance (in pixels) from the image frame to the image	0
Text	The string of characters to display	(none)
TxColor	The text color	Set by browser

Table 2–10 ImageMap Applet Settings (Continued)

Name	Description	Default
TxYOffset	The vertical distance (in pixels) from the top of the applet to the lower left corner of the text	The height of the text
TxXOffset	The horizontal distance (in pixels) from the left side of the applet to the text	0
TxHorizCenter	If true, the text is horizontally centered	false
TxVertCenter	If true, the text is vertically centered	false
TxFont	The font of the text: **TimesRoman, Helvetica, Courier, Dialog, DialogInput,** or **ZapfDingbats**	**Dialog**
TxStyle	The style of the font: **Plain, Bold, Italic,** or **BoldItalic**	**Plain**
TxPointSize	The size of the font in points	10
TxUnderLine	If true, the text is underlined	false
TxBorderWidth	The width of the text border (must be greater than 0 in order for a border to be drawn)	0
TxBorderColor	The color of the text border	black
TxBorderMargin	The distance (in pixels) from the text border to the text on all sides	0
TxFrameThickness	The thickness of the text frame (must be greater than 0 in order for a frame to be drawn)	0
TxFrameType	The type of text frame: **ShadowIn, ShadowOut, ShadowEtchedIn,** or **ShadowEtchedOut**	**ShadowIn**
TxFrameMargin	The distance (in pixels) from the text frame to the text	0
AppBGColor	The background color of the applet	Set by browser
AppBorderWidth	The width of the applet border (must be greater than 0 in order for a border to be drawn)	0
AppBorderColor	The color of the applet border	black
AppFrameThickness	The thickness of the applet frame (must be greater than 0 in order for a frame to be drawn)	0
AppFrameType	The type of applet frame: **ShadowIn, ShadowOut, ShadowEtchedIn,** or **ShadowEtchedOut**	**ShadowIn**

See Also

Related applets:

URLAudImgTxtBG on page 46
URLAudImgTxt on page 42

AudioImageText on page 37
BasicImage on page 27
BasicText on page 22

URL for **ImageMap**:   `http://www.vivids.com/ij2/fund/ImageMap.html`

CHAPTER

3

Text
Applets

A Web page conveys information. That information can be displayed in many ways, but one of the most common and useful is through text—characters, words, titles, paragraphs and so forth.

This chapter introduces some new and interesting ways to display text that will grab the attention of your visitor. Using the applets in this chapter, you will be able to create text with shadows and depth as well as characters that are embossed, engraved, or transparent.

All the applets in this chapter share the characteristic of the **ImageMap** applet described in the previous chapter. This means that all the **ImageMap** parameters are inherited by these applets. If you want to play an audio file when the pointer enters the text of any of the applets in this chapter, use the **TxAudio** parameter; if you want to load a URL when the user presses a mouse button, use the **TxURL** parameter; if you want a background image displayed beneath the text you are displaying, use the **AppBGImage** parameter; if you want to draw a border or frame, use the **TxFrameThickness** or **TxBorderWidth** parameters; if you want image maps, use the **MapN_** parameters.

Common Settings

Table 3–1 lists parameters that are common to all the applets in this chapter.

Table 3–1 Common Settings for All Text Applets

Name	Description	Default
AppNumMaps	The number of image maps (must be set to use image maps)	0
Map$N$_X1	The left horizontal coordinate for map N	0
Map$N$_Y1	The top vertical coordinate for map N	0
Map$N$_X2	The right horizontal coordinate for map N	0
Map$N$_Y2	The bottom vertical coordinate for map N	0
Map$N$_URL	The URL for map N	(none)
TestMode	If true, the pointer position is displayed in the status line	false
AudioMap$N$	The audio file to play when the pointer enters map N	(none)
AudioMapLoop$N$	If true, play the audio file for map N continuously in a loop	false
AppBGImage	The background image	(none)
AppBGImageXOffset	The horizontal offset at which to position the background image	0
AppBGImageYOffset	The vertical offset at which to position the background image	0
AppTile	If true, tile the background image	false
TxURL	The URL to load when the pointer is within the text and any mouse button is pressed	(none)
ImgURL	The URL to load when the pointer is within the image and any mouse button is pressed	(none)
TxAudio	The audio file to play when the pointer enters the text	(none)
TxAudioLoop	If true, continuously play the audio file for the text	false
ImgAudio	The audio file to play when the pointer enters the image	(none)
ImgAudioLoop	If true, continuously play the audio file for the image	false
Image	The image to display	(none)
ImgLoadWait	If true, the image is not displayed until it is completely loaded	false
ImgXOffset	The horizontal distance (in pixels) from the left side of the applet to the image	0

Table 3–1 Common Settings for All Text Applets (Continued)

Name	Description	Default
ImgYOffset	The vertical distance (in pixels) from the top of the applet to the image	0
ImgHorizCenter	If true, the image is horizontally centered	false
ImgVertCenter	If true, the image is vertically centered	false
ImgBorderWidth	The width of the image border (must be greater than 0 in order for a border to be drawn)	0
ImgBorderColor	The color of the image border	Set by browser
ImgBorderMargin	The distance (in pixels) from the image border to the image on all sides	0
ImgFrameThickness	The thickness of the image frame (must be greater than 0 in order for a frame to be drawn)	0
ImgFrameType	The type of image frame: **ShadowIn**, **ShadowOut**, **ShadowEtchedIn**, or **ShadowEtchedOut**	**ShadowIn**
ImgFrameMargin	The distance (in pixels) from the image frame to the image	0
Text	The string of characters to display	(none)
TxColor	The text color	Set by browser
TxBGColor	The text background color	transparent
TxYOffset	The vertical distance (in pixels) from the top of the applet to the lower left corner of the text	The height of the text
TxXOffset	The horizontal distance (in pixels) from the left side of the applet to the text	0
TxHorizCenter	If true, the text is horizontally centered	false
TxVertCenter	If true, the text is vertically centered	false
TxFont	The font of the text: **TimesRoman**, **Helvetica**, **Courier**, **Dialog**, **DialogInput**, or **ZapfDingbats**	**Dialog**
TxStyle	The style of the font: **Plain**, **Bold**, **Italic**, or **BoldItalic**	**Plain**
TxPointSize	The size of the font in points	10
TxUnderLine	If true, the text is underlined	false
TxBorderWidth	The width of the text border (must be greater than 0 in order for a border to be drawn)	0
TxBorderColor	The color of the text border	black
TxBorderMargin	The distance (in pixels) from the text border to the text on all sides	0
TxFrameThickness	The thickness of the text frame (must be greater than 0 in order for a frame to be drawn)	0

Table 3-1 Common Settings for All Text Applets (Continued)

Name	Description	Default
TxFrameType	The type of text frame: **ShadowIn**, **ShadowOut**, **ShadowEtchedIn**, or **ShadowEtchedOut**	**ShadowIn**
TxFrameMargin	The distance (in pixels) from the text frame to the text	0
AppBGColor	The background color of the applet	Set by browser
AppBorderWidth	The width of the applet border (must be greater than 0 in order for a border to be drawn)	0
AppBorderColor	The color of the applet border	black
AppFrameThickness	The thickness of the applet frame (must be greater than 0 in order for a frame to be drawn)	0
AppFrameType	The type of applet frame: **ShadowIn**, **ShadowOut**, **ShadowEtchedIn**, or **ShadowEtchedOut**	**ShadowIn**

The only new parameter is **TxBGColor**. This parameter is needed because the applets in this chapter use a different mechanism to draw characters on the screen.

When you use these applets, the characters are actually drawn into a rectangular image. This image is then displayed on the screen with a transparent background, allowing the background color (**AppBGColor**) or image (**AppBGImage**) to show through. This produces the same effect that we saw in the previous chapter.

It is possible to make the text background non-transparent, however. When you specify **TxBGColor**, the text's background is the color you specify, rather than being transparent.

Text

Displays a string of characters

Description

The **Text** applet displays a string of characters.

This applet may appear to be just like the **BasicText** on page 22. It is implemented differently, however, and will be useful later in the book when filters are used.

Using Text in HTML Code

The following HTML code uses the **Text** applet to display the string *Enter Here* in blue characters with a **ShadowEtchedIn** frame:

```
<applet
    archive  = Text2.zip
    codebase = Text2
    code     = Text.class
    width    = 300
    height   = 100>
<param name=Text               value="Enter Here">
<param name=TxPointSize        value=48>
<param name=TxColor            value=blue>
<param name=TxFont             value=Helvetica>
<param name=TxHorizCenter      value=true>
<param name=TxVertCenter       value=true>
<param name=TxFrameThickness value=2>
<param name=TxFrameMargin      value=4>
<param name=TxFrameType        value=ShadowEtchedIn>
</applet>
```

Settings

See Table 3–1 on page 60 for common settings that apply to this applet.

See Also

URL for **Text**: http://www.vivids.com/ij2/text/Text.html

Shadow

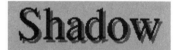

Adds a shadow to a string of characters

Description

The **Shadow** applet displays a string of characters with a shadow behind it. The offset or position of the shadow can be controlled using parameters. The position of the shadow creates the impression of illumination from a particular direction.

Using Shadow in HTML Code

The following HTML code uses the **Shadow** applet to display the string *Members Only!* with a border against a tiled background:

```
<applet
    archive  = Shadow2.zip
    codebase = Shadow2
    code     = Shadow.class
    width    = 450
    height   = 120>
<param name=Text            value="Members Only!">
<param name=TxPointSize     value=48>
<param name=TxStyle         value=BoldItalic>
<param name=TxColor         value=white>
<param name=ShadowColor     value=black>
<param name=TxHorizCenter   value=true>
<param name=TxVertCenter    value=true>
<param name=ShadowXOffset   value=-8>
<param name=ShadowYOffset   value=10>
<param name=AppBgImage      value=Shadow2/pattern.gif>
<param name=AppTile         value=true>
<param name=TxBorderWidth   value=2>
<param name=TxBorderMargin value=4>
</applet>
```

Here's another example that uses **Shadow** to display the string *Camping Season* against a background image of mountains and trees.

```
<applet
    archive  = Shadow3.zip
    codebase = Shadow3
    code     = Shadow.class
    width    = 312
    height   = 179>
<param name=text          value="Camping Season">
<param name=Txstyle       value=bold>
<param name=TxPointSize    value=24>
<param name=ShadowXOffset value=4>
<param name=ShadowYOffset value=-3>
<param name=TxHorizCenter value=true>
<param name=ShadowColor   value=black>
<param name=TxColor       value=white>
<param name=AppBGImage    value=Shadow3/forest.gif>
</applet>
```

Settings

See Table 3–1 on page 60 for common settings that apply to this applet. Three additional parameters set the color and offset of the shadow.

Table 3–2 Shadow Applet Settings

Name	Description	Default
ShadowXOffset	The horizontal offset (in pixels) of the shadow	2
ShadowYOffset	The vertical offset (in pixels) of the shadow	2
ShadowColor	The color of the shadow	gray (#646464)

See Also

Related applets: **SoftShadow** on page 66
MultiColorShadow on page 89

URL for **Shadow**: `http://www.vivids.com/ij2/text/Shadow.html`

SoftShadow

Adds a soft shadow to a string of characters

Description

The **SoftShadow** applet displays a string of characters with a soft shadow behind it. The soft shadow differs from that produced by the **Shadow** applet in that its outline is less well-defined. This effect is produced by using more than one color to draw the shadow; a lighter shade is used around the edges.

The offset, or position, of the shadow can be controlled using parameters. The position creates the impression of illumination from a particular direction and of distance between the text and the background.

Using SoftShadow in HTML Code

The following HTML code uses the **SoftShadow** applet to display the string *Sale!* against a white background. The **ShadowXOffset** and **ShadowYOffset** parameters are used to make the characters appear to be illuminated from the lower right.

```
<applet
    archive   = SoftShadow2.zip
    codebase = SoftShadow2
    code      = SoftShadow.class
    width     = 330
    height    = 88>
<param name=text           value="Sale!">
<param name=AppBGColor     value=#ffffff>
<param name=TxFont         value=Helvetica>
<param name=TxStyle        value=bold>
<param name=TxPointSize    value=72>
<param name=ShadowYOffset value=-6>
<param name=ShadowXOffset value=-6>
<param name=SoftThickness value=4>
<param name=TxHorizCenter value=True>
<param name=TxVertCenter  value=True>
</applet>
```

Settings

See Table 3–1 on page 60 for common settings that apply to this applet. Four additional parameters set the color and offset of the shadow as seen previously with the **Shadow** applet.

The **SoftThickness** parameter determines the softness of the shadow. The greater the value, the softer (or blurrier) the shadow appears.

Table 3–3 SoftShadow Applet Settings

Name	Description	Default
ShadowXOffset	The horizontal offset (in pixels) of the shadow	2
ShadowYOffset	The vertical offset (in pixels) of the shadow	2
ShadowColor	The color of the shadow	gray (#646464)
SoftThickness	The size (in pixels) of the blurring used to create the soft shadow effect	2

The **SoftThickness** parameter should be adjusted based on the size of the text displayed. For small text, you should probably set **SoftThickness** to 1. For very large text, you may want **SoftThickness** to be greater than the default of 2.

See Also

Related applets: **Shadow** on page 64
                          MultiColorShadow on page 89

URL for **SoftShadow**:   `http://www.vivids.com/ij2/text/SoftShadow.html`

SmoothText

Smooths a string of characters

Description

The **SmoothText** applet displays a string of characters which have been *anti-aliased*. Anti-aliasing removes the jagged appearance of lines and characters that appear on the computer screen.

To understand the need for anti-aliasing, look at the following uppercase A, which has been magnified many times:

The jagged appearance of the character is due to the fact that computer displays have limited resolution. Lines that are not perfectly vertical or horizontal exhibit this effect. Anti-aliasing is a technique that replaces the pixels along the edges with various shades of color to make the edge look smoother. Here is the same character after it has been anti-aliased:

Although the anti-aliased character looks a little fuzzy at this magnification, its appearance is clean and smooth when viewed at regular size.

The different shades of color that are used to create the smoothing effect are based on the foreground and the background colors. Even if you specify a background image with this applet, the shades used are based on the background color you specify, not on the background image. (If you do not specify a background color, the default background color is used.)

If the color of the background image is very different from the specified background color, the characters may appear to have a slight outline or ghost around them. For this reason, if you do place anti-aliased text on a background image you will probably want to pick a background color that matches the color of your image.

Using SmoothText in HTML Code

It's difficult to fully appreciate the anti-aliased effect on the printed page because printed resolution is so much greater than that on the screen. The effects are, however, quite noticeable when viewed on your computer display.

The following HTML code uses the **SmoothText** applet to display the string *JAVA!* against a white background.

```
<applet
    archive  = SmoothText2.zip
    codebase = SmoothText2
    code     = SmoothText.class
    width    = 250
    height   = 120>
<param name=Text           value=JAVA!>
<param name=TxPointSize     value=72>
<param name=TxFont          value=Helvetica>
<param name=TxStyle         value=Bold>
<param name=AppBGColor      value=#ffffff>
<param name=TxVertCenter    value=true>
<param name=TxHorizCenter   value=true>
<param name=TxBorderWidth   value=2>
<param name=TxBorderMargin value=8>
</applet>
```

Settings

See Table 3–1 on page 60 for common settings that apply to this applet.

See Also

URL for **SmoothText**:   http://www.vivids.com/ij2/text/SmoothText.html

WaveText

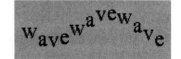

Arranges a string of characters in a sine wave

Description

The **WaveText** applet displays a string of characters arranged in a sine wave. Adjust the
Amplitude and **WaveLength** parameters to determine the exact shape of the wave.

Using WaveText in HTML Code

The following HTML code uses the **WaveText** applet to display the string *Life has its little
ups and downs*. The amplitude and wavelength are set to place the word *ups* at the top of the
wave and the word *downs* toward the bottom.

```
<applet
    archive  = WaveText2.zip
    codebase = WaveText2
    code     = WaveText.class
    width    = 250
    height   = 100>
<param name=Text            value="Life has its little ups and downs">
<param name=TxPointSize     value=18>
<param name=TxFont          value=TimesRoman>
<param name=TxHorizCenter   value=true>
<param name=TxVertCenter    value=true>
<param name=Amplitude       value=25>
<param name=WaveLength      value=30>
</applet>
```

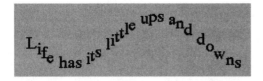

Here's another example using the **WaveText** applet. This time we set the **BeginRange** and
EndRange parameters so that the wave pattern appears only on the characters within the
range specified.

```
<applet
    archive  = WaveText3.zip
    codebase = WaveText3
    code     = WaveText.class
    width    = 350
```

```
        height    = 120>
<param name=Text        value="Life has its little ups and downs, doesn't
it?">
<param name=TxPointSize  value=18>
<param name=TxFont       value=TimesRoman>
<param name=TxHorizCenter value=true>
<param name=TxVertCenter  value=true>
<param name=Amplitude    value=25>
<param name=WaveLength   value=20>
<param name=BeginRange   value=15>
<param name=EndRange     value=31>
<param name=XTranslate   value=30>
</applet>
```

Life has its little ups and downs, doesn't it?

Settings

See Table 3–1 on page 60 for common settings that apply to this applet. Six additional parameters set the wave's characteristics.

The **Amplitude** parameter sets the height of the wave. The **WaveLength** parameter sets the horizontal length of the wave. The **XTranslate** and **YTranslate** parameters translate the wave in the horizontal and vertical directions respectively. The **BeginRange** and **EndRange** parameters set the range of characters to which the wave function applies.

Table 3–4 WaveText Applet Setting

Name	Description	Default
Amplitude	The amplitude of the wave	10
WaveLength	The wavelength of the wave	10
XTranslate	The horizontal translation of the wave	0
YTranslate	The vertical translation of the wave	0
BeginRange	The character with which to begin the wave	Beginning of line
EndRange	The character with which to end the wave	End of line

See Also

URL for **WaveText**: `http://www.vivids.com/ij2/text/WaveText.html`

Depth

Adds 3-dimensional depth to a string of characters

Description

The **Depth** applet displays a string of characters that appear to have 3-dimensional depth. The depth can be set to any reasonable degree.

Using **Depth** in HTML Code

The following HTML code uses the **Depth** applet to display the string *Enter Here* with green text, purple background, and black depth.

```
<applet
    archive  = Depth2.zip
    codebase = Depth2
    code     = Depth.class
    width    = 400
    height   = 120>
<param name=Text           value="Enter Here">
<param name=AppBGColor     value=#ff00ff>
<param name=TxPointSize     value=72>
<param name=TxColor        value=#00ff00>
<param name=TxFont         value=Helvetica>
<param name=TxHorizCenter value=true>
<param name=TxVertCenter  value=true>
<param name=DepthColor     value=#000000>
<param name=DepthXOffset  value=10>
<param name=DepthYOffset  value=-10>
</applet>
```

Here's one more example of the **Depth** applet. It displays the string *WOW!!* in white against a black background, with depth offsets of –20.

```
<applet
    archive   = Depth3.zip
    codebase  = Depth3
    code      = Depth.class
    width     = 300
    height    = 120>
<param name=Text          value="WOW!!">
<param name=TxPointSize    value=48>
<param name=TxColor        value=#ffffff>
<param name=AppBGColor     value=#000000>
<param name=TxFont         value=TimesRoman>
<param name=TxHorizCenter  value=true>
<param name=TxVertCenter   value=true>
<param name=DepthXOffset   value=-20>
<param name=DepthYOffset   value=-20>
</applet>
```

Settings

See Table 3–1 on page 60 for common settings that apply to this applet. Three additional parameters set the color of the depth, and the horizontal and vertical offsets of the depth.

Table 3–5 Depth Applet Settings

Name	Description	Default
DepthXOffset	The horizontal offset (in pixels) of the depth	-10
DepthYOffset	The vertical offset (in pixels) of the depth	-10
DepthColor	The color of the depth	The text color darkened by 50%

The **DepthColor** defaults to a shade of the text color that is 50% darker. Thus, if the foreground color is black, the depth color will also be black. You will probably want to explicitly select another color for the depth if you are using black or any other dark color as your foreground.

See Also

Related applets: **DepthFade** on page 74
                                 DepthShade on page 77

URL for **Depth**:   `http://www.vivids.com/ij2/text/Depth.html`

DepthFade

Adds fading 3-dimensional depth to a string of characters

Description

The **DepthFade** applet displays a string of characters that appear to have 3-dimensional depth, fading into the background. By default the depth fades from the foreground color to the background color. You can also specify a contrasting outline for the characters themselves, which is sometimes helpful in distinguishing between the characters and their depth.

Using DepthFade in HTML Code

The following HTML code uses the **DepthFade** applet to display the string *WOW!!* with a **FGColor** of white and a **BGColor** of black.

```
<applet
    archive  = DepthFade2.zip
    codebase = DepthFade2
    code     = DepthFade.class
    width    = 300
    height   = 120>
<param name=Text           value="WOW!!">
<param name=TxPointSize    value=48>
<param name=TxColor        value=#ffffff>
<param name=AppBGColor     value=#000000>
<param name=TxFont         value=TimesRoman>
<param name=TxHorizCenter  value=true>
<param name=TxVertCenter   value=true>
<param name=DepthXOffset   value=-20>
<param name=DepthYOffset   value=-20>
</applet>
```

You may prefer to add an outline. If so, set the **OutlineColor** parameter. The following code adds the **OutlineColor** parameter to set the outline to black.

```
<applet
    archive  = DepthFade3.zip
    codebase = DepthFade3
    code     = DepthFade.class
    width    = 300
    height   = 120>
<param name=Text           value="WOW!!">
<param name=TxPointSize    value=48>
```

```
<param name=TxColor        value=#ffffff>
<param name=AppBGColor     value=#000000>
<param name=TxFont         value=TimesRoman>
<param name=TxHorizCenter  value=true>
<param name=TxVertCenter   value=true>
<param name=DepthXOffset   value=-20>
<param name=DepthYOffset   value=-20>
<param name=OutlineColor   value=#000000>
</applet>
```

You can do some interesting things by changing the **DepthColor** parameter. The next example uses the default background color (gray in this case), a black foreground, and a yellow **DepthColor**. The effect is much more dramatic on a color display.

```
<applet
    archive  = DepthFade4.zip
    codebase = DepthFade4
    code     = DepthFade.class
    width    = 400
    height   = 120>
<param name=Text           value="Acme Tools">
<param name=TxPointSize     value=48>
<param name=TxFont          value=TimesRoman>
<param name=TxColor         value=#000000>
<param name=DepthColor      value=#ffff00>
<param name=TxHorizCenter  value=true>
<param name=TxVertCenter   value=true>
<param name=DepthXOffset   value=30>
<param name=DepthYOffset   value=-30>
</applet>
```

Settings

See Table 3–1 on page 60 for common settings that apply to this applet. Four additional parameters set the color of the depth, the outline color, and the horizontal and vertical offsets of the depth.

Table 3–6 DepthFade Applet Settings

Name	Description	Default
DepthXOffset	The horizontal offset (in pixels) of the depth	-10
DepthYOffset	The vertical offset (in pixels) of the depth	-10
DepthColor	The color of the depth	**AppBGColor**
OutlineColor	The color of the outline	(none)

The depth changes gradually from the text color (**TxColor**) to the depth color (**DepthColor**). **DepthColor** defaults to the background color (**AppBGColor**), so if you do not explicitly specify **DepthColor** the depth fades directory from the text color to the background color.

See Also

Related applets: **Depth** on page 72
                                      DepthShade on page 77

URL for **DepthFade**:   `http://www.vivids.com/ij2/text/DepthFade.html`

DepthShade

Adds a 3-dimensional shadow that fades toward a string of characters

Description

The **DepthShade** applet, like the **DepthFade** applet, displays a string of characters that appear to be 3-dimensional. The difference, however, is that the depth of the characters fades in the reverse direction, from the background color to the foreground color, producing an effect of shadowed depth.

Using **DepthShade** in HTML Code

The following HTML code uses the **DepthShade** applet to display the string *WOW!!* with a **FGColor** of white and a **BGColor** of black.

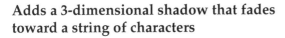

```
<applet
    archive  = DepthShade2.zip
    codebase = DepthShade2
    code     = DepthShade.class
    width    = 300
    height   = 120>
<param name=Text          value="WOW!!">
<param name=TxPointSize   value=48>
<param name=TxColor       value=white>
<param name=AppBGColor    value=black>
<param name=TxFont        value=TimesRoman>
<param name=TxHorizCenter value=true>
<param name=TxVertCenter  value=true>
<param name=DepthXOffset  value=-20>
<param name=DepthYOffset  value=-20>
<param name=TxURL         value=http://www.vivids.com>
</applet>
```

Here's the Acme Tools example from the **DepthFade** applet using **DepthShade** instead. Compare it with the earlier version.

```
<applet
    archive  = DepthShade3.zip
    codebase = DepthShade3
    code     = DepthShade.class
    width    = 340
    height   = 120>
<param name=Text          value="Acme Tools">
```

```
<param name=TxPointSize   value=48>
<param name=TxFont        value=TimesRoman>
<param name=TxColor       value=#000000>
<param name=DepthColor    value=#ffff00>
<param name=TxHorizCenter value=true>
<param name=TxVertCenter  value=true>
<param name=DepthXOffset  value=30>
<param name=DepthYOffset  value=-30>
</applet>
```

Settings

See Table 3–1 on page 60 for common settings that apply to this applet. Three additional parameters set the color of the depth, and the horizontal and vertical offsets of the depth.

Table 3–7 DepthShade Applet Settings

Name	Description	Default
DepthXOffset	The horizontal offset (in pixels) of the depth	-10
DepthYOffset	The vertical offset (in pixels) of the depth	-10
DepthColor	The color of the depth	**AppBGColor**

See Also

Related applets: **Depth** on page 72
                                    DepthFade on page 74

URL for **DepthShade**:   http://www.vivids.com/ij2/text/DepthShade.html

Emboss

Embosses a string of characters on the background

Description

The **Emboss** applet displays a string of characters that appear to be embossed on the background. By default, the background is a solid color.

Using **Emboss** in HTML Code

The following HTML code uses the **Emboss** applet to display the string *Back to Home Page* against a gray background. The characters are displayed with an intensity of 75. The **Contrast** parameter determines the shades of color that are used to create the embossed look.

```
<applet
    archive  = Emboss2.zip
    codebase = Emboss2
    code     = Emboss.class
    width    = 300
    height   = 100>
<param name=text              value="Back to Home Page">
<param name=Txstyle           value=bold>
<param name=TxPointSize        value=24>
<param name=TxFont             value=Dialog>
<param name=TxFrameThickness  value=2>
<param name=TxFrameType        value=ShadowEtchedOut>
<param name=TxFrameMargin       value=5>
<param name=TxHorizCenter      value=true>
<param name=TxVertCenter       value=true>
<param name=TxUnderLine        value=true>
<param name=Contrast           value=75>
</applet>
```

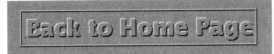

You can emboss text over a background image. The embossed text appears transparent over the background image.

The following example displays the string *Cruise, Anyone?* against a background image of some sailboats.

```
<applet
    archive  = Emboss3.zip
    codebase = Emboss3
    code     = Emboss.class
    width    = 336
    height   = 226>
<param name=text        value="Cruise, Anyone?">
<param name=Txstyle     value=bold>
<param name=AppBGImage  value=Emboss3/sailboat.gif>
<param name=TxPointSize value=24>
<param name=Depth       value=1>
<param name=TxFont      value=Dialog>
<param name=TxYOffset   value=40>
<param name=TxXOffset   value=20>
<param name=Contrast    value=75>
</applet>
```

Settings

See Table 3–1 on page 60 for common settings that apply to this applet. Two additional parameter set the intensity and the depth of the embossed look.

Table 3–8 Emboss Applet Settings

Name	Description	Default
Depth	The depth of the embossing	1
Contrast	The contrast of the colors used to create the embossed effect	50

Contrast can be any value between 0 and 100. The stronger the contrast, the greater the contrast in the colors that are used to produce the embossed effect, and the more intense the effect itself.

Embossing a string on a very dark or very light background may produce poor results.

See Also

Related applets: **Engrave** on page 82
                     EmbossImage on page 131

URL for **Emboss**:   `http://www.vivids.com/ij2/text/Emboss.html`

Engrave

Engraves a string of characters into the
background image

Description

The **Engrave** applet displays a string of characters that appear to be engraved into the background. By default, the background is a solid color.

Using **Engrave** in HTML Code

The following HTML code uses the **Engrave** applet to display the string *Congratulations* against a gray background. The characters are displayed using a **Contrast** of 90 and are enclosed in a **ShadowOut** frame.

```
<applet
    archive  = Engrave2.zip
    codebase = Engrave2
    code     = Engrave.class
    width    = 400
    height   = 80>
<param name=text              value="Congratulations">
<param name=Txstyle           value=BoldItalic>
<param name=TxPointSize        value=48>
<param name=TxFont             value=Helvetica>
<param name=TxFrameThickness  value=1>
<param name=TxFrameMargin      value=6>
<param name=TxFrameType        value=ShadowOut>
<param name=TxHorizCenter      value=true>
<param name=TxVertCenter       value=true>
<param name=Contrast           value=90>
</applet>
```

Engraving text over an image poses a problem because the text itself is not transparent. Furthermore, the colors used to create the engraved effect are calculated based on the background color of the applet (**AppBGColor**) not the colors in the image. If you are able to select a background color that closely matches the color of your image, the results can be satisfying, as shown in the next example.

```
<applet
    archive   = Engrave3.zip
    codebase  = Engrave3
    code      = Engrave.class
    width     = 336
    height    = 226>
<param name=text         value="Cruise, Anyone?">
<param name=Txstyle      value=bold>
<param name=AppBGImage   value=Engrave3/sailboat.gif>
<param name=AppBGColor   value=#a5d6f7>
<param name=TxPointSize  value=24>
<param name=Depth        value=1>
<param name=TxFont       value=Dialog>
<param name=TxYOffset    value=40>
<param name=TxXOffset    value=20>
</applet>
```

Settings

See Table 3–1 on page 60 for common settings that apply to this applet. Two additional parameters set the contrast and the depth of the engraved look.

Table 3–9 Engrave Applet Settings

Name	Description	Default
Depth	The depth of the engraving	1
Contrast	The intensity of the engraving	50

Contrast can be any value between 0 and 100. The stronger the intensity, the greater the contrast in the colors that are used to produce the engraved effect, and the more intense the effect itself.

Engraving a string into a very dark or very light background may produce poor results.

See Also

Related applets: **Emboss** on page 79

URL for **Engrave**: `http://www.vivids.com/ij2/text/Engrave.html`

Stencil

Stencil

Draws a string of characters using the background image

Description

The **Stencil** applet displays a string of characters that are drawn using the background image rather than a text color and thus appear to be transparent.

Using the **Stencil** applet without a background image produces text which cannot be seen.

Using **Stencil** in HTML Code

The following HTML code uses the **Stencil** applet to display the string *Money* against a background image of currency:

```
<applet
    archive  = Stencil2.zip
    codebase = Stencil2
    code     = Stencil.class
    width    = 400
    height   = 100>
<param name=text          value=" MONEY   ">
<param name=Txstyle       value=bold>
<param name=TxFont        value=Helvetica>
<param name=AppBGImage    value=Stencil2/money.gif>
<param name=AppTile       value=true>
<param name=TxPointSize   value=96>
<param name=AppBGColor    value=black>
<param name=TxColor       value=white>
<param name=TxVertCenter value=true>
</applet>
```

Although the text color is not displayed by the **Stencil** applet, it must be different from the background color. If you specify a black background, for example, and leave the foreground color to default to black, only the background image displays.

Settings

See Table 3–1 on page 60 for common settings that apply to this applet.

See Also

Related applets: **TransColor** on page 133

                        Transparent on page 139

URL for **Stencil**:   `http://www.vivids.com/ij2/text/Stencil.html`

MultiColor

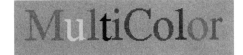

Draws a string of characters using different colors

Description

The **MultiColor** applet displays a string of characters in which each character is a different color. You may specify one or more colors to be used in succession to color the characters. If you specify fewer colors than there are characters, the colors are reused, starting with the first one specified.

Using MultiColor in HTML Code

The following HTML code uses the **MultiColor** applet to display the string *Colorful* using red, yellow, and blue. The characters are enclosed in a **ShadowEtchedOut** frame and drawn against a tiled background. Note that the colors repeat, starting with the fourth character.

```
<applet
    archive  = MultiColor2.zip
    codebase = MultiColor2
    code     = MultiColor.class
    width    = 400
    height   = 200>
<param name=AppBgImage       value=MultiColor2/pattern.gif>
<param name=AppTile          value=true>
<param name=Text             value="Colorful">
<param name=TxPointSize      value=72>
<param name=Colors           value="red yellow blue">
<param name=TxFont           value=Helvetica>
<param name=TxStyle          value=Bold>
<param name=TxHorizCenter    value=true>
<param name=TxVertCenter     value=true>
<param name=TxFrameThickness value=4>
<param name=TxFrameMargin    value=12>
<param name=TxFrameType      value=ShadowEtchedOut>
</applet>
```

Settings

See Table 3–1 on page 60 for common settings that apply to this applet. One additional parameter sets the colors used to draw the characters.

Table 3–10 MultiColor Applet Settings

Name	Description	Default
Colors	The colors to use for the characters	black

To set the **Colors** parameter, enclose a list of all the colors you want to use in double quotes, separated by spaces. This is shown in the sample HTML code where the **Colors** parameter is set.

See Also

URL for **MultiColor**:   http://www.vivids.com/ij2/text/MultiColor.html

MultiColorShadow

Draws a string of characters using different colors and a shadow

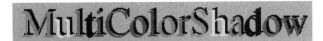

Description

The **MultiColorShadow** applet displays a string of characters in which each character is a different color and with a shadow behind it. You may specify one or more colors to be used in succession to color the characters. If you specify fewer colors than there are characters, the colors are reused, starting with the first one specified. The offset of position of the shadow can be controlled using parameters. The position of the shadow creates the impression of illumination from a particular direction.

Using **MultiColorShadow** in HTML Code

The following HTML code uses the **MultiColorShadow** applet to display the string *Colorful* using red, yellow, and blue, and a gray shadow. The characters are enclosed in a **ShadowEtchedOut** frame and drawn against a tiled background. Note that the colors repeat, starting with the fourth character.

```
<applet
    archive  = MultiColorShadow2.zip
    codebase = MultiColorShadow2
    code     = MultiColorShadow.class
    width    = 400
    height   = 200>
<param name=AppBgImage        value=MultiColorShadow2/pattern.gif>
<param name=AppTile           value=true>
<param name=Text              value="Colorful">
<param name=TxPointSize       value=72>
<param name=Colors            value="red yellow blue">
<param name=TxFont            value=Helvetica>
<param name=TxStyle           value=Bold>
<param name=TxHorizCenter     value=true>
<param name=TxVertCenter      value=true>
<param name=TxFrameThickness  value=4>
<param name=TxFrameMargin     value=12>
<param name=TxFrameType       value=ShadowEtchedOut>
<param name=ShadowXOffset     value=8>
<param name=ShadowYOffset     value=8>
</applet>
```

Settings

See Table 3–1 on page 60 for common settings that apply to this applet. Four additional parameters set the offset and color of the shadow and set the colors used to draw the characters.

Table 3–11 MultiColorShadow Applet Settings

Name	Description	Default
ShadowXOffset	The horizontal offset (in pixels) of the shadow	2
ShadowYOffset	The vertical offset (in pixels) of the shadow	2
ShadowColor	The color of the shadow	gray (#646464)
Colors	The colors to use for the characters	black

To set the **Colors** parameter, enclose a list of all the colors you want to use in double quotes, separated by spaces. This is shown in the sample HTML code where the **Colors** parameter is set.

See Also

Related applets: **MultiColor** on page 87
                     Shadow on page 64

URL for **MultiColorShadow**:

                     http://www.vivids.com/ij2/text/MultiColorShadow.html

MultiText

Draws multiple strings of characters

Description

The **MultiText** applet displays multiple strings of characters. Each string may be displayed using any of the techniques seen in this chapter. You could, for example, display three strings: one multicolored, one embossed, and one with a shadow.

Each string has its own characteristics, such as font, pointsize, offsets, border, frame, audio file, URL and so forth. For each string you can specify any of the parameters that are used in this chapter.

All the parameters that begin with **Tx** can be specified independently for each string. Each **Tx** parameter must instead begin with **Tx*N***, however, where ***N*** is the number that identifies the text string. For example, to set the font for string 2 to TimesRoman, use **Tx2Font**. To set the horizontal offset for string 1 use **Tx1XOffset**.

Using MultiText in HTML Code

To display multiple strings you must specify the **TxCount** parameter, which specifies the number of strings to be displayed. To display three strings, set **TxCount** as follows:

```
<param name=TxCount value=3>
```

To draw a string using one of the techniques discussed in the chapter, use the **Tx*N*Filter** parameter. You will learn more about **Tx*N*Filter** in Chapter 4. The **Tx*N*Filter** parameter can be used to manipulate string and images in many interesting ways. For now, you will use it to invoke one of the string display techniques that have been introduced in this chapter.

Suppose that you wanted the first string to be drawn with a shadow and the second to be drawn with an engraved look. You would specify the **Tx*N*Filter** parameter as follows:

```
<param name=Tx1Filter value=shadow>
<param name=Tx2Filter value=engrave>
```

By default, this would display the first string with the default values for the three shadow parameters—**ShadowXOffset**, **ShadowYOffset**, and **ShadowColor** (see **Shadow** on page 54). To set one or more of these parameters, supply arguments to the **Tx1Filter** value. For example, to display a shadow with a horizontal offset of -4, a vertical offset of 3, and a shadow color of green, use the following parameter settings:

```
<param name=Tx1Filter value="shadow -4 3 green">
```

The arguments must be specified in the exact order in which they were described in the Settings section for the applet that corresponds to the filter you are calling.

To set the engraved depth and intensity of the second string to 1 and 90, respectively, use the following settings:

```
<param name=Tx2Filter value="engrave 1 90">
```

Note that you must specify the **Depth** value first and then the **Contrast** value, as indicated for **Engrave** on page 82.

The following HTML code uses the **MultiText** applet to display three strings, each drawn using a different filter. The first string is drawn using **emboss**, the second is drawn using **multicolor**, and the third uses **depthshade**.

```
<applet
    archive  = MultiText2.zip
    codebase = MultiText2
    code     = MultiText.class
    width    = 320
    height   = 240>
<param name=AppTile               value=true>
<param name=AppBgImage            value=MultiText2/starfill.gif>
<param name=AppBgColor            value=black>

<param name=TxCount               value=3>

<param name=Text1                 value="Embossed Text">
<param name=Tx1PointSize          value=48>
<param name=Tx1Font               value=TimesRoman>
<param name=Tx1Style              value=BoldItalic>
<param name=Tx1HorizCenter        value=true>
<param name=Tx1YOffset            value=10>
<param name=Tx1Filter             value="emboss 1 90">
<param name=Tx1Audio              value=MultiText2/embossed.au>
<param name=Tx1URL                value=http://www.sun.com>

<param name=Text2                 value="Colorful">
<param name=Tx2PointSize          value=48>
<param name=Tx2Font               value=Helvetica>
<param name=Tx2Style              value=Bold>
<param name=Tx2HorizCenter        value=true>
<param name=Tx2YOffset            value=80>
<param name=Tx2FrameThickness value=4>
<param name=Tx2FrameMargin        value=12>
<param name=Tx2FrameType          value=ShadowEtchedOut>
<param name=Tx2Filter        value="multicolor yellow green cyan salmon azure">
<param name=Tx2Audio              value=MultiText2/colorful.au>
```

```
<param name=Tx2URL                 value=http://www.vivids.com>

<param name=Text3                  value="DepthShade">
<param name=Tx3PointSize           value=48>
<param name=Tx3Font                value=TimesRoman>
<param name=Tx3Style               value=Bold>
<param name=Tx3HorizCenter         value=true>
<param name=Tx3Color               value=lightpink>
<param name=Tx3YOffset             value=160>
<param name=Tx3Filter              value="depthshade 20 -10">
<param name=Tx3Audio               value=MultiText2/depthsh.au>
<param name=Tx3URL                 value=http://www.adobe.com>
</applet>
```

Settings

See Table 3–1 on page 60 for common settings that apply to this applet. However, the parameters that begin with **Tx** must instead begin with **Tx*N***, where ***N*** specifies the string involved. The **Tx*N*Filter** parameter is used to specify the program (or filter) that is used to draw the string. In addition, the **TxCount** parameter must be specified to indicate the number of strings to display, as shown here.

Table 3–12 MultiText Applet Settings

Name	Description	Default
TxCount	The number of text strings to display	0
Tx*N*Filter	The program to use to generate the *N*th string	0

See Also

URL for **MultiText**:   `http://www.vivids.com/ij2/text/MultiText.html`

Tips for Programmers

The applets in this chapter are implemented by extending the **ImgFilt** class defined in the classes directory. The **ImgFilt** class is an abstract class that requires any subclass to supply a `filter` method. To create a text generating filter (like the ones discussed in this chapter), you create a class that subclasses **ImgFilt** and write the `filter` method that creates the text.

We'll go over the steps in detail and show an example. The benefit of following this procedure is that you can create your own text generating filter that will work with the rest of the applets and filters described in this book.

To begin, let's look at the source code for the **shadow** filter. The filter naming convention is to prepend a lower-case 'f', so the **shadow** filter is in a file named **fshadow.java**, and the name of the class is **fshadow**:

```
1    import java.awt.*;
2    import java.awt.image.*;
3
4    class fshadow extends ImgFilt {
5        int shadow_xoffset = 2;
6        int shadow_yoffset = 2;
7        Color shadow_color = new Color(100, 100, 100);
8
9        public void setparameter(String str, int i) {
10           switch(i) {
11           case 0:
12               shadow_xoffset = Integer.parseInt(str);
13               break;
14           case 1:
15               shadow_yoffset = Integer.parseInt(str);
16               break;
17           case 2:
18               shadow_color = String2Color(str);
19               break;
20           }
21       }
22
23       public int[] filter(int[] p1, int w, int h) {
24           int x, y;
25           Image image;
26           Graphics g;
27           int ascent, descent;
28           FontMetrics fontmetrics;
29           int pixels[];
30           boolean retval;
31           ftransp tp;
```

```
32
33          // Ignore p1, w, and h
34
35          fontmetrics = applet.getFontMetrics(font);
36          ascent = fontmetrics.getAscent();
37          descent = fontmetrics.getDescent();
38          new_width = fontmetrics.stringWidth(tx) +
39                                      Math.abs(shadow_xoffset);
40          new_height = fontmetrics.getHeight() +
41                                      Math.abs(shadow_yoffset);
42
43          image = applet.createImage(new_width, new_height);
44          g = image.getGraphics();
45          g.setFont(font);
46          g.setColor(bg);
47          g.fillRect(0, 0, new_width, new_height);
48
49          x = (shadow_xoffset < 0) ? Math.abs(shadow_xoffset) : 0;
50          y = (shadow_yoffset < 0) ? Math.abs(shadow_yoffset) : 0;
51
52          // Draw text in shadow color offset by xoffset, yoffset
53          g.setColor(shadow_color);
54          g.drawString(tx, x+shadow_xoffset,
55                          y+ascent+shadow_yoffset);
56          drawUnderline(g, fontmetrics, x+shadow_xoffset,
57                          y+ascent+shadow_yoffset+
58                          Math.max(1, (descent/4)),
59                          new_width, shadow_color);
60
61          // Now draw the main foreground text
62          g.setColor(fg);
63          g.drawString(tx, x, y+ascent);
64          drawUnderline(g, fontmetrics, x,
65                          y+ascent+Math.max(1, (descent/4)),
66                          new_width, fg);
67
68          // Grab the pixels
69          pixels = ImgGetr.getPixels(image, applet);
70          if(transparent) {
71              tp = new ftransp();
72              tp.setTransparentColor(bg);
73              pixels = tp.filter(pixels, new_width, new_height);
74          }
75          return pixels;
76      }
77  }
```

All text generating filters draw text into an off-screen image, retrieve the array of pixels that represent the image, and return the array to the calling object. Here is a list of requirements for filters that are to work in this environment:

- The `filter` method must return an array of pixels which represent the image
- The filter must set the `new_width` instance variable to the width of the image
- The filter must set the `new_height` instance variable to the height of the image

In addition, the filter may also elect to do the following:

- Define a `setparameter` method to set customizable options

The **fshadow** filter demonstrates each of these features.

The setparameter method

On line 9 the `setparameter` method is declared. The setparameter method is automatically called when the filter is specified as a **TxFilter**. For each argument specified in the HTML file, the `setparameter` method is called. The `i` parameter specifies the position at which the argument was supplied. If, for example, the HTML file includes this line,

```
<param name=TxFilter value="shadow 2 -2 green">
```

then `setparameter` is called three times because there are three arguments to shadow. The first time it is called, the `str` parameter is 2 (the first argument to shadow) and the `i` parameter is 0 (representing the first parameter). The second time, the `str` parameter is –2 and the `i` parameter is 1. The third time, the `str` parameter is `green` and the `i` parameter is 2.

The code in the `setparameter` method sets the appropriate variables that correspond to the filter parameter being set. In this example the horizontal shadow offset is 2, the vertical shadow offset is –2, and the shadow color is green. It is important to specify default values in case the HTML author does not specify an argument.

The filter method

The `filter` method contains the code that generates the text. The arguments passed to the `filter` method are ignored for all text generating filters. The arguments are used when manipulating an image, as seen in Chapter 4. None of the filters is this chapter, however, use the filter arguments.

Variables

After the parameters are set, the `filter` method is called. This is where the real work of generating the text is done. There are several instance variables defined in `ImgFilt` that are set automatically (when invoked using the **TxFilter** parameter). You can use these variables within your filter method:

`bg`	A Color object. The background color.
`fg`	A Color object. The foreground color.
`font`	A Font object. The specified font.
`tx`	A String object. The specified text.
`applet`	An Applet object. The current applet.
`underline`	A boolean variable. If true, underline the text.
`transparent`	A boolean variable. If true, make the background transparent.

Exactly what you do in the `filter` method will be up to you, but here is a general outline for a generic text generating filter:

- Determine the dimensions that the text will require

- Create an image

- Retrieve the `Graphics` context for the image

- Draw the text into the image using the `Graphics` context

- Get the array of integers representing the pixels of the image

- Set the `new_width` and `new_height` variables

- If specified, make the background transparent

- Return the pixel array

Let's look at each of these steps in the code example shown above.

Determine the dimensions that the text will require

On lines 35 through 37 the `FontMetrics` class is used to determine the size of the string based on the font. Because this code draws a shadow, we must allow some extra horizontal and vertical space for the shadow, as shown on lines 38 through 41:

```
35          fontmetrics = applet.getFontMetrics(font);
36          ascent = fontmetrics.getAscent();
37          descent = fontmetrics.getDescent();
38          new_width = fontmetrics.stringWidth(tx) +
39                                          Math.abs(shadow_xoffset);
40          new_height = fontmetrics.getHeight() +
41                                          Math.abs(shadow_yoffset);
```

Create an image

This step will probably be the same for most filters. Use the width and height that you calculated for your image and call `createImage` to create a new, empty image of the specified dimensions. Line 43 of the example performs this step.

```
43          image = applet.createImage(new_width, new_height);
```

Retrieve the Graphics context for the image

Simply call the `getGraphics` method of the image object to retrieve the `Graphics` object as shown on line 44.

```
44          g = image.getGraphics();
```

Draw the text into the image using the Graphics context

You will probably want to set the font and fill the background with the background color before drawing into the image, as shown on lines 45 and 46.

```
45          g.setFont(font);
46          g.setColor(bg);
47          g.fillRect(0, 0, new_width, new_height);
```

Then perform the filter specific tasks. In this case we will draw the string once in the shadow color with the appropriate offset, and again in the foreground color.

```
49          x = (shadow_xoffset < 0) ? Math.abs(shadow_xoffset) : 0;
50          y = (shadow_yoffset < 0) ? Math.abs(shadow_yoffset) : 0;
51
52          // Draw text in shadow color offset by xoffset, yoffset
53          g.setColor(shadow_color);
54          g.drawString(tx, x+shadow_xoffset,
55                          y+ascent+shadow_yoffset);
56          drawUnderline(g, fontmetrics, x+shadow_xoffset,
57                          y+ascent+shadow_yoffset+
58                          Math.max(1, (descent/4)),
59                          new_width, shadow_color);
60
61          // Now draw the main foreground text
62          g.setColor(fg);
63          g.drawString(tx, x, y+ascent);
64          drawUnderline(g, fontmetrics, x,
65                          y+ascent+Math.max(1, (descent/4)),
66                          new_width, fg);
```

Get the array of integers representing the pixels of the image

Simply call the getPixels method from the ImgGetr class. The getPixels method is static so you don't need to worry about instantiating ImgGetr.

```
69              pixels = ImgGetr.getPixels(image, applet);
```

Set the new_width and new_height variables

We already took care of this step when we calculated the dimensions of the image, back on lines 38 through 41.

```
38              new_width = fontmetrics.stringWidth(tx) +
39                                          Math.abs(shadow_xoffset);
40              new_height = fontmetrics.getHeight() +
41                                          Math.abs(shadow_yoffset);
```

If specified, make the background transparent

Most text generating filters will have the transparent variable set to true unless the user explicitly specified a text background color using the **TxBGColor** parameter. Check the transparent variable to determine if the background should be made transparent. For most cases you can simply use these lines of code:

```
70              if(transparent) {
71                  tp = new ftransp();
72                  tp.setTransparentColor(bg);
73                  pixels = tp.filter(pixels, new_width, new_height);
74              }
```

These lines invoke the ftransp filter, which makes transparent all pixels that match the color specified as the argument to setTransparentColor.

Return the pixel array

Finally, return the array of pixels.

```
75              return pixels;
```

What's Next?

Now you're ready to compile and install your filter. After you compile it, just put it in the same directory as the other filters. There is no other action required. The class loader will automatically find the filter at run time.

CHAPTER 4

Image
Applets

Text and images are the two most common components of any Web page. Chapter 3 covered text; this chapter covers images. The techniques developed in the last chapter applied specifically to text. In this chapter we develop new techniques to apply to images, but these can also be applied to text.

All the applets in this chapter are intended to display a single image. They are all derived from the applets in the **Fundamental Applets** and the **Text Applets** chapters. This allows you to do all the things you have learned about, including playing audio, loading URLs, using image maps, and displaying a background image behind your primary image. Even though this chapter focuses on manipulating images, you can always include an audio file that is played when the pointer enters the applet, or a URL that is loaded when the mouse button is pressed while the pointer is within the text or image.

When you are done with this chapter you will be able to display both images and text in a variety of ways, including rotated, mirrored, slanted, waved, blurred, or embossed effects. In addition to using these individual techniques, you will be able to combine most of them to produce interesting and useful results. Remember that the text capabilities of the previous chapter are all still available when displaying images.

Common Settings

Table 4–1 lists parameters that are common to all the applets in this chapter.

Table 4–1 Common Settings for All Image Applets

Name	Description	Default
AppNumMaps	The number of image maps (must be set to use image maps)	0
Map*N*_X1	The left horizontal coordinate for map *N*	0
Map*N*_Y1	The top vertical coordinate for map *N*	0
Map*N*_X2	The right horizontal coordinate for map *N*	0
Map*N*_Y2	The bottom vertical coordinate for map *N*	0
Map*N*_URL	The URL for map *N*	(none)
TestMode	If true, the pointer position is displayed in the status line	false
AudioMap*N*	The audio file to play when the pointer enters map *N*	(none)
AudioMapLoop*N*	If true, play the audio file for map *N* continuously in a loop	false
AppBGImage	The background image	(none)
AppBGImageXOffset	The horizontal offset at which to position the background image	0
AppBGImageYOffset	The vertical offset at which to position the background image	0
AppTile	If true, tile the background image	false
ImgFilter	The programs to use to manipulate the image	(none)
TxFilter	The programs to use to generate and manipulate the string	(none)
TxURL	The URL to load when the pointer is within the text and any mouse button is pressed	(none)
ImgURL	The URL to load when the pointer is within the image and any mouse button is pressed	(none)
TxAudio	The audio file to play when the pointer enters the text	(none)
TxAudioLoop	If true, continuously play the audio file for the text	false
ImgAudio	The audio file to play when the pointer enters the image	(none)
ImgAudioLoop	If true, continuously play the audio file for the image	false
Image	The image to display	(none)
ImgLoadWait	If true, the image is not displayed until it is completely loaded	false

Table 4–1 Common Settings for All Image Applets (Continued)

Name	Description	Default
ImgXOffset	The horizontal distance (in pixels) from the left side of the applet to the image	0
ImgYOffset	The vertical distance (in pixels) from the top of the applet to the image	0
ImgHorizCenter	If true, the image is horizontally centered	false
ImgVertCenter	If true, the image is vertically centered	false
ImgBorderWidth	The width of the image border (must be greater than 0 in order for a border to be drawn)	0
ImgBorderColor	The color of the image border	Set by browser
ImgBorderMargin	The distance (in pixels) from the image border to the image on all sides	0
ImgFrameThickness	The thickness of the image frame (must be greater than 0 in order for a frame to be drawn)	0
ImgFrameType	The type of image frame: **ShadowIn, ShadowOut, ShadowEtchedIn,** or **ShadowEtchedOut**	**ShadowIn**
ImgFrameMargin	The distance (in pixels) from the image frame to the image	0
Text	The string of characters to display	(none)
TxColor	The text color	Set by browser
TxBGColor	The text background color	transparent
TxYOffset	The vertical distance (in pixels) from the top of the applet to the lower left corner of the text	The height of the text
TxXOffset	The horizontal distance (in pixels) from the left side of the applet to the text	0
TxHorizCenter	If true, the text is horizontally centered	false
TxVertCenter	If true, the text is vertically centered	false
TxFont	The font of the text: **TimesRoman, Helvetica, Courier, Dialog, DialogInput,** or **ZapfDingbats**	**Dialog**
TxStyle	The style of the font: **Plain, Bold, Italic,** or **BoldItalic**	**Plain**
TxPointSize	The size of the font in points	10
TxUnderLine	If true, the text is underlined	false
TxBorderWidth	The width of the text border (must be greater than 0 in order for a border to be drawn)	0
TxBorderColor	The color of the text border	black
TxBorderMargin	The distance (in pixels) from the text border to the text on all sides	0
TxFrameThickness	The thickness of the text frame (must be greater than 0 in order for a frame to be drawn)	0

Table 4–1 Common Settings for All Image Applets (Continued)

Name	Description	Default
TxFrameType	The type of text frame: **ShadowIn, ShadowOut, ShadowEtchedIn,** or **ShadowEtchedOut**	**ShadowIn**
TxFrameMargin	The distance (in pixels) from the text frame to the text	0
AppBGColor	The background color of the applet	Set by browser
AppBorderWidth	The width of the applet border (must be greater than 0 in order for a border to be drawn)	0
AppBorderColor	The color of the applet border	black
AppFrameThickness	The thickness of the applet frame (must be greater than 0 in order for a frame to be drawn)	0
AppFrameType	The type of applet frame: **ShadowIn, ShadowOut, ShadowEtchedIn,** or **ShadowEtchedOut**	**ShadowIn**

Using Filters

In the last chapter, you learned about the **Tx*N*Filter** parameter in the description of the **MultiText** on page 91. The **Tx*N*Filter** parameter was used to specify which filter should be used to draw a particular string, so each string could be drawn uniquely. Most of the applets in this chapter display a single text and image, so the **N** is not needed in the parameter name. The **Tx*N*Filter** parameter will be used again in the **MultiImage** on page 155.

In this chapter we extend the definition and usage of the **TxFilter** parameter and introduce the **ImgFilter** parameter. Let's begin by defining what a filter is.

A filter is not actually an applet, although it corresponds to one; applets are self-contained programs that can run in a browser. The filters described in this book are actually just classes—that's objected oriented programming terminology meaning a piece of code that performs some function—that are the bases of the functional cores of applets. The applets in Chapter 3 and in this chapter are simple programs that actually just invoke a filter, which then does all the work.

In general, a filter takes an image and manipulates it in some way. Therefore, we can manipulate an image any number of times by invoking a series of filters on the same image. This is true of all the filters discussed in this chapter.

The filters introduced in the previous chapter, **Text Applets,** are slightly different in that they *generate* an image rather than manipulating an existing one. The filters introduced in this chapter require an image that already exists. In either case, the result is an image which can be further manipulated by invoking yet another filter.

To further understand this concept, suppose that you want to display smooth text that had been rotated some number of degrees. You would generate the text using the **smooth** filter and then invoke the **rotate** filter (**rotate** is introduced later in this chapter). Here's the HTML code:

```
<param name=Text        value="Some smooth text">
<param name=TxPointSize value=36>
<param name=TxFilter    value="smooth|rotate 45">
```

The **Text** parameter specifies the text to be displayed and **TxPointSize** specifies its size. The | (vertical bar) is used to join a sequence of filters, so the **TxFilter** value of "smooth|rotate 45" invokes the **smoothtext** filter, which generates text, and sends the output to the **rotate** filter. The result is smooth text that has been rotated 45 degrees.

Let's take this one step further. Suppose that you want the smoothed rotated text to also be slanted 28 degrees to the right and blurred. To accomplish all of this you would use the following **TxFilter** parameter:

```
<param name=TxFilter value="smoothtext|rotate 45|slantright 28|blur">
```

The **ImgFilter** parameter works the same way as **TxFilter**, except that it is used with images instead of text. The text generating filters described in Chapter 3 will not work with images. If you specify one of the text generating filters from Chapter 3 with an image, there is no result.

Most of the applets in this chapter automatically invoke one of the image filters. The **Mirror** applet, for example, displays the mirror image of the specified image; the **Scale** applet displays the image after scaling it horizontally and vertically.

All the applets in this chapter support text as well as images. In order to display text that appears over an image or background image, you must specify some **TxFilter**. If you want just plain text use the **Text** filter. If you do not specify a **TxFilter**, the text is displayed on a rectangular area the color of the background, which obscures the image.

Here's an example that displays an image that is slanted right 20 degrees with text that is embossed and mirrored:

```
<param name=Text        value="Engraved & mirrored">
<param name=TxPointSize value=24>
<param name=TxFilter    value="engrave|mirror">
<param name=Image       value=sailboat.gif>
<param name=ImgFilter   value="slantright 20">
```

Img

Displays an image

Description

The **Img** applet displays an unaltered image.

This applet may appear to be just like the **BasicImage** on page 27. It is implemented using filters, however, as described at the beginning of this chapter.

Using Img in HTML Code

The following HTML code display a company logo:

```
<applet
    archive  = Img2.zip
    codebase = Img2
    code     = Img.class
    width    = 179
    height   = 179>
<param name=Image      value=Img2/vivid.gif>
<param name=AppBGColor value=white>
<param name=ImgXOffset value=10>
<param name=ImgYOffset value=10>
</applet>
```

Settings

See Table 4–1 on page 104 for common settings that apply to this applet.

See Also

URL for **Img**:   http://www.vivids.com/ij2/image/Img.html

ImageShadow

Displays an image with a shadow

Description

The **ImageShadow** applet displays an image with a shadow.

The **ImageShadow** applet creates the shadow based on the opaque portion of the image. If the image has transparent pixels, only the non-transparent pixels are used to create the shadow.

Using ImageShadow in HTML Code

The following HTML code displays a bouquet image that has a transparent background. Notice the shadow is created only around the flowers and text.

```
<applet
    archive  = ImageShadow2.zip
    codebase = ImageShadow2
    code     = ImageShadow.class
    width    = 216
    height   = 180>
<param name=Image           value=ImageShadow2/bouquet.gif>
<param name=AppBGColor      value=white>
<param name=ShadowXOffset value=6>
<param name=ShadowYOffset value=-6>
<param name=ShadowColor     value=#dddddd>
</applet>
```

Settings

See Table 4–1 on page 104 for common settings that apply to this applet. Three additional parameters set the color and offset of the shadow.

Table 4–2 ImageShadow Applet Settings

Name	Description	Default
ShadowXOffset	The horizontal offset (in pixels) of the shadow	2
ShadowYOffset	The vertical offset (in pixels) of the shadow	2
ShadowColor	The color of the shadow	gray (#444444)

See Also

Related applets: **Shadow** on page 64
                     SoftShadow on page 66
                     MultiColorShadow on page 89

URL for **ImageShadow**:   `http://www.vivids.com/ij2/image/ImageShadow.html`

Rotate

Rotates an image counter clockwise

Description

The **Rotate** applet rotates the image an arbitrary number of degrees counter clockwise.

Using **Rotate** in HTML Code

The following HTML code rotates the company logo −10 degrees against a background image.

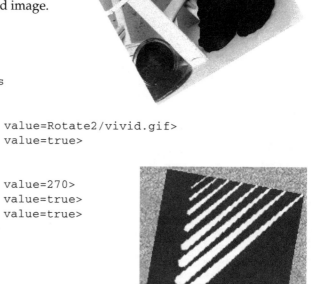

```
<applet
    archive  = Rotate2.zip
    codebase = Rotate2
    code     = Rotate.class
    width    = 240
    height   = 240>
<param name=Image          value=Rotate2/vivid.gif>
<param name=AppTile        value=true>
<param name=AppBGImage
value=Rotate2/pattern.gif>
<param name=Degree         value=270>
<param name=ImgVertCenter  value=true>
<param name=ImgHorizCenter value=true>
</applet>
```

Settings

See Table 4–1 on page 104 for common settings that apply to this applet. One other parameter sets the degree of rotation.

Table 4–3 Rotate Applet Settings

Name	Description	Default
Degree	The degree of rotation	0

See Also

URL for **Rotate**:   http://www.vivids.com/ij2/image/Rotate.html

Mirror

Mirrors an image

Description

The **Mirror** applet flips the image around its vertical center line.

Using Mirror in HTML Code

The following HTML code mirrors the company logo. The applet also displays the string *VIVID,* which is drawn using the **depthfade** text generating filter.

```
<applet
    archive  = Mirror2.zip
    codebase = Mirror2
    code     = Mirror.class
    width    = 220
    height   = 220>
<param name=Image           value=Mirror2/vivid.gif>
<param name=ImgVertCenter   value=true>
<param name=ImgHorizCenter  value=true>
<param name=ImgAudio        value=Mirror2/welcome.au>
<param name=AppBGColor      value=white>
<param name=Text            value="VIVID">
<param name=TxPointSize     value=36>
<param name=TxStyle         value=Bold>
<param name=TxXOffset       value=10>
<param name=TxYOffset       value=135>
<param name=TxColor         value=black>
<param name=TxFilter        value="depthfade 10 -10 #00849c">
</applet>
```

Settings

See Table 4–1 on page 104 for common settings that apply to this applet.

See Also

URL for **Mirror**:   http://www.vivids.com/ij2/image/Mirror.html

SlantRight

Slant an image to the right

Description

The **SlantRight** applet slants the image to the right.

Using SlantRight in HTML Code

The following HTML code slants the company logo 45 degrees.

```
<applet
    archive  = SlantRight2.zip
    codebase = SlantRight2
    code     = SlantRight.class
    width    = 440
    height   = 200>
<param name=Image           value=SlantRight2/vivid.gif>
<param name=ImgVertCenter   value=true>
<param name=ImgHorizCenter  value=true>
<param name=AppBGColor      value=white>
<param name=Angle           value=45>
</applet>
```

Settings

See Table 4–1 on page 104 for common settings that apply to this applet. One other parameter sets the slant angle.

Table 4–4 SlantRight Applet Settings

Name	Description	Default
Angle	The slant angle	45

See Also

Related applets:

SlantLeft on page 115
SlantUp on page 117
SlantDown on page 118

URL for **SlantRight**:

http://www.vivids.com/ij2/image/SlantRight.html

SlantLeft

Slants an image to the left

Description

The **SlantLeft** applet slants the image to the left.

Using **SlantLeft** in HTML Code

The following HTML code slants the company logo 25 degrees. The image is enclosed in a **ShadowEtchedOut** frame and displayed against a background color that closely matches the background color of the image.

```
<applet
    archive  = SlantLeft2.zip
    codebase = SlantLeft2
    code     = SlantLeft.class
    width    = 350
    height   = 200>
<param name=Image             value=SlantLeft2/vivid.gif>
<param name=ImgVertCenter     value=true>
<param name=ImgHorizCenter    value=true>
<param name=Angle             value=25>
<param name=AppBGColor        value=#00849c>
<param name=ImgFrameThickness value=6>
<param name=ImgFrameType      value=ShadowEtchedIn>
<param name=ImgFrameMargin    value=2>
</applet>
```

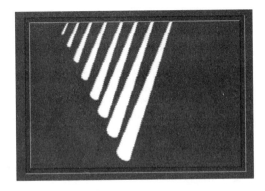

Note that the frame in the example is not slanted. Frames and borders are drawn independent of any image processing.

Settings

See Table 4–1 on page 104 for common settings that apply to this applet. One other parameter sets the slant angle.

Table 4–5 SlantLeft Applet Settings

Name	Description	Default
Angle	The slant angle	45

See Also

Related applets:

SlantRight on page 114
SlantUp on page 117
SlantDown on page 118

URL for **SlantLeft**:

`http://www.vivids.com/ij2/image/SlantLeft.html`

SlantUp

Slants an image up

Description

The **SlantUp** applet slants the image up.

Using SlantUp in HTML Code

The following HTML code slants the logo up 20 degrees and also slants it right 20 degrees.

```
<applet
    archive  = SlantUp2.zip
    codebase = SlantUp2
    code     = SlantUp.class
    width    = 260
    height   = 300>
<param name=Image          value=SlantUp2/vivid.gif>
<param name=ImgVertCenter  value=true>
<param name=ImgHorizCenter value=true>
<param name=Angle          value=20>
<param name=AppBGColor     value=#ffffff>
<param name=ImgFilter      value="slantright 20">
</applet>
```

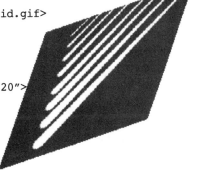

Settings

See Table 4–1 on page 104 for common settings that apply to this applet. One other parameter sets the slant angle.

Table 4–6 SlantUp Applet Settings

Name	Description	Default
Angle	The slant angle	45

See Also

Related applets:

SlantRight on page 114
SlantLeft on page 115
SlantDown on page 118

URL for **SlantUp**:

`http://www.vivids.com/ij2/image/SlantUp.html`

SlantDown

Slants an image down

Description

The **SlantDown** applet slants the image down.

Using SlantDown in HTML Code

The following HTML code slants the logo against a black background. The text has the same slant as the image. The horizontal and vertical offsets of the text result in the text overlapping the image and the background.

```
<applet
     archive  = SlantDown2.zip
     codebase = SlantDown2
     code     = SlantDown.class
     width    = 200
     height   = 250>
<param name=Image        value=SlantDown2/vivid.gif>
<param name=ImgXOffset   value=20>
<param name=ImgYOffset   value=20>
<param name=Angle        value=10>
<param name=AppBGColor   value=#000000>
<param name=TxColor      value=#ffffff>
<param name=Text         value=VIVID>
<param name=TxPointSize  value=36>
<param name=TxFont       value=Helvetica>
<param name=TxStyle      value=Bold>
<param name=TxXOffset    value=50>
<param name=TxYOffset    value=168>
<param name=TxFilter     value="text|slantdown 10">
</applet>
```

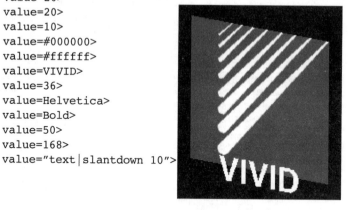

Settings

See Table 4–1 on page 104 for common settings that apply to this applet. One other parameter sets the slant angle.

Table 4–7 SlantDown Applet Settings

Name	Description	Default
Angle	The slant angle	45

See Also

Related applets: **SlantRight** on page 114
SlantLeft on page 115
SlantUp on page 117

URL for **SlantDown**:   `http://www.vivids.com/ij2/image/SlantDown.html`

SqueezeRight

Squeeze the right side of an image

Description

The **SqueezeRight** applet squeezes an image in the direction of the right side. The image may be squeezed toward the top right, center right, or bottom right.

Using SqueezeRight in HTML Code

The following HTML code squeeze the logo 90% up and to the right.

```
<applet
    archive  = SqueezeRight2.zip
    codebase = SqueezeRight2
    code     = SqueezeRight.class
    width    = 159
    height   = 159>
<param name=Image      value=SqueezeRight2/vivid.gif>
<param name=SqueezePerc value=90>
<param name=Direction   value=Up>
</applet>
```

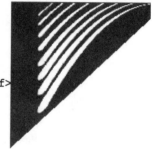

The next example squeeze the logo 100% down and to the right.

```
<applet
    archive  = SqueezeRight3.zip
    codebase = SqueezeRight3
    code     = SqueezeRight.class
    width    = 159
    height   = 159>
<param name=Image      value=SqueezeRight3/vivid.gif>
<param name=SqueezePerc value=100>
<param name=Direction   value=Down>
</applet>
```

Settings

See Table 4–1 on page 104 for common settings that apply to this applet. Two other parameters sets the squeeze percentage and the direction of the squeeze.

Table 4–8 SqueezeRight Applet Settings

Name	Description	Default
SqueezePerc	The squeeze percentage	100
Direction	The direction of the squeeze: **Up, Center, Down**	Center

See Also

Related applets: **SqueezeLeft** on page 122
SqueezeUp on page 124
SqueezeDown on page 126

URL for **SqueezeRight**: http://www.vivids.com/ij2/image/SqueezeRight.html

SqueezeLeft

Squeeze the left side of an image

Description

The **SqueezeLeft** applet squeezes the left side of an image. The image may be squeezed toward the top left, center left, or bottom left.

Using SqueezeLeft in HTML Code

The following HTML code squeeze the logo 90% up and to the left.

```
<applet
    archive  = SqueezeLeft2.zip
    codebase = SqueezeLeft2
    code     = SqueezeLeft.class
    width    = 159
    height   = 159>
<param name=Image       value=SqueezeLeft2/vivid.gif>
<param name=SqueezePerc value=90>
<param name=Direction   value=Up>
</applet>
```

The next example squeeze the logo 100% down and to the left.

```
<applet
    archive  = SqueezeLeft3.zip
    codebase = SqueezeLeft3
    code     = SqueezeLeft.class
    width    = 159
    height   = 159>
<param name=Image       value=SqueezeLeft3/vivid.gif>
<param name=SqueezePerc value=100>
<param name=Direction   value=Down>
</applet>
```

Settings

See Table 4–1 on page 104 for common settings that apply to this applet. Two other parameters sets the squeeze percentage and the direction of the squeeze.

Table 4–9 SqueezeLeft Applet Settings

Name	Description	Default
SqueezePerc	The squeeze percentage	100
Direction	The direction of the squeeze: **Up, Center, Down**	Center

See Also

Related applets: **SqueezeRight** on page 120
SqueezeUp on page 124
SqueezeDown on page 126

URL for **SqueezeLeft**: `http://www.vivids.com/ij2/image/SqueezeLeft.html`

SqueezeUp

Squeeze the top side of an image

Description

The **SqueezeUp** applet squeezes the top side of an image.
The image may be squeezed toward the top left, top center,
or top right.

Using SqueezeUp in HTML Code

The following HTML code squeeze the logo 90% left and to
the top.

```
<applet
    archive  = SqueezeUp2.zip
    codebase = SqueezeUp2
    code     = SqueezeUp.class
    width    = 159
    height   = 159>
<param name=Image       value=SqueezeUp2/vivid.gif>
<param name=SqueezePerc value=90>
<param name=Direction   value=Left>
</applet>
```

The next example squeeze the logo 100% left and to the top.

```
<applet
    archive  = SqueezeUp3.zip
    codebase = SqueezeUp3
    code     = SqueezeUp.class
    width    = 159
    height   = 159>
<param name=Image       value=SqueezeUp3/vivid.gif>
<param name=SqueezePerc value=100>
<param name=Direction   value=Right>
</applet>
```

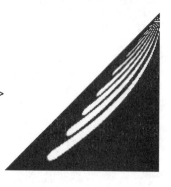

Settings

See Table 4–1 on page 104 for common settings that apply to this applet. Two other parameters sets the squeeze percentage and the direction of the squeeze.

Table 4–10 SqueezeUp Applet Settings

Name	Description	Default
SqueezePerc	The squeeze percentage	100
Direction	The direction of the squeeze: **Left, Center, Right**	Center

See Also

Related applets: **SqueezeRight** on page 120
SqueezeLeft on page 122
SqueezeDown on page 126

URL for **SqueezeUp**:   `http://www.vivids.com/ij2/image/SqueezeUp.html`

SqueezeDown

Squeeze the bottom side of an image

Description

The **SqueezeDown** applet squeezes the left side of an image. The image may be squeezed toward the top left, center left, or bottom left.

Using SqueezeDown in HTML Code

The following HTML code squeezes the logo 90% left and to the bottom.

```
<applet
    archive  = SqueezeDown2.zip
    codebase = SqueezeDown2
    code     = SqueezeDown.class
    width    = 159
    height   = 159>
<param name=Image       value=SqueezeDown2/vivid.gif>
<param name=SqueezePerc value=90>
<param name=Direction   value=Left>
</applet>
```

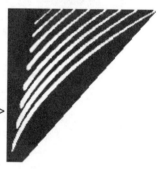

The next example squeezes the logo 100% left and to the bottom.

```
<applet
    archive  = SqueezeDown3.zip
    codebase = SqueezeDown3
    code     = SqueezeDown.class
    width    = 159
    height   = 159>
<param name=Image       value=SqueezeDown3/vivid.gif>
<param name=SqueezePerc value=100>
<param name=Direction   value=Right>
</applet>
```

Settings

See Table 4–1 on page 104 for common settings that apply to this applet. Two other parameters sets the squeeze percentage and the direction of the squeeze.

Table 4–11 SqueezeDown Applet Settings

Name	Description	Default
SqueezePerc	The squeeze percentage	100
Direction	The direction of the squeeze: **Left, Center, Right**	Center

See Also

Related applets: **SqueezeRight** on page 120
                       SqueezeLeft on page 122
                       SqueezeUp on page 124

URL for **SqueezeDown**:   http://www.vivids.com/ij2/image/SqueezeDown.html

WaveImage

Alters an image along a sine wave

Description

The **WaveImage** applet creates a sine wave pattern in the image. It is similar to the **WaveText** on page 70.

Using WaveImage in HTML Code

The following HTML code uses the **WaveImage** applet to distort the company logo by setting **Amplitude** to 35 and **WaveLength** to 8.

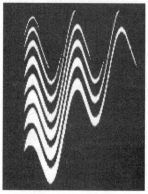

```
<applet
    archive  = WaveImage2.zip
    codebase = WaveImage2
    code     = WaveImage.class
    width    = 250
    height   = 250>
<param name=Image      value=WaveImage2/vivid.gif>
<param name=Amplitude  value=35>
<param name=WaveLength value=8>
<param name=ImgXOffset value=20>
<param name=ImgYOffset value=20>
<param name=AppBGColor value=#00849c>
</applet>
```

The following example uses the **BeginRange**, **EndRange**, and **XTranslate** parameters to create an ocean wave effect through part of an image of sailboats.

```
<applet
    archive  = WaveImage3.zip
    codebase = WaveImage3
    code     = WaveImage.class
    width    = 360
    height   = 280>
<param name=Image      value=WaveImage3/sailboat.gif>
<param name=Amplitude  value=10>
<param name=WaveLength value=8>
<param name=BeginRange value=22>
<param name=EndRange   value=200>
<param name=XTranslate value=-2>
<param name=AppBGColor value=white>
</applet>
```

Settings

See Table 4–1 on page 104 for common settings that apply to this applet. Six additional parameters set the amplitude, wavelength, horizontal and vertical translation, and the begin and end range.

Table 4–12 WaveImage Applet Settings

Name	Description	Default
Amplitude	The amplitude of the wave (in pixels)	10
WaveLength	The wave length of the wave	10
XTranslate	The horizontal translation (in pixels)	0
YTranslate	The vertical translation (in pixels)	0
BeginRange	The pixel at which to begin the sinewave function	0
EngRange	The pixel at which to end the sinewave function	width of image

See Also

Related applets:	**WaveText** on page 70
URL for **WaveImage**:	http://www.vivids.com/ij2/image/WaveImage.html

Blur

Blurs an image

Description

The **Blur** applet blurs the image by sampling surrounding pixels.

Using **Blur** in HTML Code

The following HTML code uses the **Blur** applet to blur the company logo four times in all. This produces an extremely blurred image.

```
<applet
    archive  = Blur2.zip
    codebase = Blur2
    code     = Blur.class
    width    = 200
    height   = 200>
<param name=Image        value=Blur2/vivid.gif>
<param name=ImgVertCenter  value=true>
<param name=ImgHorizCenter value=true>
</applet>
```

Settings

See Table 4–1 on page 104 for common settings that apply to this applet. One additional parameter sets the blur amount.

Table 4–13 Blur Applet Settings

Name	Description	Default
Blur	The amount of the blur	1

See Also

URL for **Blur**: http://www.vivids.com/ij2/image/Blur.html

EmbossImage

Creates an embossed effect in an image

Description

The **EmbossImage** applet displays the image with a directional edge enhancement for an embossed effect.

Using EmbossImage in HTML Code

The following HTML code uses the **EmbossImage** applet to emboss the image to the **NorthWest**:

```
<applet
    archive  = EmbossImage2.zip
    codebase = EmbossImage2
    code     = EmbossImage.class
    width    = 180
    height   = 180>
<param name=Image          value=EmbossImage2/vivid.gif>
<param name=ImgVertCenter  value=true>
<param name=ImgHorizCenter value=true>
<param name=AppBGColor     value=#ffffff>
<param name=Direction      value=NorthWest>
</applet>
```

The next example displays the same image but sets the direction to **SouthWest**.

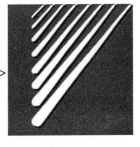

```
<applet
    archive  = EmbossImage3.zip
    codebase = EmbossImage3
    code     = EmbossImage.class
    width    = 180
    height   = 180>
<param name=Image          value=EmbossImage3/vivid.gif>
<param name=ImgVertCenter  value=true>
<param name=ImgHorizCenter value=true>
<param name=AppBGColor     value=#ffffff>
<param name=Direction      value=SouthEast>
</applet>
```

Settings

See Table 4–1 on page 104 for common settings that apply to this applet. One additional parameter sets the direction of the embossing.

Table 4–14 EmbossImage Applet Settings

Name	Description	Default
Direction	The direction of the embossing: **North, South, East, West, NorthWest, NorthEast, SouthWest, SouthEast**	**West**

See Also

Related applets: **Emboss** on page 79

URL for **EmbossImage**:   `http://www.vivids.com/ij2/image/EmbossImage.html`

TransColor

Makes one or more of an image's colors transparent

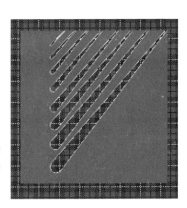

Description

The **TransColor** applet removes the specified colors from the image, creating transparency instead. There is no limit to the number of colors that can be made transparent.

Using **TransColor** in HTML Code

The following HTML code uses the **TransColor** applet to make the image partially transparent. The solid color in the logo is actually a composite of several colors. The **Colors** parameter includes several but not all of the colors which constitute the logo's background color, resulting in a partially transparent look.

```
<applet
    archive   = TransColor2.zip
    codebase  = TransColor2
    code      = TransColor.class
    width     = 200
    height    = 200>
<param name=Image          value=TransColor2/vivid.gif>
<param name=AppBGImage     value=TransColor2/plaid.gif>
<param name=AppTile        value=true>
<param name=ImgVertCenter  value=true>
<param name=ImgHorizCenter value=true>
<param name=Colors      value="#088ca5 #0884a5 #008ca5 #0084a5 #007b9c">
</applet>
```

The next example makes transparent all the colors in the logo's background. Only the white solids from the logo remain, displayed over the background image.

```
<applet
    archive  = TransColor3.zip
    codebase = TransColor3
    code     = TransColor.class
    width    = 200
    height   = 200>
<param name=Image           value=TransColor3/vivid.gif>
<param name=AppBGImage      value=TransColor3/plaid.gif>
<param name=AppTile         value=true>
<param name=ImgVertCenter   value=true>
<param name=ImgHorizCenter value=true>
<param name=Colors          value="#088ca5 #0884a5 #008ca5 #0084a5 #00849c
#007b9c">
</applet>
```

Settings

See Table 4–1 on page 104 for common settings that apply to this applet. One additional parameter sets the colors that are to be made transparent. Each color in the list is separated by a space. The list of colors must be enclosed in double quotes, with spaces separating the colors.

Table 4–15 TransColor Applet Settings

Name	Description	Default
Colors	The colors to make transparent	(none)

See Also

Related applets: **Stencil** on page 85
Transparent on page 139

URL for **TransColor**:   http://www.vivids.com/ij2/image/TransColor.html

Scale

Alters the horizontal or vertical scale of an image

Description

The **Scale** applet horizontally or vertically scales an image. You can scale one or the other dimension, or both. You can scale one amount in one dimension and another in the other dimension. The picture at right is scaled 50% in the horizontal dimension only.

Using Scale in HTML Code

The following HTML code uses the **Scale** applet to rescale the logo 300% horizontally and 50% vertically.

```
<applet
    archive  = Scale2.zip
    codebase = Scale2
    code     = Scale.class
    width    = 500
    height   = 100>
<param name=Image          value=Scale2/vivid.gif>
<param name=ImgVertCenter  value=true>
<param name=ImgHorizCenter value=true>
<param name=AppBGColor     value=#ffffff>
<param name=ScaleX         value=300>
<param name=ScaleY         value=50>
</applet>
```

Settings

See Table 4–1 on page 104 for common settings that apply to this applet. Three additional parameters set the scale factors.

Table 4–16 Scale Applet Settings

Name	Description	Default
ScaleX	The percentage to rescale in the horizontal direction	100
ScaleY	The percentage to rescale in the vertical direction	100
Scale	The percentage to rescale in both directions (overrides **ScaleX** and **ScaleY)**	100

The **ScaleX** and **ScaleY** parameters are for setting the horizontal and vertical scale factors respectively. The scale factor is a percentage where 100 represents no rescaling, 50 represents half size, and 200 represents double size.

The **Scale** parameter overrides both the **ScaleX** and **ScaleY** parameters. Using **Scale** always preserves the original aspect ratio.

See Also

URL for **Scale**:   `http://www.vivids.com/ij2/image/Scale.html`

Negative

Displays an image with negative colors

Description

The **Negative** applet displays an image with negative colors. Each component (red, green, blue) of each color is subtracted from 255—the maximum color intensity—to produce the negative color. The effect is similar to that of looking at the negative of a color photograph.

Using Negative in HTML Code

The following HTML code uses the **Negative** applet to display the company logo with negative colors.

```
<applet
    archive  = Negative2.zip
    codebase = Negative2
    code     = Negative.class
    width    = 159
    height   = 159>
<param name=Image          value=Negative2/vivid.gif>
<param name=ImgVertCenter  value=true>
<param name=ImgHorizCenter value=true>
</applet>
```

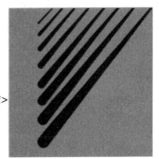

Settings

See Table 4–1 on page 104 for common settings that apply to this applet. One additional parameter sets the number (default is 255) from which to subtract the color components.

Table 4–17 Negative Applet Settings

Name	Description	Default
SubFrom	The number from which to subtract each color component	255

Setting the **SubFrom** parameter to 0 will produce the original unaltered image. **SubFrom** values greater than 255 produce unpredictable (though interesting) results.

See Also

URL for **Negative**:　　　　http://www.vivids.com/ij2/image/Negative.html

Fade

Displays an image with faded colors

Description

The **Fade** applet fades an image. This fading is accomplished by altering the colors of the image toward one specific color. By default, the image is faded toward the background color. You can also specify another color to which the image is faded.

Using Fade in HTML Code

The following HTML code uses the **Fade** applet to fade the company logo 75 percent toward white. Note the washed out appearance.

```
<applet
    archive  = Fade2.zip
    codebase = Fade2
    code     = Fade.class
    width    = 159
    height   = 159>
<param name=Image     value=Fade2/vivid.gif>
<param name=Percent   value=75>
<param name=FadeColor value=white>
</applet>
```

Settings

See Table 4–1 on page 104 for common settings that apply to this applet. Two additional parameters set the color to which to fade and the percent fade.

Table 4–18 Fade Applet Settings

Name	Description	Default
Percent	The percentage (0 to 100) to fades the image's colors	0
FadeToColor	The color to which the image is faded	AppBgColor

Fading an image 100% turns the image into a solid area of the **FadeToColor** specified. Fading 0% leaves the image unaltered.

See Also

Related applets: **SlideShowFade** on page 260

URL for **Fade**: http://www.vivids.com/ij2/image/Fade.html

Transparent

Displays an image with a degree of transparency

Description

The **Transparent** applet displays an image with the specified percentage transparency. The higher the percentage transparency, the more transparent the image. A transparency of 100% will cause the image to completely disappear.

Using Transparent in HTML Code

The following HTML code uses the **Transparent** applet to display the company logo against a plaid background and with a yellow frame. The **Transparency** parameter is set to 40.

```
<applet
    archive  = Transparent2.zip
    codebase = Transparent2
    code     = Transparent.class
    width    = 200
    height   = 200>
<param name=AppBGImage       value=Transparent2/plaid.gif>
<param name=Image            value=Transparent2/vivid.gif>
<param name=Transparency     value=40>
<param name=ImgHorizCenter   value=true>
<param name=ImgVertCenter    value=true>
<param name=ImgFrameThickness value=2>
<param name=ImgFrameType     value=ShadowEtchedOut>
<param name=ImgFrameMargin   value=5>
<param name=AppBGColor       value=yellow>
<param name=AppTile          value=true>
</applet>
```

Settings

See Table 4–1 on page 104 for common settings that apply to this applet. One additional parameter sets the transparency percentage.

Table 4–19 Transparent Applet Settings

Name	Description	Default
Transparency	The percentage transparency	0

See Also

Related applets: **TransColor** on page 133

URL for **Transparent**:   `http://www.vivids.com/ij2/image/Transparent.html`

ReplaceColor

Displays an image with colors replaced

Description

The **ReplaceColor** applet displays an image with specified colors replaced. One or more colors can be replaced with a different color. A closeness factor is also available so that colors are replaced if they are *close* to the color specified.

Colors are specified by listing a pair of colors separated by an equals sign. For example,

```
white=black
```

indicates that all white pixels be replaced with black. You may specify multiple colors to be replaced by providing multiple color pairs as shown in the second example below.

Using **ReplaceColor** in HTML Code

The following HTML code uses the **ReplaceColor** applet to display the company logo. All white pixels are replaced with black pixels.

```
<applet
    archive  = ReplaceColor2.zip
    codebase = ReplaceColor2
    code     = ReplaceColor.class
    width    = 159
    height   = 159>
<param name=Image           value=ReplaceColor2/vivid.gif>
<param name=ImgVertCenter   value=true>
<param name=ImgHorizCenter  value=true>
<param name=Colors          value="white=black">
</applet>
```

The next example displays a sailboat. The white in the clouds and sails is replaced with black. The orange in the sun is replaced with red. The **Closeness** parameter is set to 10 which means that colors that are within 10% closeness to the colors to be replaced (white and #f7ce08) are replaced.

```
<applet
    archive  = ReplaceColor3.zip
    codebase = ReplaceColor3
    code     = ReplaceColor.class
    width    = 336
```

```
        height    = 226>
    <param name=Image        value=ReplaceColor3/sailboat.gif>
    <param name=Closeness    value=10>
    <param name=Colors       value="white=black #f7ce08=red">
    </applet>
```

Settings

See Table 4–1 on page 104 for common settings that apply to this applet. Two additional parameters set the closeness percentage and the colors to replace.

Table 4–20 ReplaceColor Applet Settings

Name	Description	Default
Closeness	The percentage within which a color must be in order to be considered a match. 0 means it must be an exact match	0
Colors	The colors to replace	(none)

See Also

Related applets: **TransColor** on page 133

URL for **ReplaceColor**:   http://www.vivids.com/ij2/image/ReplaceColor.html

BlackAndWhite

Displays an image with a degree of black and white

Description

The **BlackAndWhite** applet displays a color image with a percentage black and white. The higher the percentage black and white, the more black and white the image. When the black and white percentage is specified at 100, the image is completely without color. A black and white percentage of 0 means that the colors are displayed without alteration.

Using BlackAndWhite in HTML Code

The following HTML code uses the **BlackAndWhite** applet to display a sailboat against a plaid background and with a yellow frame. The **Percent** parameter defaults to 100.

```
<applet
    archive  = BlackAndWhite2.zip
    codebase = BlackAndWhite2
    code     = BlackAndWhite.class
    width    = 336
    height   = 226>
<param name=Image value=BlackAndWhite2/sailboat.gif>
</applet>
```

Settings

See Table 4–1 on page 104 for common settings that apply to this applet. One additional parameter sets the black and white percentage.

Table 4–21 BlackAndWhite Applet Settings

Name	Description	Default
Percent	The percentage black and white	100

See Also

URL for **BlackAndWhite**:   http://www.vivids.com/ij2/image/BlackAndWhite.html

CropRectangle

Crops an image to a rectangular region

Description

The **CropRectangle** applet displays an image that has been cropped to fit the specified rectangular region. The image area outside the cropped region reveals the background color or image behind it.

Using CropRectangle in HTML Code

The following HTML code uses the **CropRectangle** applet to display the cropped company logo against a plaid background.

```
<applet
    archive  = CropRectangle2.zip
    codebase = CropRectangle2
    code     = CropRectangle.class
    width    = 159
    height   = 159>
<param name=AppBGImage  value=CropRectangle2/plaid.gif>
<param name=Image       value=CropRectangle2/vivid.gif>
<param name=CropXOffset value=25>
<param name=CropYOffset value=25>
<param name=CropWidth   value=75>
<param name=CropHeight  value=125>
<param name=AppTile     value=true>
</applet>
```

Settings

See Table 4–1 on page 104 for common settings that apply to this applet. Four additional parameters set the horizontal and vertical position, and the width and height of the crop region.

Table 4–22 CropRectangle Applet Settings

Name	Description	Default
CropXOffset	The horizontal offset of the crop region (in pixels)	0
CropYOffset	The vertical offset of the crop region (in pixels)	0
CropWidth	The width of the crop region (in pixels)	The width of the image
CropHeight	The height of the crop region (in pixels)	The height of the image

See Also

Related applets:

RemoveRectangle on page 145
CropOval on page 147
RemoveOval on page 149
CropRoundRect on page 151
RemoveRoundRect on page 153

URL for **CropRectangle**: `http://www.vivids.com/ij2/image/CropRectangle.html`

RemoveRectangle

Removes a rectangular region from an image

Description

The **RemoveRectangle** applet removes a rectangular region
from an image. The removed part of the image reveals the
background color or image behind it.

Using **RemoveRectangle** in HTML Code

The following HTML code uses the **RemoveRectangle** applet
to display the altered company logo against a plaid background.

```
<applet
    archive  = RemoveRectangle2.zip
    codebase = RemoveRectangle2
    code     = RemoveRectangle.class
    width    = 159
    height   = 159>
<param name=AppBGImage   value=RemoveRectangle2/plaid.gif>
<param name=AppTile      value=true>
<param name=Image        value=RemoveRectangle2/vivid.gif>
<param name=CropXOffset value=25>
<param name=CropYOffset value=25>
<param name=CropWidth    value=75>
<param name=CropHeight   value=125>
</applet>
```

Settings

See Table 4–1 on page 104 for common settings that apply to
this applet. Four additional parameters set the horizontal and
vertical position, and the width and height of the crop region.

Table 4–23 RemoveRectangle Applet Settings

Name	Description	Default
CropXOffset	The horizontal offset of the crop region (in pixels)	0
CropYOffset	The vertical offset of the crop region (in pixels)	0
CropWidth	The width of the crop region (in pixels)	The width of the image
CropHeight	The height of the crop region (in pixels)	The height of the image

See Also

Related applets:

CropRectangle on page 143
CropOval on page 147
RemoveOval on page 149
CropRoundRect on page 151
RemoveRoundRect on page 153

URL for **RemoveRectangle**: `http://www.vivids.com/ij2/image/RemoveRectangle.html`

CropOval

Crops an image to an oval region

Description

The **CropOval** applet displays an image that has been cropped to fit the specified oval region. The image area outside the cropped region reveals the background color or image behind it.

Using CropOval in HTML Code

The following HTML code uses the **CropOval** applet to display the cropped company logo against a plaid background.

```
<applet
    archive  = CropOval2.zip
    codebase = CropOval2
    code     = CropOval.class
    width    = 159
    height   = 159>
<param name=AppBGImage  value=CropOval2/plaid.gif>
<param name=AppTile     value=true>
<param name=Image       value=CropOval2/vivid.gif>
<param name=CropXOffset value=25>
<param name=CropYOffset value=25>
<param name=CropWidth   value=75>
<param name=CropHeight  value=125>
</applet>
```

Settings

See Table 4–1 on page 104 for common settings that apply to this applet. Four additional parameters set the horizontal and vertical position, and the width and height of the crop region.

Table 4–24 CropOval Applet Settings

Name	Description	Default
CropXOffset	The horizontal offset of the crop region (in pixels)	0
CropYOffset	The vertical offset of the crop region (in pixels)	0
CropWidth	The width of the crop region (in pixels)	The width of the image
CropHeight	The height of the crop region (in pixels)	The height of the image

If the **CropWidth** and **CropHeight** parameters are identical the cropped region will be a circle.

See Also

Related applets:

CropRectangle on page 143
RemoveRectangle on page 145
RemoveOval on page 149
CropRoundRect on page 151
RemoveRoundRect on page 153

URL for **CropOval**:

`http://www.vivids.com/ij2/image/CropOval.html`

RemoveOval

Removes an oval region from an image

Description
The **RemoveOval** applet removes an oval region from an image. The removed part of the image reveals the background color or image behind it.

Using RemoveOval in HTML Code
The following HTML code uses the **RemoveOval** applet to display the altered company logo against a plaid background.

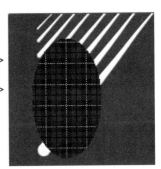

```
<applet
    archive  = RemoveOval2.zip
    codebase = RemoveOval2
    code     = RemoveOval.class
    width    = 159
    height   = 159>
<param name=AppBGImage  value=RemoveOval2/plaid.gif>
<param name=AppTile     value=true>
<param name=Image       value=RemoveOval2/vivid.gif>
<param name=CropXOffset value=25>
<param name=CropYOffset value=25>
<param name=CropWidth   value=75>
<param name=CropHeight  value=125>
</applet>
```

Settings
See Table 4–1 on page 104 for common settings that apply to this applet. Four additional parameters set the horizontal and vertical position, and the width and height of the crop region.

Table 4–25 RemoveOval Applet Settings

Name	Description	Default
CropXOffset	The horizontal offset of the crop region (in pixels)	0
CropYOffset	The vertical offset of the crop region (in pixels)	0
CropWidth	The width of the crop region (in pixels)	The width of the image
CropHeight	The height of the crop region (in pixels)	The height of the image

If the **CropWidth** and **CropHeight** parameters are identical the cropped region will be a circle.

See Also

Related applets:

CropRectangle on page 143
RemoveRectangle on page 145
CropOval on page 147
CropRoundRect on page 151
RemoveRoundRect on page 153

URL for **RemoveOval**:

`http://www.vivids.com/ij2/image/RemoveOval.html`

CropRoundRect

Crops an image to a rounded rectangular region

Description

The **CropRoundRect** applet displays an image that has been cropped to fit the specified rounded rectangular region. The image area outside the cropped region reveals the background color or image behind it.

Using CropRoundRect in HTML Code

The following HTML code uses the **CropRoundRect** applet to display the cropped company logo against a plaid background.

```
<applet
    archive  = CropRoundRect2.zip
    codebase = CropRoundRect2
    code     = CropRoundRect.class
    width    = 159
    height   = 159>
<param name=AppBGImage  value=CropRoundRect2/plaid.gif>
<param name=AppTile     value=true>
<param name=Image       value=CropRoundRect2/vivid.gif>
<param name=CropXOffset value=25>
<param name=CropYOffset value=25>
<param name=CropWidth   value=75>
<param name=CropHeight  value=125>
<param name=ArcWidth    value=20>
<param name=ArcHeight   value=60>
</applet>
```

Settings

See Table 4–1 on page 104 for common settings that apply to this applet. Six additional parameters set the horizontal and vertical position, the width and height of the crop region, and the horizontal and vertical diameters of the arcs at the four corners.

Table 4–26 CropRoundRect Applet Settings

Name	Description	Default
CropXOffset	The horizontal offset of the crop region (in pixels)	0
CropYOffset	The vertical offset of the crop region (in pixels)	0
CropWidth	The width of the crop region (in pixels)	The width of the image

Table 4–26 CropRoundRect Applet Settings (Continued)

Name	Description	Default
CropHeight	The height of the crop region (in pixels)	The height of the image
ArcWidth	The horizontal diameter of the arc at the four corners (in pixels)	One half the width of the image
ArcHeight	The vertical diameter of the arc at the four corners (in pixels)	One half the height of the image

See Also

Related applets:

CropRectangle on page 143
RemoveRectangle on page 145
CropOval on page 147
RemoveOval on page 149
RemoveRoundRect on page 153

URL for **CropRoundRect**: `http://www.vivids.com/ij2/image/CropRoundRect.html`

RemoveRoundRect

Removes a rounded rectangular region from an image

Description

The **RemoveRoundRect** applet removes a rounded rectangular region from an image. The removed part of the image reveals the background color or image behind it.

Using **RemoveRoundRect** in HTML Code

The following HTML code uses the **RemoveRoundRect** applet to display the altered company logo against a plaid background.

```
<applet
    archive  = RemoveRoundRect2.zip
    codebase = RemoveRoundRect2
    code     = RemoveRoundRect.class
    width    = 159
    height   = 159>
<param name=AppBGImage  value=RemoveRoundRect2/plaid.gif>
<param name=AppTile     value=true>
<param name=Image       value=RemoveRoundRect2/vivid.gif>
<param name=CropXOffset value=25>
<param name=CropYOffset value=25>
<param name=CropWidth   value=75>
<param name=CropHeight  value=125>
<param name=ArcWidth    value=20>
<param name=ArcHeight   value=60>
</applet>
```

Settings

See Table 4–1 on page 104 for common settings that apply to this applet. Six additional parameters set the horizontal and vertical position, the width and height of the crop region, and the horizontal and vertical diameters of the arcs at the four corners.

Table 4–27 RemoveRoundRect Applet Settings

Name	Description	Default
CropXOffset	The horizontal offset of the crop region (in pixels)	0
CropYOffset	The vertical offset of the crop region (in pixels)	0

Table 4–27 RemoveRoundRect Applet Settings (Continued)

Name	Description	Default
CropWidth	The width of the crop region (in pixels)	The width of the image
CropHeight	The height of the crop region (in pixels)	The height of the image
ArcWidth	The horizontal diameter of the arc at the four corners (in pixels)	One half the width of the image
ArcHeight	The vertical diameter of the arc at the four corners (in pixels)	One half the height of the image

See Also

Related applets:

CropRectangle on page 143
RemoveRectangle on page 145
CropOval on page 147
RemoveOval on page 149
CropRoundRect on page 151

URL for **RemoveRoundRect**:

```
http://www.vivids.com/ij2/image/RemoveRoundRect.html
```

MultiImage

Displays multiple images

Caledonia Railroad

Martin Canter
Vice President

1138 Bespin Drive
Suite 94
San Rafael, CA 94912

415/555-5555
415/555-4444 FAX

Description

The **MultiImage** applet displays more than one image.
Each image may be displayed using any of the techniques
seen in this chapter. Furthermore, one or more strings may
also be displayed, as described for the **MultiText** applet on
page 91.

Each image and string has its own characteristics that may
be uniquely set. You can, for example, rotate one image,
scale another, and slant and blur yet another. Use the filter
technique described at the beginning of this chapter to
manipulate the image or images as desired.

All parameters that begin with **Img** can be specified independently for each image. Each
Img parameter must instead begin with **Img$N$**, however, where **N** is the number that identifies the image. For example, to scale the second image 50%, use the **Img2Filter** parameter
and specify the **scale** filter as shown here:

```
<param name=Image2      value=bluejava.gif>
<param name Img2Filter value="scale 50 50">
```

Using **MultiImage** in HTML Code

You must specify the **ImgCount** parameter, which specifies the number of images the
applet displays. To indicate three images, set **ImgCount** to 3:

```
<param name=ImgCount value=3>
```

The following HTML code uses the **MultiImage** applet to display three images.

```
<applet
    archive  = MultiImage2.zip
    codebase = MultiImage2
    code     = MultiImage.class
    width    = 400
    height   = 420>
<param name=AppBGImage      value=MultiImage2/pattern.gif>
<param name=AppTile         value=true>

<param name=ImgCount        value=3>
```

```
<param name=Image1          value=MultiImage2/pie.gif>
<param name=Img1XOffset     value=160>
<param name=Img1YOffset     value=240>
<param name=Img1Filter      value="slantright 10">

<param name=Image2          value=MultiImage2/key.gif>
<param name=Img2XOffset     value=20>
<param name=Img2YOffset     value=130>

<param name=Image3          value=MultiImage2/wndlcup.gif>
<param name=Img3YOffset     value=10>
<param name=Img3HorizCenter value=true>
<param name=Img3Filter      value="scale 60 60">

</applet>
```

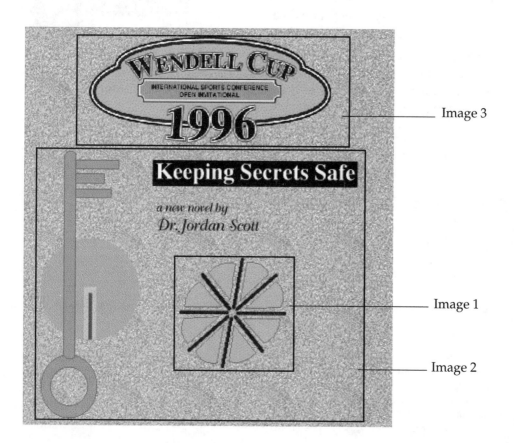

Image 3

Image 1

Image 2

Settings

See Table 4–1 on page 104 for common settings that apply to this applet. However, the parameters that begin with **Img** must instead begin with **ImgN**, where *N* specifies the string involved. The **ImgNFilter** parameter is used to specify the program (or filter) that is used to draw the string. In addition, the **ImgCount** parameter must be specified to indicate the number of strings to display.

Table 4–28 MultiImage Applet Settings

Name	Description	Default
ImgCount	The number of images to display	0
ImgNFilter	The filters for image *N*	0

See Also

Related applets:	**MultiText** on page 91
URL for **MultiImage**:	http://www.vivids.com/ij2/image/MultiImage.html

Tips for Programmers

The applets in this chapter are implemented by extending the **ImgFilt** class. The filters in this chapter each manipulate an image. The method is similar to that discussed in Chapter 3, except that rather than generating text you will be taking an existing image and processing it in some way.

You should become familiar with the Tips for Programmers section in Chapter 3 on page 95. The techniques for image manipulation have some similarities to text generating filters. You must, for example, return an array on integers which represent the image. You must also set the new_width and new_height variables.

To understand image filters let's look at the **negative** filter. The conventions for filter naming are identical to those discussed in Chapter 3. The **negative** filter is in a file named **fnegative.java**, and the name of the class is **fnegative**:

```
1   public class fnegative extends ImgFilt {
2       int subfrom = 255;
3
4       public void setparameter(String str, int i) {
5           switch(i) {
6           case 0:
7               subfrom = Integer.parseInt(str);
8               break;
9           }
10      }
11
12      public int[] filter(int[] p1, int w, int h) {
13          int x, y, i;
14          int index, new_index;
15          int alpha, red, green, blue;
16          int nalpha, nred, ngreen, nblue;
17
18          if(p1.length != (w*h)) {
19            System.out.println("negative filter: wrong size array");
20              System.out.println("p1.length = " + p1.length +
21                              " (w,h) = " + w + "," + h);
22              return null;
23          }
24
25          newpixels = new int[h * w];
26
27          new_index = 0;
28          for(y=0;y<h;y++) {
29              for(x=0;x<w;x++) {
30                  index = (y*w) + x;
```

```
31                    alpha = (p1[index] & 0xff000000) >>> 24;
32                    red   = (p1[index] & 0x00ff0000) >> 16;
33                    green = (p1[index] & 0x0000ff00) >> 8;
34                    blue  = (p1[index] & 0x000000ff);
35
36                    nred   = Math.abs(subfrom - red);
37                    ngreen = Math.abs(subfrom - green);
38                    nblue  = Math.abs(subfrom - blue);
39                    newpixels[new_index++] =
40                        (alpha << 24)|(nred << 16)|(ngreen << 8)|nblue;
41                }
42            }
43        new_width  = w;
44        new_height = h;
45        return newpixels;
46    }
47 }
```

Image filters have the same requirements as do text generating filters.

- The `filter` method must return an array of pixels which represent the image
- The filter must set the `new_width` instance variable to the width of the image
- The filter must set the `new_height` instance variable to the height of the image

In addition, the filter may also elect to do the following:

- Define a `setparameter` method to set customizable options

When image filters are invoked, an existing image is passed to the `filter` method. The first argument, `p1`, is the array of pixels containing the image. The two other arguments, `w` and `h`, represent the width and height of the image. The image may or may not have already passed through other image filters, or it may have been generated by a text generating filter. It doesn't matter where it came from; we simply treat it as an array of integers.

Image filters may have a `setparameter` method to set customizable features. Setting parameters for image filters is identical to setting parameters for text generating filters. For more information, see the discussion on page 95.

The setparameter method

The setparameter method for image filters is identical to that for text. The **negative** filter gets the `subfrom` variable from the setparameter method as shown here:

```
4       public void setparameter(String str, int i) {
5           switch(i) {
6           case 0:
7               subfrom = Integer.parseInt(str);
```

```
 8                    break;
 9              }
10       }
```

Basic Steps

The procedure for processing an image is even easier than that for generating text. Of course, the algorithm used to process the image may be more complex, but the procedure is very straightforward. Here are the steps:

- Verify the array size

- Determine the dimensions that your processed image will require

- Create an array of integers for the new image (optional)

- Process the image

- Set the new_width and new_height variables

- Return the pixel array

Let's look at each of these steps in the code example shown above.

Verify the array size

The first thing to check in the filter method is the size of the image. The size of the array should match the width multiplied by the height. If it doesn't, the image data has been corrupted.

```
18          if(p1.length != (w*h)) {
19             System.out.println("negative filter: wrong size array");
20                System.out.println("p1.length = " + p1.length +
21                            " (w,h) = " + w + "," + h);
22             return null;
23          }
```

Determine the dimensions that your text will require

The **negative** filter simply replaces the pixels in the image without changing the size. Therefore, we do not have to calculate new dimensions.

Create an array of integers for the new image

Depending on the type of image processing being done, you may need to create a new array in which to store the new image. This is particularly true if the size of the image is changing. If you are rotating the image, for example, you will probably end up with a new image size. So, before processing the image, create a new array:

```
25              newpixels = new int[h * w];
```

Process the image

This is where the real work gets done. Depending on the complexity of the image processing, this may be a few lines of code or several hundred. The **negative** filter simply calculates a new color value for each pixel based on the previous value.

```
27              new_index = 0;
28              for(y=0;y<h;y++) {
29                  for(x=0;x<w;x++) {
30                      index = (y*w) + x;
31                      alpha = (p1[index] & 0xff000000) >>> 24;
32                      red   = (p1[index] & 0x00ff0000) >> 16;
33                      green = (p1[index] & 0x0000ff00) >> 8;
34                      blue  = (p1[index] & 0x000000ff);
35
36                      nred   = Math.abs(subfrom - red);
37                      ngreen = Math.abs(subfrom - green);
38                      nblue  = Math.abs(subfrom - blue);
39                      newpixels[new_index++] =
40                          (alpha << 24)|(nred << 16)|(ngreen << 8)|nblue;
41                  }
42              }
```

Set the new_width and new_height variables

You must set the `new_width` and `new_height` variables to the new values of the width and height. Even if the width and height do not change, set the `new_width` and `new_height` variables.

```
43              new_width  = w;
44              new_height = h;
```

Return the pixel array

Finally, return the array of pixels.

```
45              return newpixels;
```

Array Format

It's essential to understand exactly how the array of integers is organized to represent the image. The array is a single dimensional array and images are two-dimensional entities. The array maintains the pixels of the image in row order. Each row of the image is placed in the image back-to-back. For example, an image that is 5 pixels in width by 3 pixels in length is be contained in an array of size 15. The first row of the image is contained in positions 0 through 4, the second row of the image is contained in array positions 5 through 9, and so on.

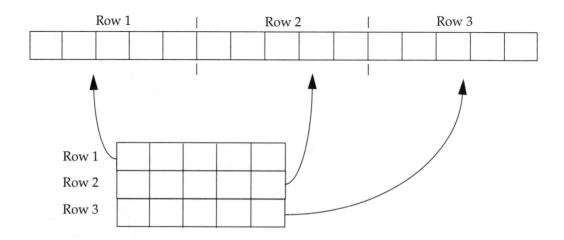

Pixel Format

To better understand the image processing capabilities, one needs to understand the pixel data and how it is used. Each integer (a 32-bit value) represents the red, green, and blue components of a single pixel in the image. The low order 8 bits represent blue, the next 8 bits represent green, and the next 8 bits represent red. The high order 8 pixels represent the alpha component of the color.

alpha	red	green	blue

The values of each of these color components can range from 0 to 255.

The red, green, and blue components of the pixel represent the intensity of the respective color in the pixel. The alpha component controls the transparency of the color. A value of 255 indicates that the pixel is fully opaque. A value of 0 indicates that the pixel is full transparent. Values between 0 and 255 represent a percentage of transparency.

CHAPTER

5

Animation
Applets

I n Chapters 3 and 4 you learned many different techniques for displaying text and
images. In this chapter you will use what you learned to produce animation.

Animation Defined

Let's begin with a definition. Animation is a series of images that are displayed in rapid succession to simulate live action. On television and in movies, this is accomplished by displaying many images per second.

Animation on a computer screen also involves a series of images displayed in rapid succession. The conventional method for creating computer animation is to use some independent
means to generate the images required, and then use an animation application to display
them.

Figure 5–1 illustrates a typical use of this sort of animation. Ten different images of a company logo are displayed in rapid sequence to produce an animated effect.

If you have or can make such a series of images, you can use the Java applets in this chapter
to create animation by this familiar method.

You can also use them to create animation by another method, however, one that does not
require you to start out with a prepared series of images.

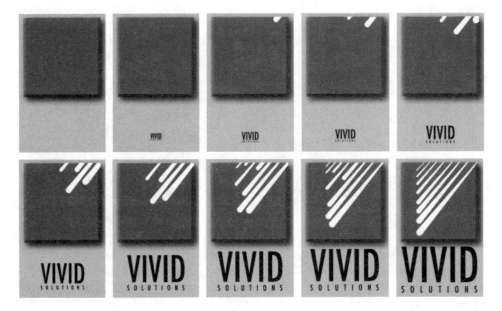

Figure 5-1: Vivid Solutions animated logo

How Do I Animate?

One of the challenges of traditional animation is that you must have some means of creating the series of images to be animated. If you are a graphic artist, or a whiz with an animation program, this may be easy for you. If you can afford a professional animator you will be able to come up with some dazzling animation sequences.

The rest of us are stuck wanting to create animation, but at a loss as to how to produce anything effective.

Self-Animation

To solve this problem, you are going to use the techniques for generating and displaying text and images introduced in Chapters 3 and 4 to create the needed series of images *on the fly*. This is called self-animation. In self-animation, a single image—or text that is generated and maintained as an image—is manipulated in any of a variety of ways to produce multiple images. These images are then displayed in sequence to create animation.

Suppose you have a single image of your company logo. You would like to create some kind of animation, but don't have the means to generate the sort of multiple images shown in the previous example.

Instead, you can use the filters you learned about in Chapter 4 to alter an image numerous times. For example, suppose you use the **scale** filter to produce a sequence of 10 images, each a different size. You could then display them in rapid succession to create the effect of a growing logo, as shown in Figure 5–2.

Figure 5–2: Self-animation by rescaling

You can apply several filters to an image to create more complex self-animation. Figure 5–3 both rescales and rotates the image in 10 steps.

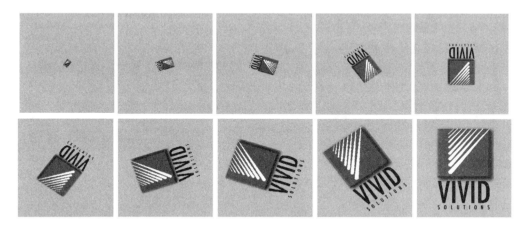

Figure 5–3: Self-animation by rescaling and rotating

Animation Without Images

By using the text-generating techniques introduced in Chapter 3 you can even animate strings. You could use the **multicolor** filter, for example, to display a string of characters in which each character is a different color, changing the colors to create animated colored text like a neon sign, as shown in Figure 5–4.

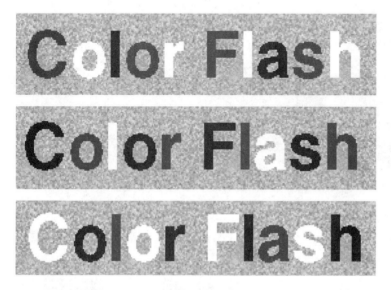

Figure 5–4: Self-animation using Text only

Another example of text animation is embossed text with gradually increasing contrast, which creates an effect of characters emerging from the screen, as shown in Figure 5–5.

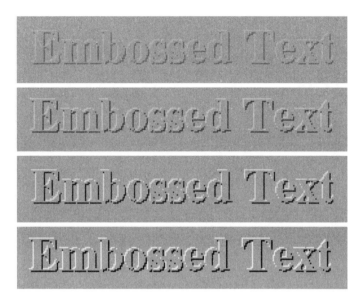

Figure 5–5: Self-animation using embossed text

In addition to using filters to manipulate text or images, you can also position each image in the animation sequence by specifying explicit horizontal and vertical coordinates. This allows you to animate with movement alone, or to combine image movement with other forms of self-animation.

Which Method to Use?

Remember that you can use the applets in this chapter to create either type of animation. If you have, or can create, a series of separate images, you can use these applets to produce conventional animation. But you can always take advantage of self-animation to create exciting animated effects.

The Animation Applets in this Chapter

There are seven applets in this chapter. The first six can display and animate one string and one image at the same time. These six applets share almost identical settings.

The last applet in this chapter can display multiple text and image animations simultaneously. Its settings are slightly expanded.

The first seven applets each animate in a slightly different manner. Here is a list of those applets, with a brief description of what they do:

- **AnimateContinuous**

  Continuous animation in one direction. The images are displayed in order from first to last, at which time a specified pause may take effect. The animation then begins again with the first image.

- **AnimateTwoWay**

  Continuous animation in two directions. The images are displayed in order from first to last, at which time a specified pause may take effect. The animation then reverses itself, displaying the images from last to first.

- **AnimateOnButton**

  One forward animation when the visitor presses a mouse button within the image or text. If the visitor presses a mouse button again, the animation repeats.

- **AnimateOnButtonTwoWay**

  One forward or backward animation when the visitor presses a mouse button within the image or text. If the visitor presses a mouse button again, the animation reverses itself.

- **AnimateOnEntry**

  Continuous forward animation when the pointer enters the text or image area. The animation continues until the pointer leaves the area.

- **AnimateOnEntryTwoWay**

  One forward animation when the pointer enters the text or image area. When the pointer leaves the area, the animation reverses itself.

- **AnimateOnPressRelease**

  One forward animation when the visitor presses a mouse button within the text or image area. When the mouse button is released, the animation reverses itself.

The settings for these applets are almost identical.

Using the Animation Applets in this Chapter

Before describing the settings for these applets, let's look at an example illustrating the fundamental concepts you will use throughout this chapter.

The basic idea is that you use parameters to specify the sources and filters that will generate a series of images for animation. These images will be displayed in succession, at a rate (the fixed delay between images) that you specify.

Let's begin with the applet settings that produced the animation shown in Figure 5–1. This was actually a series of 10 separate images; no filters were involved. Here is the HTML code:

```
<applet
    codebase = AnimateContinuous
    code     = AnimateContinuous.class
    width    = 187
    height   = 288>

<! Delay between images >
<param name=ImgDelayBetweenImages value=200>
<! Delay between runs >
<param name=ImgDelayBetweenRuns   value=5000>

<param name=ImgNumImages value=10>
<param name=Image1         value=../images/vivid0.gif>
<param name=Image2         value=../images/vivid1.gif>
<param name=Image3         value=../images/vivid2.gif>
<param name=Image4         value=../images/vivid3.gif>
<param name=Image5         value=../images/vivid4.gif>
<param name=Image6         value=../images/vivid5.gif>
<param name=Image7         value=../images/vivid6.gif>
<param name=Image8         value=../images/vivid7.gif>
<param name=Image9         value=../images/vivid8.gif>
<param name=Image10        value=../images/vivid9.gif>
</applet>
```

The **ImgNumImages** parameter specifies the number of images included in the animation sequence. If you specify **ImgNumImages** to be less than the actual number of images you include in the code, only the number of images you specify is displayed. If you specify **ImgNumImages** to be greater than the actual number of images you have, the applet will not run.

The parameter for specifying the images is **Image*N***, where *N* represents the sequence number of the image. The images are displayed according to sequence number: **Image1** is first, **Image2** second, and so forth.

The **ImgDelayBetweenImages** parameter specifies the number of milliseconds between images. This controls the rate of animation. The **ImgDelayBetweenRuns** parameter specifies the number of milliseconds between animation runs. If you specify identical values for **ImgDelayBetweenRuns** and **ImgDelayBetweenImages**, the animation is continuous, with no discernible pause between runs.

Reusing an Image

You may want to use an image more than once in a given animation sequence. To do this you can specify the image repeatedly, but this means that Java will reload the image each time. This is unnecessary, and slows the animation. To reuse an image in an animation sequence, you can instead employ a special identifier when specifying the value for the **Image**_N_ parameter. To reuse **Image3** as the 7th image in the animation sequence, specify **$3** as the value for **Image7**:

```
<param name=Image7 value=$3>
```

This indicates "Reuse **Image3** as **Image7**."

To demonstrate the use of this feature, let's rewrite the previous example to display images 5, 6, and 7 a few extra times during the animation. By using the **$**_N_ identifier, we avoid taking any time to reload the images. Here's the modified HTML code:

```
<applet
    code    = AnimateContinuous.class
    width   = 300
    height  = 400>

<! Delay between images >
<param name=ImgDelayBetweenImages value=200>
<! Delay between runs >
<param name=ImgDelayBetweenRuns    value=5000>

<param name=ImgNumImages value=15>
<param name=Image1         value=../images/vivid0.gif>
<param name=Image2         value=../images/vivid1.gif>
<param name=Image3         value=../images/vivid2.gif>
<param name=Image4         value=../images/vivid3.gif>
<param name=Image5         value=../images/vivid4.gif>
<param name=Image6         value=../images/vivid5.gif>
<param name=Image7         value=../images/vivid6.gif>
<param name=Image8         value=$7>
<param name=Image9         value=$6>
<param name=Image10        value=$5>
<param name=Image11        value=$6>
<param name=Image12        value=$7>
<param name=Image13        value=../images/vivid7.gif>
<param name=Image14        value=../images/vivid8.gif>
<param name=Image15        value=../images/vivid9.gif>
</applet>
```

Note that while there are now 15 images in our sequence, we had to load only 10 unique image sources as shown in Figure 5–6.

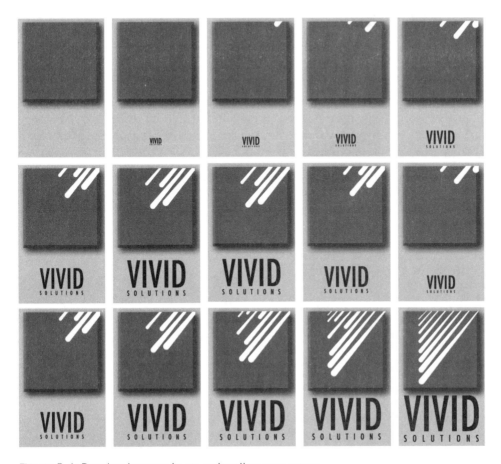

Figure 5–6: Reusing images in an animation sequence

Displaying an Image During Loading

It is often time consuming to load and manipulate multiple images. By default, the animation does not begin until all necessary images have been loaded and manipulated. You may, however, want to provide something for your viewer to look at while waiting for the animation to begin. You can use the **ImgDisplayFirst** parameter to specify that you want the initial image in the sequence to display while waiting for the rest to load. To activate this feature, set **ImgDisplayFirst** to true:

```
<param name=ImgDisplayFirst value=true>
```

Setting the Initial Image

The **ImgInitialImage** parameter is available to specify which image should begin the animation sequence. If you specify image 4 as the initial image, then images 1, 2, and 3 are not included in the sequence.

This feature is useful for several reasons. If, for example, you want to display an image while the animation sequence is being loaded and manipulated, but the first image in the sequence is not the one you want to display, you can specify image #1 as the **ImgDisplay-First** image, but start your animation with image 2.

In the previous example, if you wanted to display the complete company logo (vivid9.gif) during load time, but have vivid0.gif begin the animation sequence, you would use the following HTML code:

```
<applet
    code    = AnimateContinuous.class
    width   = 300
    height = 400>

<! Delay between images >
<param name=ImgDelayBetweenImages value=200>
<! Delay between runs >
<param name=ImgDelayBetweenRuns    value=5000>

<param name=ImgDisplayFirst value=true>
<param name=ImgInitialImage value=2>
<param name=ImgNumImages    value=11>
<param name=Image1              value=../images/vivid9.gif>
<param name=Image2              value=../images/vivid0.gif>
<param name=Image3              value=../images/vivid1.gif>
<param name=Image4              value=../images/vivid2.gif>
<param name=Image5              value=../images/vivid3.gif>
<param name=Image6              value=../images/vivid4.gif>
<param name=Image7              value=../images/vivid5.gif>
<param name=Image8              value=../images/vivid6.gif>
<param name=Image9              value=../images/vivid7.gif>
<param name=Image10             value=../images/vivid8.gif>
<param name=Image11             value=$1>
</applet>
```

Moving Images

One of the easiest ways to create animation is to move an image repeatedly. Such movement is independent of any other action being taken. Whether you are using multiple images or generating images by manipulation, you can create movement by specifying the horizontal and vertical positions of the images in your sequence (see Figure 5–7).

The following example moves an image from right to left by changing the **ImgXOffset*N***
parameter, where ***N*** represents the image sequence number.

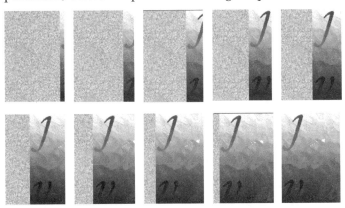

Figure 5–7: Moving an image

Note that the code specifies just one image and uses the **ImgXOffset*N*** parameter to move it.
You can also move an image vertically by using the **ImgYOffset*N*** parameter.

```
<applet
    codebase = AnimateContinuous
    code     = AnimateContinuous.class
    width    = 96
    height   = 144>
<param name=AppBGImage          value=../images/pattern.gif>
<param name=AppTile             value=true>

<param name=ImgDelayBetweenRuns   value=750>
<param name=ImgDelayBetweenImages value=750>

<param name=ImgNumImages        value=11>
<param name=Image1              value=../images/bluejava.gif>
<param name=ImgXOffset1         value=100>
<param name=ImgXOffset2         value=90>
<param name=ImgXOffset3         value=80>
<param name=ImgXOffset4         value=70>
<param name=ImgXOffset5         value=60>
<param name=ImgXOffset6         value=50>
<param name=ImgXOffset7         value=40>
<param name=ImgXOffset8         value=30>
<param name=ImgXOffset9         value=20>
<param name=ImgXOffset10        value=10>
<param name=ImgXOffset11        value=0>
</applet>
```

You can simplify these parameter by using the **ImgAutoMove** parameter. Rather than specifying the coordinates for each and every position, specify just the end points and the applet will calculate the intermediate points. For example, you can accomplish the exact same animation as shown in Figure 5–7 using the following code:

```
<applet
    codebase = AnimateContinuous
    code     = AnimateContinuous.class
    width    = 96
    height   = 144>
<param name=AppBGImage              value=../images/pattern.gif>
<param name=AppTile                 value=true>

<param name=ImgDelayBetweenRuns     value=750>
<param name=ImgDelayBetweenImages   value=750>

<param name=ImgNumImages            value=11>
<param name=Image1                  value=../images/bluejava.gif>
<param name=ImgAutoMove             value=true>
<param name=ImgXOffset1             value=100>
<param name=ImgXOffset11            value=0>
</applet>
```

Using Filters for Self-Animation

Now let's look at the HTML code that generated the animation sequence shown in Figure 5–2. This is the first self-animation example we've seen:

```
<applet
    codebase = AnimateContinuous
    code     = AnimateContinuous.class
    width    = 187
    height   = 288>

<param name=ImgDelayBetweenRuns     value=2000>
<param name=ImgDelayBetweenImages   value=200>
<param name=ImgVertCenter           value=true>
<param name=ImgHorizCenter          value=true>

<param name=ImgNumImages            value=10>
<param name=Image1                  value=../images/vivid9.gif>
<param name=ImgFilter1              value="scale 10 10">
<param name=ImgFilter2              value="scale 20 20">
<param name=ImgFilter3              value="scale 30 30">
<param name=ImgFilter4              value="scale 40 40">
<param name=ImgFilter5              value="scale 50 50">
```

```
<param name=ImgFilter6          value="scale 60 60">
<param name=ImgFilter7          value="scale 70 70">
<param name=ImgFilter8          value="scale 80 80">
<param name=ImgFilter9          value="scale 90 90">
<param name=ImgFilter10         value="scale 100 100">
</applet>
```

Only one image source (**Image1**) is specified, yet **ImgNumImages** is set to 10. This is because the example manipulates one image 10 times by using the **ImgFilter*N*** parameter. Since only one image is specified, the specified filters all must apply to that image. This is the filter rule:

Filters operate on the last specified image of the same or smaller sequence number.

In the example, all the filters apply to **Image1** because it is the last image specified and its number is the same as or smaller than those of the filter numbers. If another image had been specified as **Image5**, **ImgFilter1** through **ImgFilter4** would have manipulated **Image1**, and **ImgFilter5** through **ImgFilter10** would have manipulated **Image5**.

Animation with Multiple Filters

There is no limit to the number of filters you can specify for an image. Let's look at the HTML code that generated Figure 5–3, another example of self-animation. The same image is used as in the previous example; this time however, the image is sent through two filters, **scale** and **rotate**, to create a rotating, growing animation. Here's the HTML code:

```
<applet
    codebase = AnimateContinuous
    code     = AnimateContinuous.class
    width    = 187
    height   = 288>

<param name name=AppBGColor              value=#cecece>
<param name=ImgDelayBetweenRuns          value=2000>
<param name=ImgDelayBetweenImages value=100>
<param name=ImgVertCenter                value=true>
<param name=ImgHorizCenter               value=true>

<param name=ImgNumImages                 value=10>
<param name=Image1                       value=../images/vivid9.gif>
<param name=ImgFilter1                   value="scale 10 10|rotate 324">
<param name=ImgFilter2                   value="scale 20 20|rotate 288">
<param name=ImgFilter3                   value="scale 30 30|rotate 252">
<param name=ImgFilter4                   value="scale 40 40|rotate 216">
<param name=ImgFilter5                   value="scale 50 50|rotate 180">
<param name=ImgFilter6                   value="scale 60 60|rotate 144">
<param name=ImgFilter7                   value="scale 70 70|rotate 108">
```

```
<param name=ImgFilter8        value="scale 80 80|rotate 72">
<param name=ImgFilter9        value="scale 90 90|rotate 36">
<param name=ImgFilter10       value="scale 100 100">
</applet>
```

Reusing Filtered Images

Sometimes you may want to reuse an image after it has been processed through a filter. Just as you reused an image so that you did not have to reload it, you can also reuse an image after it has passed through filters so that you don't need to filter it again.

The following example uses the **removerectangle** filter to selectively remove rectangular regions of a photograph as shown in Figure 5–8. By reusing the last image in the sequence each time, we can slowly make the image entirely disappear.

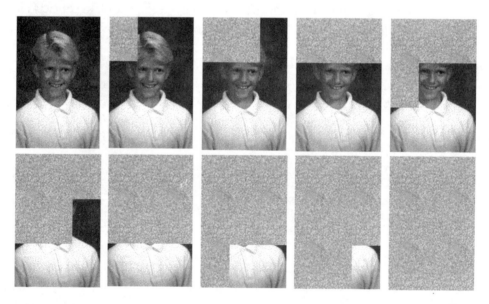

Figure 5–8: Reusing a filtered image

You have already seen how to reuse an unaltered image by specifying the **$N** identifier. It can be employed in just the same way to reuse a previously manipulated image—one that has already been filtered. For example, to reuse the 3rd filtered image for image number 7, use the following parameter setting:

```
<param name=ImgFilter7 value=$3>
```

Here's the HTML code used to generate the disappearing Jeffrey animation shown above:

```
<applet
    codebase = AnimateTwoWay
    code     = AnimateTwoWay.class
    width    = 140
    height   = 209>
<param name=AppBGImage              value=../images/pattern.gif>
<param name=AppTile                 value=true>

<param name=ImgDelayBetweenRuns     value=3000>
<param name=ImgDelayBetweenImages   value=150>

<param name=ImgNumImages    value=10>
<param name=Image1          value=../images/jeff.gif>
<param name=ImgFilter2      value="$1|removerectangle 0 0 47 70">
<param name=ImgFilter3      value="$2|removerectangle 47 0 47 70">
<param name=ImgFilter4      value="$3|removerectangle 94 0 47 70">
<param name=ImgFilter5      value="$4|removerectangle 0 70 47 70">
<param name=ImgFilter6      value="$5|removerectangle 47 70 47 70">
<param name=ImgFilter7      value="$6|removerectangle 94 70 47 70">
<param name=ImgFilter8      value="$7|removerectangle 0 140 47 70">
<param name=ImgFilter9      value="$8|removerectangle 47 140 47 70">
<param name=ImgFilter10     value="$9|removerectangle 94 140 47 70">
</applet>
```

If you reuse an image by specifying the value of **ImageN** as **$M**, you are reusing unaltered image **M**. If you reuse a filtered image by specifying the value of **ImgFilterN** as **$M**, you are reusing image **M** which has been filtered. If you reuse a filtered image by specifying the value of **ImageFilterN** as **$M**, and filter **M** has not been specified, then unaltered image **M** is reused instead.

Animating Text

The examples so far have shown image animation only. However, text animation is created in very similar fashion. You must, of course, specify a text generating filter as the primary (first) filter, because this generates the text that is then manipulated by any other filters you use. Most parameter settings are the same for text as for images, except that the parameter names begin with **Tx** rather than **Img**.

To demonstrate the use of self-animation with text, let's look at the HTML code that generated the animation shown in Figure 5–4. Here we use the **multicolor** text generating filter to produce three images:

```
<applet
    codebase = AnimateContinuous
    code     = AnimateContinuous.class
    width    = 350
```

```
     height   = 100>
<param name=AppBGImage            value=../images/pattern.gif>
<param name=AppTile               value=true>

<param name=Text                  value="Color Flash">
<param name=TxFont                value=Helvetica>
<param name=TxStyle               value=Bold>
<param name=TxPointSize           value=48>
<param name=TxDelayBetweenRuns    value=200>
<param name=TxDelayBetweenImages value=200>
<param name=TxNumImages           value=3>
<param name=TxFilter1             value="multicolor white blue red">
<param name=TxFilter2             value="multicolor blue red white">
<param name=TxFilter3             value="multicolor red white blue">
<param name=TxXOffset1            value=20>
<param name=TxYOffset1            value=20>
</applet>
```

There is no reason to limit ourselves to text filters with generated text. Let's expand the last example to add rotation to the flashing like that shown in Figure 5–9. In addition, we'll use some of the other techniques we've already learned about, such as setting the initial image and reusing filtered images.

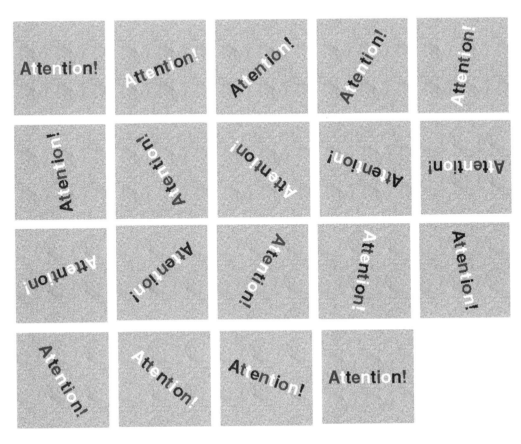

Figure 5-9: Complex animation using text

```
<applet
    archive  = AnimateContinuous.zip
    codebase = AnimateContinuous
    code     = AnimateContinuous.class
    width    = 200
    height   = 150>
<param name=AppBGImage            value=AnimateContinuous/pattern.gif>
<param name=AppTile               value=true>

<param name=Text                  value="Attention!">
<param name=TxFont                value=TimesRoman>
<param name=TxHorizCenter         value=true>
<param name=TxVertCenter          value=true>
<param name=TxStyle               value=Bold>
<param name=TxPointSize           value=36>
<param name=TxDelayBetweenRuns    value=50>
```

```
<param name=TxDelayBetweenImages value=50>
<param name=TxNumImages         value=21>
<param name=TxInitialImage      value=4>
<param name=TxFilter1           value="multicolor white blue red">
<param name=TxFilter2           value="multicolor blue red white">
<param name=TxFilter3           value="multicolor red white blue">
<param name=TxFilter4           value="$1">
<param name=TxFilter5           value="$2|rotate 20">
<param name=TxFilter6           value="$3|rotate 40">
<param name=TxFilter7           value="$1|rotate 60">
<param name=TxFilter8           value="$2|rotate 80">
<param name=TxFilter9           value="$3|rotate 100">
<param name=TxFilter10          value="$1|rotate 120">
<param name=TxFilter11          value="$2|rotate 140">
<param name=TxFilter12          value="$3|rotate 160">
<param name=TxFilter13          value="$1|rotate 180">
<param name=TxFilter14          value="$2|rotate 200">
<param name=TxFilter15          value="$3|rotate 220">
<param name=TxFilter16          value="$1|rotate 240">
<param name=TxFilter17          value="$2|rotate 260">
<param name=TxFilter18          value="$3|rotate 280">
<param name=TxFilter19          value="$1|rotate 300">
<param name=TxFilter20          value="$2|rotate 320">
<param name=TxFilter21          value="$3|rotate 340">
</applet>
```

Because we set **ImgInitialImage** to 4, the first three images are not included in the animation sequence. However, the images are created according to **TxFilter1**, **TxFilter2**, and **TxFilter3**, which specify the **multicolor** filter. By creating these three image we save time; for images 3 through 21 we have only to rotate existing images, rather than creating new ones. This speeds up the image manipulation phase of the animation.

Changing Text

Another text animation method involves changing the actual text itself during the animation sequence. For example, an animation could consist of a word being printed out one character at a time. This is easily accomplished by using the **TextN** parameter to specify a unique text string for each frame of animation.

The following example displays the string "Welcome", one character at a time.

```
<applet
    codebase = AnimateContinuous
    code     = AnimateContinuous.class
    width    = 200
    height   = 60>
<param name=AppBGColor      value=white>

<param name=TxNumImages     value=8>
<param name=Text1           value=" ">
<param name=Text2           value="W">
<param name=Text3           value="We">
<param name=Text4           value="Wel">
<param name=Text5           value="Welc">
<param name=Text6           value="Welco">
<param name=Text7           value="Welcom">
<param name=Text8           value="Welcome">
<param name=TxFont          value="TimesRoman">
<param name=TxPointSize1    value=30>
<param name=TxVertCenter    value=true>
<param name=TxXOffset1      value=10>
</applet>
```

W

We

Wel

Welc

Welco

Welcom

Welcome

Changing Text Attributes

In addition to altering the actual string itself, you can also alter the font, style, pointsize, and color of the text for each frame of animation. To change the font, style, or pointsize, use the **TxFontN**, **TxStyleN**, or **TxPointsizeN** parameters respectively. To change the color, use the **TxColorN** parameter.

The following example demonstrates using the **TxPointsizeN** parameter to alter the size of the "Welcome" string.

```
<applet
    codebase = AnimateContinuous
    code     = AnimateContinuous.class
    width    = 200
    height   = 60>
<param name=AppBGColor      value=white>

<param name=TxNumImages     value=4>
<param name=Text1       value="Welcome">
<param name=TxFont      value="TimesRoman">
<param name=TxPointSize1    value=10>
<param name=TxPointSize2    value=20>
<param name=TxPointSize3    value=30>
<param name=TxPointSize4    value=40>
<param name=TxVertCenter    value=true>
<param name=TxHorizCenter   value=true>
</applet>
```

Welcome

Welcome

Welcome

Welcome

Controlling Animation Speed

The speed of each applet in this chapter can be controlled by the user. There are two delay speeds which can be controlled: **DelayBetweenImages** and **DelayBetweenRuns**. By changing the delay times the animation can be sped up or slowed down. The **DelayBetweenRuns** setting affects only those applets which run continuously. Animation applets which run once and stop (such as **AnimateOnButton**) do not use the **DelayBetweenRuns** parameter.

The applets in this chapter respond to the following keyboard input:

f   Animation 10% faster (**DelayBetweenImages** decreases)

s   Animation 10% slower (**DelayBetweenImages** increased)

F   Animation sequences repeat 10% more rapidly (**DelayBetweenRuns** decreases)

S   Animation sequences repeat 10% more slowly (**DelayBetweenRuns** increased)

Common Settings

Table 5–1 lists parameters that are common to all the applets in this chapter.

Table 5–1 Common Settings for All Animation Applets

Name	Description	Default
TxNumImages	The number of text images in the text animation sequence	0
ImgNumImages	The number of images in the image animation sequence	0
ImgFilter*N*	The filter with which to manipulate the *N*th image in the image animation sequence	(none)
TxFilter*N*	The filter with which to manipulate the *N*th image in the text animation sequence	(none)
WaitForEverything	If true, wait for all the images in the text and image animation sequence to load before displaying anything	false
TxDelayBetweenImages	The delay (in milliseconds) between images in the text animation sequence	100
TxDelayBetweenRuns	The delay (in milliseconds) between text animation sequences	2000
ImgDelayBetweenImages	The delay (in milliseconds) between images in the image animation sequence	100
ImgDelayBetweenRuns	The delay (in milliseconds) between image animation sequences	2000
TxInitialImage	The sequence number of the first image to display in the text animation sequence	1
ImgInitialImage	The sequence number of the first image to use in the image animation sequence	1
ImgDisplayFirst	If true, display Image1 while the rest of the images in the image animation sequence are being loaded and filtered	false
TxXOffset*N*	The horizontal distance (in pixels) from the top of the applet to the upper left corner of the *N*th image in the text animation sequence	0
TxYOffset*N*	The vertical distance (in pixels) from the top of the applet to the upper left corner of the *N*th image in the text animation sequence	0
TxAutoMove	If true, automatically calculate the X and Y offset between specified positions of the text in the text animation sequence	false
ImgXOffset*N*	The horizontal distance (in pixels) from the top of the applet to the upper left corner of the *N*th image in the image animation sequence	0

Table 5–1 Common Settings for All Animation Applets (Continued)

Name	Description	Default
ImgYOffset*N*	The vertical distance (in pixels) from the top of the applet to the upper left corner of the *N*th image in the image animation sequence	0
ImgAutoMove	If true, automatically calculate the X and Y offset between specified positions of the image in the image animation sequence	false
AppNumMaps	The number of image maps (required for use of image maps)	0
Map*N***_X1**	The left X coordinate for map *N*	0
Map*N***_Y1**	The top Y coordinate for map *N*	0
Map*N***_X2**	The right X coordinate for map **N**	0
Map*N***_Y2**	The bottom Y coordinate for map *N*	0
Map*N***_URL**	The URL for map *N*	(none)
TestMode	If true, the pointer position is displayed in the status line	false
AppBGImage	The background image	(none)
AppBGImageXOffset	The horizontal offset at which to position the background image	0
AppBGImageYOffset	The vertical offset at which to position the background image	0
AppTile	If true, tile the background image	false
TxURL	The URL to load when the pointer is within the text and any mouse button is pressed	(none)
ImgURL	The URL to load when the pointer is within the image and any mouse button is pressed	(none)
TxAudio	The audio file to play when the pointer enters the text	(none)
TxAudioLoop	If true, continuously play the audio file for the text	false
ImgAudio	The audio file to play when the pointer enters the image	(none)
ImgAudioLoop	If true, continuously play the audio file for the image	false
TxAudio*N*	The audio file to play when the *N*th text in the animation sequence is displayed	(none)
ImgAudio*N*	The audio file to play when the *N*th image in the animation sequence is displayed	(none)
Image*N*	The *N*th image to display	(none)
ImgXOffset	The horizontal distance (in pixels) from the left side of the applet to the image	0

Table 5–1 Common Settings for All Animation Applets (Continued)

Name	Description	Default
ImgYOffset	The vertical distance (in pixels) from the top of the applet to the image	0
ImgHorizCenter	If true, the image is horizontally centered	false
ImgVertCenter	If true, the image is vertically centered	false
ImgBorderWidth	The width of the image border (must be greater than 0 in order for a border to be drawn)	0
ImgBorderColor	The color of the image border	Set by browser
ImgBorderMargin	The distance (in pixels) from the image border to the image on all sides	0
ImgFrameThickness	The thickness of the image frame (must be greater than 0 in order for a frame to be drawn)	0
ImgFrameType	The type of image frame: **ShadowIn**, **ShadowOut**, **ShadowEtchedIn**, or **ShadowEtchedOut**	**ShadowIn**
ImgFrameMargin	The distance (in pixels) from the image frame to the image	0
Text	The string of characters to display	(none)
Text*N*	The *N*th string of characters to display	**Text** or **Text*N-1***
TxColor	The text color	Set by browser
TxColor*N*	The color of the *N*th text	**TxColor** or **TxColor*N-1***
TxBGColor	The text background color	transparent
TxHorizCenter	If true, the text is horizontally centered	false
TxVertCenter	If true, the text is vertically centered	false
TxFont	The font of the text: **TimesRoman**, **Helvetica**, **Courier**, **Dialog**, **DialogInput**, or **ZapfDingbats**	**Dialog**
TxFont*N*	The font of the *N*th text: **TimesRoman**, **Helvetica**, **Courier**, **Dialog**, **DialogInput**, or **ZapfDingbats**	**TxFont** or **TxFont*N-1***
TxStyle	The style of the font: **Plain**, **Bold**, **Italic**, or **BoldItalic**	**Plain**
TxStyle*N*	The style of the *N*th font: **Plain**, **Bold**, **Italic**, or **BoldItalic**	**TxStyle** or **TxStyleN-1**
TxPointSize	The size of the font in points	10
TxPointSize*N*	The size of the *N*th font in points	**TxPointSize** or **TxPointSize*N-1***
TxUnderLine	If true, the text is underlined	false

Table 5–1 Common Settings for All Animation Applets (Continued)

Name	Description	Default
TxBorderWidth	The width of the text border (must be greater than 0 in order for a border to be drawn)	0
TxBorderColor	The color of the text border	black
TxBorderMargin	The distance (in pixels) from the text border to the text on all sides	0
TxFrameThickness	The thickness of the text frame (must be greater than 0 in order for a frame to be drawn)	0
TxFrameType	The type of text frame: **ShadowIn, ShadowOut, ShadowEtchedIn,** or **ShadowEtchedOut**	**ShadowIn**
TxFrameMargin	The distance (in pixels) from the text frame to the text	0
AppBGColor	The background color of the applet	Set by browser
AppBorderWidth	The width of the applet border (must be greater than 0 in order for a border to be drawn)	0
AppBorderColor	The color of the applet border	black
AppFrameThickness	The thickness of the applet frame (must be greater than 0 in order for a frame to be drawn)	0
AppFrameType	The type of applet frame: **ShadowIn, ShadowOut, ShadowEtchedIn,** or **ShadowEtchedOut**	**ShadowIn**

AnimateContinuous

Continuous forward animation

Description

The **AnimateContinuous** applet animates the images in the specified sequence. When the end of the sequence is reached, animation pauses for the specified number of milliseconds and then repeats itself.

Using **AnimateContinuous** in HTML Code

The following HTML code uses the **AnimateContinuous** applet to create the animation shown at the top of this page:

```
<applet
    archive  = AnimateContinuous.zip
    codebase = AnimateContinuous
    code     = AnimateContinuous.class
    width    = 200
    height   = 150>
<param name=AppBGImage          value=AnimateContinuous/pattern.gif>
<param name=AppTile             value=true>

<param name=Text                value="Attention!">
<param name=TxFont              value=TimesRoman>
<param name=TxHorizCenter       value=true>
<param name=TxVertCenter        value=true>
<param name=TxStyle             value=Bold>
<param name=TxPointSize         value=24>
<param name=TxDelayBetweenRuns  value=50>
<param name=TxDelayBetweenImages value=50>
<param name=TxNumImages         value=8>
<param name=TxInitialImage      value=4>
<param name=TxFilter1           value="multicolor white blue red">
<param name=TxFilter2           value="multicolor blue red white">
<param name=TxFilter3           value="multicolor red white blue">
<param name=TxFilter4           value="$1">
<param name=TxFilter5           value="$2|rotate 20">
<param name=TxFilter6           value="$3|rotate 40">
<param name=TxFilter7           value="$1|rotate 60">
<param name=TxFilter8           value="$2|rotate 80">
</applet>
```

Here's another example of continuous animation using **AnimateContinuous**. This example uses the **waveimage** filter to alter the eyeball image.

```
<applet
    archive   = AnimateContinuous2.zip
    codebase  = AnimateContinuous2
    code      = AnimateContinuous.class
    width     = 100
    height    = 100>
<param name=AppBGColor              value=white>

<param name=Image1                  value=AnimateContinuous2/eyball.jpg>
<param name=ImgDelayBetweenRuns     value=40>
<param name=ImgDelayBetweenImages   value=40>
<param name=ImgVertCenter           value=true>
<param name=ImgHorizCenter          value=true>
<param name=ImgNumImages            value=12>
<param name=ImgFilter1              value="waveimage 4 4 0">
<param name=ImgFilter2              value="waveimage 4 4 2">
<param name=ImgFilter3              value="waveimage 4 4 4">
<param name=ImgFilter4              value="waveimage 4 4 6">
<param name=ImgFilter5              value="waveimage 4 4 8">
<param name=ImgFilter6              value="waveimage 4 4 10">
<param name=ImgFilter7              value="waveimage 4 4 12">
<param name=ImgFilter8              value="waveimage 4 4 14">
<param name=ImgFilter9              value="waveimage 4 4 16">
<param name=ImgFilter10             value="waveimage 4 4 18">
<param name=ImgFilter11             value="waveimage 4 4 20">
<param name=ImgFilter12             value="waveimage 4 4 22">
</applet>
```

Settings

See Table 5–1 on page 185 for common settings that apply to this applet.

See Also

Related applets: **AnimateTwoWay** on page 191

URL for **AnimateContinuous**

```
http://www.vivids.com/ij2/animate/AnimateContinuous.html
```

AnimateTwoWay

Continuous forward and backward animation

Forward

Description

The **AnimateTwoWay** applet animates the images in the specified sequence. When the end of the sequence is reached, the animation pauses the specified number of milliseconds, then reverses itself by displaying the images in reverse order. Backward and forward animation repeats continuously.

Backward

Using **AnimateTwoWay** in HTML Code

The following HTML code uses the **AnimateTwoWay** applet to create the animation shown at the top of this page:

```
<applet
    archive  = AnimateTwoWay.zip
    codebase = AnimateTwoWay
    code     = AnimateTwoWay.class
    width    = 200
    height   = 150>
<param name=AppBGImage            value=AnimateTwoWay/pattern.gif>
<param name=AppTile               value=true>
<param name=Text                  value="Attention!">
<param name=TxFont                value=TimesRoman>
<param name=TxHorizCenter         value=true>
<param name=TxVertCenter          value=true>
<param name=TxStyle               value=Bold>
<param name=TxPointSize            value=24>
<param name=TxDelayBetweenRuns    value=750>
<param name=TxDelayBetweenImages value=50>
<param name=TxNumImages           value=8>
<param name=TxInitialImage        value=4>
<param name=TxFilter1             value="multicolor white blue red">
<param name=TxFilter2             value="multicolor blue red white">
<param name=TxFilter3             value="multicolor red white blue">
<param name=TxFilter4             value="$1">
<param name=TxFilter5             value="$2|rotate 20">
<param name=TxFilter6             value="$3|rotate 40">
<param name=TxFilter7             value="$1|rotate 60">
<param name=TxFilter8             value="$2|rotate 80">
</applet>
```

Here's another example of continuous two-way animation using **AnimateTwoWay**. This animation shrinks an image using the **scale** filter.

```
<applet
    archive  = AnimateTwoWay2.zip
    codebase = AnimateTwoWay2
    code     = AnimateTwoWay.class
    width    = 120
    height   = 531>
<param name=Image1             value=AnimateTwoWay2/face.gif>
<param name=ImgHorizCenter     value=true>
<param name=ImgVertCenter      value=true>
<param name=ImgDelayBetweenRuns    value=2000>
<param name=ImgDelayBetweenImages  value=250>
<param name=ImgNumImages       value=12>
<param name=ImgFilter2         value="scale 95 90">
<param name=ImgFilter3         value="scale 90 80">
<param name=ImgFilter4         value="scale 85 70">
<param name=ImgFilter5         value="scale 80 60">
<param name=ImgFilter6         value="scale 75 50">
<param name=ImgFilter7         value="scale 70 40">
<param name=ImgFilter8         value="scale 65 30">
<param name=ImgFilter9         value="scale 60 20">
<param name=ImgFilter10        value="scale 55 10">
<param name=ImgFilter11        value="scale 50 2">
<param name=ImgFilter12        value="scale 0 0">
</applet>
```

Settings

See Table 5–1 on page 185 for common settings that apply to this applet.

See Also

Related applets: **AnimateContinuous** on page 189

URL for **AnimateTwoWay**:

```
http://www.vivids.com/ij2/animate/AnimateTwoWay.html
```

AnimateOnButton

Forward animation activated by mouse button

Description

The **AnimateOnButton** applet animates the images in the specified sequence when any mouse button is pressed in the image area or text area. The animation runs one time. When a mouse button is pressed again the animation repeats itself.

Forward on mouse press

Forward on mouse press

Using **AnimateOnButton** in HTML Code

The following HTML code uses the **AnimateOnButton** applet to create the animation shown at the top of this page.

```
<applet
    archive  = AnimateOnButton.zip
    codebase = AnimateOnButton
    code     = AnimateOnButton.class
    width    = 200
    height   = 150>
<param name=AppBGImage            value=AnimateOnButton/pattern.gif>
<param name=AppTile               value=true>

<param name=Text                  value="Attention!">
<param name=TxFont                value=TimesRoman>
<param name=TxHorizCenter         value=true>
<param name=TxVertCenter          value=true>
<param name=TxStyle               value=Bold>
<param name=TxPointSize           value=24>
<param name=TxDelayBetweenRuns    value=50>
<param name=TxDelayBetweenImages  value=50>
<param name=TxNumImages           value=9>
<param name=TxInitialImage        value=4>
<param name=TxRunOnce             value=true>
<param name=TxFilter1             value="multicolor white blue red">
<param name=TxFilter2             value="multicolor blue red white">
<param name=TxFilter3             value="multicolor red white blue">
<param name=TxFilter4             value="$1">
<param name=TxFilter5             value="$2|rotate 20">
<param name=TxFilter6             value="$3|rotate 40">
```

```
<param name=TxFilter7              value="$1|rotate 60">
<param name=TxFilter8              value="$2|rotate 80">
<param name=TxFilter22             value="$1">
</applet>
```

Here's another example using **AnimateOnButton** with a prepared series of images. This animation displays a car moving across a button. It is activated by button press.

```
<applet
    archive   = AnimateOnButton2.zip
    codebase  = AnimateOnButton2
    code      = AnimateOnButton.class
    width     = 106
    height    = 106>
<param name=AppBGImage              value=AnimateOnButton2/pattern.gif>
<param name=AppTile                 value=true>

<param name=ImgHorizCenter          value=true>
<param name=ImgVertCenter           value=true>
<param name=ImgDelayBetweenImages value=200>
<param name=ImgDisplayFirst         value=true>
<param name=ImgNumImages            value=8>
<param name=ImgInitialImage         value=1>
<param name=Image1                  value=AnimateOnButton2/car1.gif>
<param name=Image2                  value=AnimateOnButton2/car2.gif>
<param name=Image3                  value=AnimateOnButton2/car3.gif>
<param name=Image4                  value=AnimateOnButton2/car4.gif>
<param name=Image5                  value=AnimateOnButton2/car5.gif>
<param name=Image6                  value=AnimateOnButton2/car6.gif>
<param name=Image7                  value=AnimateOnButton2/car7.gif>
<param name=Image8                  value=$1>
</applet>
```

Settings

See Table 5–1 on page 185 for common settings that apply to this applet. Two additional parameters specify whether the text and image animation sequence should run once at launch time, independent of any mouse activity.

Table 12-2 AnimateOnButtonTwoWay Applet Settings

Name	Description	Default
TxRunOnce	If true, the text animation sequence runs once at launch time	false
ImgRunOnce	If true, the image animation sequence runs once at launch time	false

See Also

Related applets: **AnimateOnButtonTwoWay** on page 197

URL for **AnimateOnButton**:

    http://www.vivids.com/ij2/animate/AnimateOnButton.html

AnimateOnButtonTwoWay

Forward and backward animation activated by mouse button

Description

The **AnimateOnButtonTwoWay** applet animates the images in the specified sequence when any mouse button is pressed in the image or text area. The animation runs one time. When a mouse button is pressed again the animation reverses itself.

Forward on mouse press

Backward on mouse press

Using **AnimateOnButtonTwoWay** in HTML Code

The following HTML code uses the **AnimateOnButtonTwoWay** applet to create the animation shown at the top of this page:

```
<applet
    archive  = AnimateOnButtonTwoWay.zip
    codebase = AnimateOnButtonTwoWay
    code     = AnimateOnButtonTwoWay.class
    width    = 200
    height   = 150>
<param name=AppBGImage          value=AnimateOnButtonTwoWay/pattern.gif>
<param name=AppTile             value=true>

<param name=Text                value="Attention!">
<param name=TxFont              value=TimesRoman>
<param name=TxHorizCenter       value=true>
<param name=TxVertCenter        value=true>
<param name=TxStyle             value=Bold>
<param name=TxPointSize          value=24>
<param name=TxDelayBetweenRuns   value=50>
<param name=TxDelayBetweenImages value=50>
<param name=TxNumImages          value=8>
<param name=TxInitialImage       value=4>
<param name=TxRunOnce            value=true>
<param name=TxFilter1           value="multicolor white blue red">
<param name=TxFilter2           value="multicolor blue red white">
<param name=TxFilter3           value="multicolor red white blue">
<param name=TxFilter4           value="$1">
<param name=TxFilter5           value="$2|rotate 20">
<param name=TxFilter6           value="$3|rotate 40">
```

```
<param name=TxFilter7          value="$1|rotate 60">
<param name=TxFilter8          value="$2|rotate 80">
</applet>
```

Here's another example using **AnimateOnButtonTwoWay**. This animation displays a sign that has been processed with the **waveimage** filter.

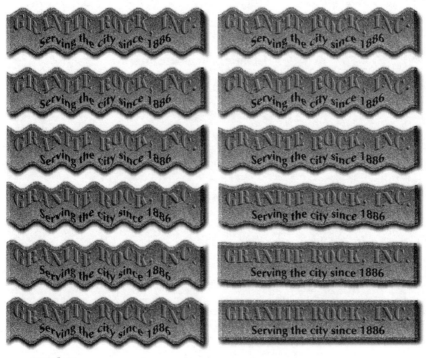

```
<applet
    archive  = AnimateOnButtonTwoWay2.zip
    codebase = AnimateOnButtonTwoWay2
    code     = AnimateOnButtonTwoWay.class
    width    = 300
    height   = 150>

<param name=Image1
value=AnimateOnButtonTwoWay2/granite2.gif>
<param name=AppBGColor              value=#ffffff>
<param name=ImgDelayBetweenImages value=75>
<param name=ImgHorizCenter          value=true>
<param name=ImgVertCenter           value=true>
<param name=ImgNumImages            value=13>
<param name=ImgInitialImage         value=2>
<param name=ImgFilter1              value="scale 60 60">
```

```
<param name=ImgFilter2              value="$1|waveimage 8 10 0">
<param name=ImgFilter3              value="$1|waveimage 8 10 10">
<param name=ImgFilter4              value="$1|waveimage 8 10 20">
<param name=ImgFilter5              value="$1|waveimage 8 10 30">
<param name=ImgFilter6              value="$1|waveimage 8 10 40">
<param name=ImgFilter7              value="$1|waveimage 8 10 50">
<param name=ImgFilter8              value="$1|waveimage 8 10 60">
<param name=ImgFilter9              value="$1|waveimage 8 10 70">
<param name=ImgFilter10             value="$1|waveimage 6 10 80">
<param name=ImgFilter11             value="$1|waveimage 4 10 90">
<param name=ImgFilter12             value="$1|waveimage 2 10 100">
<param name=ImgFilter13             value="$1">
</applet>
```

Settings

See Table 5–1 on page 185 for common settings that apply to this applet. Two additional parameters specify whether the text and image animation sequences should run once at launch time, independent of any mouse activity.

Table 12-3 AnimateOnButtonTwoWay Applet Settings

Name	Description	Default
TxRunOnce	If true, the text animation sequence runs once at launch time	false
ImgRunOnce	If true, the image animation sequence runs once at launch time	false

See Also

Related applets: **AnimateOnButton** on page 194

URL for **AnimateOnButtonTwoWay**

```
http://www.vivids.com/ij2/animate/AnimateOnButtonTwoWay.html
```

AnimateOnEntry

Continuous forward animation activated by pointer entry

Description

The **AnimateOnEntry** applet animates the images in the specified sequence when the pointer enters the text or image area. The animation runs continuously while the

Forward when pointer enters

pointer remains within the boundaries of the text or image. When the pointer leaves the area, the animation stops.

You can specify that when the pointer leaves the text or image area, the image reverts to its original state. Otherwise, the image remains as it was when the pointer left the area.

Using **AnimateOnEntry** in HTML Code

The following HTML code uses the **AnimateOnEntry** applet to create the animation shown at the top of this page:

```
<applet
    archive  = AnimateOnEntry.zip
    codebase = AnimateOnEntry
    code     = AnimateOnEntry.class
    width    = 200
    height   = 150>
<param name=AppBGImage              value=AnimateOnEntry/pattern.gif>
<param name=AppTile                 value=true>

<param name=Text                    value="Attention!">
<param name=TxFont                  value=TimesRoman>
<param name=TxHorizCenter           value=true>
<param name=TxVertCenter            value=true>
<param name=TxStyle                 value=Bold>
<param name=TxPointSize             value=24>
<param name=TxDelayBetweenRuns      value=50>
<param name=TxDelayBetweenImages    value=50>
<param name=TxNumImages             value=8>
<param name=TxInitialImage          value=4>
<param name=TxRunOnce               value=true>
<param name=TxFilter1               value="multicolor white blue red">
<param name=TxFilter2               value="multicolor blue red white">
<param name=TxFilter3               value="multicolor red white blue">
<param name=TxFilter4               value="$1">
<param name=TxFilter5               value="$2|rotate 20">
```

```
<param name=TxFilter6              value="$3|rotate 40">
<param name=TxFilter7              value="$1|rotate 60">
<param name=TxFilter8              value="$2|rotate 80">
```

The following example uses the **AnimateOnEntry** applet with a prepared series of images to "ring the telephone" when the pointer enters the image region. The "ringing" continues until the pointer leaves the region.

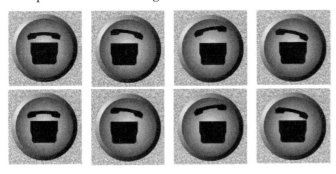

```
<applet
    archive  = AnimateOnEntry2.zip
    codebase = AnimateOnEntry2
    code     = AnimateOnEntry.class
    width    = 120
    height   = 120>
<param name=AppBGImage             value=AnimateOnEntry2/pattern.gif>
<param name=AppTile                value=true>

<param name=Image1                 value=AnimateOnEntry2/phone1.gif>
<param name=Image2                 value=AnimateOnEntry2/phone2.gif>
<param name=Image3                 value=AnimateOnEntry2/phone3.gif>
<param name=Image4                 value=AnimateOnEntry2/phone4.gif>
<param name=ImgHorizCenter         value=true>
<param name=ImgVertCenter          value=true>
<param name=ImgDelayBetweenImages  value=100>
<param name=ImgDelayBetweenRuns    value=100>
<param name=ImgNumImages           value=4>
<param name=ImgReturnStart         value=true>
<param name=ImgAudio               value=AnimateOnEntry2/phone.au>
<param name=ImgAudioLoop           value=true>
<param name=ImgURL                 value=http://www.pacbell.net>
</applet>
```

Settings

See Table 5–1 on page 185 for common settings that apply to this applet. Two additional parameters specify whether the text and image animation sequence should revert to the initial image when the pointer leaves the region.

Table 12-4 AnimateOnEntry Applet Settings

Name	Description	Default
TxReturnStart	If true, the text animation sequence reverts to the initial image when the pointer leaves the text region	false
ImgReturnStart	If true, the image animation sequence reverts to the initial image when the pointer leaves the image region	false

See Also

Related applets: **AnimateOnEntryTwoWay** on page 203

URL for **AnimateOnEntry**:
http://www.vivids.com/ij2/animate/AnimateOnEntry.html

AnimateOnEntryTwoWay

Forward animation activated by pointer entry
Backward animation activated by pointer exit

Description

The **AnimateOnEntryTwoWay** applet animates the images in the specified sequence when the pointer enters the text or image area. The animation runs once. When the pointer leaves the area, the animation reverses itself.

Forward when pointer enters

Backward when pointer leaves

Using **AnimateOnEntryTwoWay** in HTML Code

The following HTML code uses the **AnimateOnEntryTwoWay** applet to create the animation shown at the top of this page.

```
<applet
    archive  = AnimateOnEntryTwoWay.zip
    codebase = AnimateOnEntryTwoWay
    code     = AnimateOnEntryTwoWay.class
    width    = 200
    height   = 150>
<param name=AppBGImage          value=AnimateOnEntryTwoWay/pattern.gif>
<param name=AppTile             value=true>

<param name=Text                value="Attention!">
<param name=TxFont              value=TimesRoman>
<param name=TxHorizCenter       value=true>
<param name=TxVertCenter        value=true>
<param name=TxStyle             value=Bold>
<param name=TxPointSize         value=24>
<param name=TxDelayBetweenRuns  value=50>
<param name=TxDelayBetweenImages value=50>
<param name=TxNumImages         value=8>
<param name=TxInitialImage      value=4>
<param name=TxFilter1           value="multicolor white blue red">
<param name=TxFilter2           value="multicolor blue red white">
<param name=TxFilter3           value="multicolor red white blue">
<param name=TxFilter4           value="$1">
<param name=TxFilter5           value="$2|rotate 20">
<param name=TxFilter6           value="$3|rotate 40">
```

```
<param name=TxFilter7              value="$1|rotate 60">
<param name=TxFilter8              value="$1|rotate 80">
</applet>
```

Here's an example that uses both text and an image. When the pointer moves within the image, the **transparent** filter makes the image become gradually transparent. At the same time, the text gradually becomes less transparent. The effect is of the image disappearing while the text appears.

```
<applet
    archive  = AnimateOnEntryTwoWay2.zip
    codebase = AnimateOnEntryTwoWay2
    code     = AnimateOnEntryTwoWay.class
    width    = 240
    height   = 200>
<param name=AppBGImage           value=AnimateOnEntryTwoWay2/pattern.gif>
<param name=AppTile                    value=true>

<param name=Text                       value="Welcome!">
<param name=TxFont                     value=TimesRoman>
<param name=TxHorizCenter              value=true>
<param name=TxVertCenter               value=true>
<param name=TxStyle                    value=Bold>
<param name=TxPointSize                value=42>
<param name=TxDelayBetweenImages  value=250>
<param name=TxNumImages                value=7>
<param name=TxInitialImage             value=2>
<param name=TxFilter1                  value="text">
<param name=TxFilter2                  value="$1|transparent 100">
<param name=TxFilter3                  value="$1|transparent 80">
<param name=TxFilter4                  value="$1|transparent 60">
<param name=TxFilter5                  value="$1|transparent 40">
```

```
<param name=TxFilter6                    value="$1|transparent 20">
<param name=TxFilter7                    value="$1|transparent 0">

<param name=Image1                value=AnimateOnEntryTwoWay2/vivid.gif>
<param name=ImgHorizCenter         value=true>
<param name=ImgVertCenter          value=true>
<param name=ImgDelayBetweenImages value=250>
<param name=ImgNumImages           value=6>
<param name=ImgFilter2             value="transparent 20">
<param name=ImgFilter3             value="transparent 40">
<param name=ImgFilter4             value="transparent 60">
<param name=ImgFilter5             value="transparent 80">
<param name=ImgFilter6             value="transparent 100">
</applet>
```

Settings

See Table 5–1 on page 185 for common settings that apply to this applet.

See Also

Related applets: **AnimateOnEntry** on page 200

URL for **AnimateOnEntryTwoWay**:

```
http://www.vivids.com/ij2/animate/AnimateOnEntryTwoWay.html
```

AnimateOnPressRelease

Forward animation activated by button press
Backward animation activated by button release

Description

The **AnimateOnPressRelease** applet animates the images in the specified sequence when the mouse button is pressed with the pointer in the text or image area. The animation runs once. When the mouse button is released, the animation reverses itself.

Forward on button press

Backward on button release

Using **AnimateOnPressRelease** in HTML Code

The following HTML code uses the **AnimateOnPressRelease** applet to create the animation shown at the top of this page.

```
<applet
    archive  = AnimateOnPressRelease.zip
    codebase = AnimateOnPressRelease
    code     = AnimateOnPressRelease.class
    width    = 200
    height   = 150>
<param name=AppBGImage          value=AnimateOnPressRelease/pattern.gif>
pParam name=AppTile             value=true>

<param name=Text                value="Attention!">
<param name=TxFont              value=TimesRoman>
<param name=TxHorizCenter       value=true>
<param name=TxVertCenter        value=true>
<param name=TxStyle             value=Bold>
<param name=TxPointSize         value=24>
<param name=TxDelayBetweenRuns  value=50>
<param name=TxDelayBetweenImages value=50>
<param name=TxNumImages         value=22>
<param name=TxInitialImage      value=4>
<param name=TxRunOnce           value=true>
<param name=TxFilter1           value="multicolor white blue red">
<param name=TxFilter2           value="multicolor blue red white">
<param name=TxFilter3           value="multicolor red white blue">
<param name=TxFilter4           value="$1">
<param name=TxFilter5           value="$2|rotate 20">
```

```
<param name=TxFilter6          value="$3|rotate 40">
<param name=TxFilter7          value="$1|rotate 60">
<param name=TxFilter8          value="$2|rotate 80">
<param name=TxFilter9          value="$3|rotate 100">
<param name=TxFilter10         value="$1|rotate 120">
<param name=TxFilter11         value="$2|rotate 140">
<param name=TxFilter12         value="$3|rotate 160">
<param name=TxFilter13         value="$1|rotate 180">
<param name=TxFilter14         value="$2|rotate 200">
<param name=TxFilter15         value="$3|rotate 220">
<param name=TxFilter16         value="$1|rotate 240">
<param name=TxFilter17         value="$2|rotate 260">
<param name=TxFilter18         value="$3|rotate 280">
<param name=TxFilter19         value="$1|rotate 300">
<param name=TxFilter20         value="$2|rotate 320">
<param name=TxFilter21         value="$3|rotate 340">
<param name=TxFilter22         value="$1">
</applet>
```

Here's an example that displays an image with a shadow. When the mouse button is pressed, the button moves down and to the left a few pixels and the shadow darkens and its offset is altered. This gives the impression that the button is being pressed.

```
<applet
    archive  = AnimateOnPressRelease2.zip
    codebase = AnimateOnPressRelease2
    code     = AnimateOnPressRelease.class
    width    = 118
    height   = 118>
<param name=AppBGColor              value=white>

<param name=Image1                  value=AnimateOnPressRelease2/phone1.gif>
<param name=ImgDelayBetweenImages   value=50>
<param name=ImgNumImages            value=3>
<param name=ImgURL                  value="http://www.pacbell.net">
<param name=ImgFilter1              value="imageshadow 6 6 #dddddd">
<param name=ImgFilter2              value="imageshadow 4 4 #999999">
```

```
<param name=ImgFilter3         value="imageshadow 2 2 #777777">
<param name=ImgAudio         value=AnimateOnPressRelease2/phone.au>
<param name=ImgAudioLoop        value=true>
<param name=ImgXOffset1         value=3>
<param name=ImgYOffset1         value=3>
<param name=ImgXOffset2         value=5>
<param name=ImgYOffset2         value=5>
<param name=ImgXOffset3         value=7>
<param name=ImgYOffset3         value=7>
</applet>
```

Settings

See Table 5–1 on page 185 for common settings that apply to this applet.

See Also

Related applets: **AnimateOnEntry** on page 200

URL for **AnimateOnPressRelease**:

```
http://www.vivids.com/ij2/animate/AnimateOnPressRelease.html
```

AnimateMultiple
Multiple simultaneous animations

Description

The **AnimateMultiple** applet animates multiple strings and images simultaneously and is the most complex applet in the book.

If you want to create multiple animations, you always have the option of using several animation applets on the same Web page. One limitation of using multiple applets is that the animation applets cannot overlap each other. If you want several animation sequences to touch each other, overlap each other, or run on top of each other you need to use **Animate-Multiple**. Another limitation of using multiple applets is that you cannot synchronize the applets. With **AnimateMultiple** you can synchronize multiple animations.

Synchronizing animation sequences means that each frame in each animation sequence will be displayed simultaneously. **AnimateMultiple** has the capability to synchronize all image animations or all text animations. It cannot synchronize text and image animations.

The first animation (**Tx1** or **Img1**) is the controlling animation sequence. All other animation sequences will follow the first animation. This means that the speed and behavior or the first animation will be inherited by the other animation sequences of the same type. An example synchronous animation is shown later in this section.

Using **AnimateMultiple** in HTML Code

The following HTML code uses the **AnimateMultiple** applet to create the three text animations and two image animations shown in the illustration.

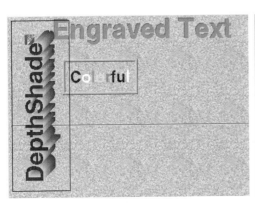
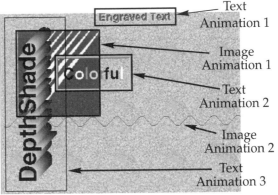

```
<applet
    archive  = AnimateMultiple.zip
    codebase = AnimateMultiple
    code     = AnimateMultiple.class
    width    = 380
    height   = 280>
<param name=AppTile                    value=true>
<param name=AppBgImage                 value=AnimateMultiple/pattern.gif>
<param name=AppFrameThickness          value=4>
<param name=AppFrameType               value=ShadowEtchedIn>

<param name=TxCount                    value=3>

<param name=Text1                      value="Engraved Text">
<param name=Text1_1                    value="Engraved Text">
<param name=Text1_2                    value="Engraved Text">
<param name=Text1_3                    value="Engraved Text">
<param name=Text1_4                    value="Engraved Text">
<param name=Tx1DelayBetweenImages      value=100>
<param name=Tx1DelayBetweenRuns        value=1000>
<param name=Tx1AnimationType           value=TwoWay>
<param name=Tx1XCenter                 value=210>
<param name=Tx1PointSize1              value=48>
<param name=Tx1PointSize2              value=44>
<param name=Tx1PointSize3              value=40>
<param name=Tx1PointSize4              value=36>
<param name=Tx1PointSize5              value=32>
<param name=Tx1PointSize6              value=28>
<param name=Tx1PointSize7              value=24>
<param name=Tx1PointSize8              value=20>
<param name=Tx1PointSize9              value=16>
<param name=Tx1Font1                   value=Helvetica>
<param name=Tx1Style1                  value=Bold>
<param name=Tx1NumImages               value=16>
<param name=Tx1Filter1                 value="engrave 1 40">
<param name=Tx1Filter2                 value="engrave 1 40">
<param name=Tx1Filter3                 value="engrave 1 40">
<param name=Tx1Filter4                 value="engrave 1 40">
<param name=Tx1Filter5                 value="engrave 1 50">
<param name=Tx1Filter6                 value="engrave 1 60">
<param name=Tx1Filter7                 value="engrave 1 70">
<param name=Tx1Filter8                 value="engrave 1 80">
<param name=Tx1Filter9                 value="engrave 1 70">
<param name=Tx1Filter10                value="engrave 1 60">
<param name=Tx1Filter11                value="engrave 1 50">
<param name=Tx1Filter12                value="engrave 1 40">
<param name=Tx1Filter13                value="engrave 1 30">
<param name=Tx1Filter14                value="engrave 1 20">
```

```
<param name=Tx1Filter15          value="engrave 1 10">
<param name=Tx1Filter16          value="engrave 1 0">
<param name=Tx1URL               value=http://www.sun.com>
<param name=Tx1XOffset1          value=10>
<param name=Tx1XOffset2          value=20>
<param name=Tx1XOffset3          value=30>
<param name=Tx1XOffset4          value=40>
<param name=Tx1XOffset5          value=50>
<param name=Tx1XOffset6          value=60>
<param name=Tx1XOffset7          value=70>
<param name=Tx1XOffset8          value=80>

<param name=Text2                value="Colorful">
<param name=Tx2DelayBetweenImages value=100>
<param name=Tx2DelayBetweenRuns  value=100>
<param name=Tx2PointSize         value=24>
<param name=Tx2Font              value=Helvetica>
<param name=Tx2Style             value=Bold>
<param name=Tx2XOffset1          value=100>
<param name=Tx2YOffset1          value=80>
<param name=Tx2FrameThickness    value=4>
<param name=Tx2FrameMargin       value=12>
<param name=Tx2FrameType         value=ShadowEtchedOut>
<param name=Tx2NumImages         value=4>
<param name=Tx2Filter1  value="multicolor yellow green blue black white salmon">
<param name=Tx2Filter2  value="multicolor green blue black white salmon yellow">
<param name=Tx2Filter3  value="multicolor blue black white salmon yellow green">
<param name=Tx2Filter4  value="multicolor black white salmon yellow green blue">
<param name=Tx2Audio       value=AnimateMultiple/sun.au>
<param name=Tx2URL         value=http://www.vivids.com>

<param name=Text3                value="DepthShade">
<param name=Tx3Color1            value="#aa00aa">
<param name=Tx3Color2            value="#990099">
<param name=Tx3Color3            value="#660066">
<param name=Tx3Color4            value="#440044">
<param name=Tx3Color5            value="#220022">
<param name=Tx3Color6            value="#000000">
<param name=Tx3DelayBetweenImages value=400>
<param name=Tx3DelayBetweenRuns  value=1000>
<param name=Tx3AnimationType     value=TwoWay>
<param name=Tx3PointSize         value=36>
<param name=Tx3Font              value=Helvetica>
<param name=Tx3Style             value=Bold>
<param name=Tx3XOffset1          value=22>
<param name=Tx3YOffset1          value=22>
<param name=Tx3BorderWidth       value=1>
<param name=Tx3BorderMargin      value=13>
```

```
<param name=Tx3NumImages            value=6>
<param name=Tx3Filter1        value="depthshade 10 10 yellow|rotate 90">
<param name=Tx3Filter2        value="depthshade 15 15 yellow|rotate 90">
<param name=Tx3Filter3        value="depthshade 20 20 yellow|rotate 90">
<param name=Tx3Filter4        value="depthshade 25 25 yellow|rotate 90">
<param name=Tx3Filter5        value="depthshade 30 30 yellow|rotate 90">
<param name=Tx3Filter6        value="depthshade 35 35 yellow|rotate 90">

<param name=ImgCount                value=2>

<param name=Img1Image1              value=AnimateMultiple/vivid.gif>
<param name=Img1DelayBetweenImages value=100>
<param name=Img1DelayBetweenRuns    value=100>
<param name=Img1XOffset1            value=30>
<param name=Img1YOffset1            value=30>
<param name=Img1NumImages           value=19>
<param name=Img1Filter1             value="scale 10 10">
<param name=Img1Filter2             value="scale 20 20">
<param name=Img1Filter3             value="scale 30 30">
<param name=Img1Filter4             value="scale 40 40">
<param name=Img1Filter5             value="scale 50 50">
<param name=Img1Filter6             value="scale 60 60">
<param name=Img1Filter7             value="scale 70 70">
<param name=Img1Filter8             value="scale 80 80">
<param name=Img1Filter9             value="scale 90 90">
<param name=Img1Image10             value=$1>
<param name=Img1Filter11            value=$9>
<param name=Img1Filter12            value=$8>
<param name=Img1Filter13            value=$7>
<param name=Img1Filter14            value=$6>
<param name=Img1Filter15            value=$5>
<param name=Img1Filter16            value=$4>
<param name=Img1Filter17            value=$3>
<param name=Img1Filter18            value=$2>
<param name=Img1Filter19            value=$1>
<param name=Img1Audio               value=AnimateMultiple/welcome.au>

<param name=Img2Image1              value=AnimateMultiple/hr.gif>
<param name=Img2DelayBetweenImages value=100>
<param name=Img2DelayBetweenRuns    value=3000>
<param name=Img2XOffset1            value=0>
<param name=Img2YOffset1            value=160>
<param name=Img2NumImages           value=10>
<param name=Img2Filter1             value="transcolor #c0c0c0">
<param name=Img2Filter2             value="$1|waveimage 2 6 10">
<param name=Img2Filter3             value="$1|waveimage 4 6 20">
<param name=Img2Filter4             value="$1|waveimage 6 6 30">
<param name=Img2Filter5             value="$1|waveimage 8 6 40">
```

```
<param name=Img2Filter6        value="$5">
<param name=Img2Filter7        value="$4">
<param name=Img2Filter8        value="$3">
<param name=Img2Filter9        value="$2">
<param name=Img2Filter10       value="$1">
<param name=Img2YOffset2       value=158>
<param name=Img2YOffset3       value=156>
<param name=Img2YOffset4       value=154>
<param name=Img2YOffset5       value=152>
<param name=Img2YOffset6       value=152>
<param name=Img2YOffset7       value=154>
<param name=Img2YOffset8       value=156>
<param name=Img2YOffset9       value=158>
<param name=Img2YOffset10      value=160>

</applet>
```

Here another example using **AnimateMultiple**. This example creates five animations, each with a different animation type.

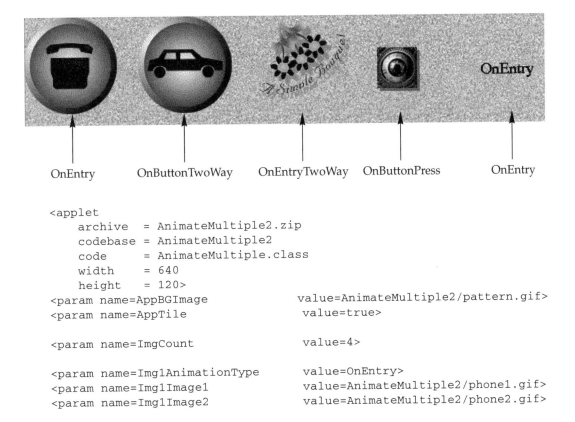

OnEntry   OnButtonTwoWay   OnEntryTwoWay   OnButtonPress   OnEntry

```
<applet
     archive   = AnimateMultiple2.zip
     codebase  = AnimateMultiple2
     code      = AnimateMultiple.class
     width     = 640
     height    = 120>
<param name=AppBGImage        value=AnimateMultiple2/pattern.gif>
<param name=AppTile            value=true>

<param name=ImgCount           value=4>

<param name=Img1AnimationType  value=OnEntry>
<param name=Img1Image1         value=AnimateMultiple2/phone1.gif>
<param name=Img1Image2         value=AnimateMultiple2/phone2.gif>
```

```
<param name=Img1Image3                 value=AnimateMultiple2/phone3.gif>
<param name=Img1Image4                 value=AnimateMultiple2/phone4.gif>
<param name=Img1XOffset1               value=0>
<param name=Img1YOffset1               value=0>
<param name=Img1DelayBetweenImages value=100>
<param name=Img1DelayBetweenRuns       value=100>
<param name=Img1NumImages              value=4>
<param name=Img1ReturnStart            value=true>
<param name=Img1Audio                  value=AnimateMultiple2/phone.au>
<param name=Img1AudioLoop              value=true>

<param name=Img2AnimationType          value=OnButtonTwoWay>
<param name=Img2Image1                 value=AnimateMultiple2/car1.gif>
<param name=Img2Image2                 value=AnimateMultiple2/car2.gif>
<param name=Img2Image3                 value=AnimateMultiple2/car3.gif>
<param name=Img2Image4                 value=AnimateMultiple2/car4.gif>
<param name=Img2Image5                 value=AnimateMultiple2/car5.gif>
<param name=Img2Image6                 value=AnimateMultiple2/car6.gif>
<param name=Img2Image7                 value=AnimateMultiple2/car7.gif>
<param name=Img2Image8                 value=$1>
<param name=Img2XOffset1               value=130>
<param name=Img2YOffset1               value=0>
<param name=Img2DelayBetweenImages value=100>
<param name=Img2DelayBetweenRuns       value=100>
<param name=Img2NumImages              value=8>
<param name=Img2ReturnStart            value=true>
<param name=Img2Audio                  value=AnimateMultiple2/movecar.au>

<param name=Img3AnimationType          value=OnEntryTwoWay>
<param name=Img3Image1                 value=AnimateMultiple2/bouquet.gif>
<param name=Img3Filter1                value="scale 50 50">
<param name=Img3Filter2                value="$1|imageshadow 5 5 #aaaaaa">
<param name=Img3Filter3                value="$1|imageshadow 3 3 #888888">
<param name=Img3Filter4                value="$1|imageshadow 1 1 #222222">
<param name=Img3Filter5                value="$1">
<param name=Img3XOffset1               value=260>
<param name=Img3YOffset1               value=0>
<param name=Img3XOffset2               value=261>
<param name=Img3YOffset2               value=1>
<param name=Img3XOffset3               value=262>
<param name=Img3YOffset3               value=2>
<param name=Img3XOffset4               value=263>
<param name=Img3YOffset4               value=3>
<param name=Img3XOffset5               value=264>
<param name=Img3YOffset5               value=4>
<param name=Img3InitialImage           value=2>
<param name=Img3DelayBetweenImages value=100>
<param name=Img3DelayBetweenRuns       value=100>
```

```
<param name=Img3NumImages            value=5>

<param name=Img4AnimationType        value=OnPressRelease>
<param name=Img4Image1               value=AnimateMultiple2/eyball.jpg>
<param name=Img4Filter1              value="imageshadow 5 5 #aaaaaa">
<param name=Img4Filter2              value="imageshadow 3 3 #888888">
<param name=Img4Filter3              value="imageshadow 1 1 #222222">
<param name=Img4Filter4              value="noop">
<param name=Img4XOffset1             value=400>
<param name=Img4YOffset1             value=35>
<param name=Img4XOffset2             value=401>
<param name=Img4YOffset2             value=36>
<param name=Img4XOffset3             value=402>
<param name=Img4YOffset3             value=37>
<param name=Img4XOffset4             value=403>
<param name=Img4YOffset4             value=38>
<param name=Img4XOffset5             value=404>
<param name=Img4YOffset5             value=39>
<param name=Img4InitialImage         value=2>
<param name=Img4DelayBetweenImages value=100>
<param name=Img4DelayBetweenRuns     value=100>
<param name=Img4NumImages            value=4>


<param name=TxCount                  value=1>

<param name=Tx1AnimationType         value=OnEntry>
<param name=Text1                    value="OnEntry">
<param name=Tx1Font1                 value="TimesRoman">
<param name=Tx1PointSize1            value=18>
<param name=Tx1PointSize2            value=24>
<param name=Tx1PointSize3            value=32>
<param name=Tx1PointSize4            value=36>
<param name=Tx1Filter5               value=$3>
<param name=Tx1Filter6               value=$2>
<param name=Tx1Filter7               value=$1>
<param name=Tx1XCenter               value=550>
<param name=Tx1YCenter               value=60>
<param name=Tx1DelayBetweenImages  value=100>
<param name=Tx1DelayBetweenRuns    value=100>
<param name=Tx1NumImages             value=6>
<param name=Tx1ReturnStart           value=true>
</applet>
```

The next example uses the **TxSynchronous** parameter to synchronize two text animations. When the first animation is activated (by a button click) the second animation is also activated. Each animation sequence is then displayed simultaneously.

Press Here

This text will grow

See

This text will grow

See what

This text will grow

See what happens?

This text has grown

Press Here

This text has grown

```
<applet
    archive  = AnimateMultiple3.zip
    codebase = AnimateMultiple3
    code     = AnimateMultiple.class
    width    = 300
    height   = 80>
<param name=AppBGColor              value=white>

<param name=TxSynchronous           value=true>
<param name=TxCount                 value=2>

<param name=Tx1AnimationType        value=OnButton>
<param name=Tx1NumImages            value=5>
<param name=Text1_1                 value="Press Here">
<param name=Text1_2                 value="See">
<param name=Text1_3                 value="See what">
<param name=Text1_4                 value="See what happens?">
<param name=Text1_5                 value="Press Here">
```

```
<param name=Tx1Font1                value="TimesRoman">
<param name=Tx1PointSize1           value=18>
<param name=Tx1XOffset1             value=20>
<param name=Tx1YCenter              value=20>
<param name=Tx1DelayBetweenImages   value=500>
<param name=Tx1DelayBetweenRuns     value=500>
<param name=Tx1ReturnStart          value=true>

<param name=Tx2AnimationType        value=OnEntry>
<param name=Tx2NumImages            value=4>
<param name=Text2_1                 value="This text will grow">
<param name=Text2_2                 value="This text will grow">
<param name=Text2_3                 value="This text will grow">
<param name=Text2_4                 value="This text has grown">
<param name=Tx2Font1                value="TimesRoman">
<param name=Tx2PointSize1           value=18>
<param name=Tx2PointSize2           value=22>
<param name=Tx2PointSize3           value=26>
<param name=Tx2PointSize4           value=30>
<param name=Tx2XOffset1             value=20>
<param name=Tx2YCenter              value=58>
<param name=Tx2ReturnStart          value=true>
</applet>
```

Settings

See Table 5–1 on page 185 for common settings that apply to this applet. However, the parameters that begin with **Tx** must instead begin with **TxN**, and parameters that begin with **Img** must instead begin with **ImgN**. The **N** specifies the text or image animation involved.

The parameters that specify filters include two numbers: one that specifies the animation number, and the other the filter number. **TxNFilterM** specifies the **N**th text animation and the **M**th filter for that animation sequence. **Img2Filter1**, for example, specifies the filter for the first image in image animation sequence 2. The parameters that specify the text, font, style, pointsize, and color also include two numbers: one for the animation number (**N**), and the other the text sequence number in that animation sequence (**M**).

Table 12-5 AnimateMultiple Applet Settings

Name	Description	Default
TxCount	The number of text animation sequences	0
ImgCount	The number of image animation sequences	0
ImgNimageM	The **M**th image of the **N**th image animation sequence	
TxNAnimationType	The animation type of the Nth text animation: **Continuous, TwoWay, OnButton, OnButtonTwoWay, OnEntry, OnEntryTwoWay**	**Continuous**

Table 12-5 AnimateMultiple Applet Settings

Name	Description	Default
Img*N*AnimationType	The animation type of the Nth image animation: **Continuous, TwoWay, OnButton, OnButtonTwoWay, OnEntry, OnEntryTwoWay, On PressRelease**	**Continuous**
Tx*N*XCenter	The horizontal position at which to center the *N*th text animation sequence	(do not center)
Tx*N*YCenter	The vertical position at which to center the *N*th text animation sequence	(do not center)
Img*N*XCenter	The horizontal position at which to center the *N*th image animation sequence	(do not center)
Img*N*YCenter	The vertical position at which to center the *N*th image animation sequence	(do not center)
Tx*N*ReturnStart	If true, the *N*th text animation sequence reverts to the initial image when the pointer leaves the text region	false
Img*N*ReturnStart	If true, the *N*th image animation sequence reverts to the initial image when the pointer leaves the image region	false
Tx*N*Filter*M*	The filter with which to manipulate the *M*th text in the **N**th text animation sequence	(none)
Img*N*Filter*M*	The filter with which to manipulate the *M*th image in the **N**th image animation sequence	(none)
TxSynchronous	If true, synchronize all text animation sequences	false
ImgSynchronous	If true, synchronize all image animation sequences	false
Text*N*_*M*	The *M*th text in the **N**th text animation sequence	**Text*N*** or **Text*N*_*M-1***
TxColor*N*_*M*	The *M*th color in the **N**th text animation sequence	**TxColor*N*** or **TxColor*N*_*M-1***
TxFont*N*_*M*	The *M*th font in the **N**th text animation sequence	**TxFont*N*** or **TxFont*N*_*M-1***
TxStyle*N*_*M*	The *M*th style in the **N**th text animation sequence	**TxStyle*N*** or **TxStyle*N*_*M-1***
TxPointsize*N*_*M*	The *M*th pointsize in the **N**th text animation sequence	**TxPointsize*N*** or **TxPointsize*N*_*M-1***

See Also

URL for **AnimateMultiple**:

```
http://www.vivids.com/ij2/animate/AnimateMultiple.html
```

CHAPTER

6

Assorted Applets

The applets in this chapter are presented together because they don't fit into any particular category. They are, however, some of the most useful and interesting applets in the book.

These applets fit into two categories: string animation and slide shows.

The string animation applets are useful for displaying text in an eye-catching manner. They are not as flexible as the ones introduced in the previous chapters—you can't, for example, play an audio file or load a URL, or combine them as with filters—but they are not as complicated and have less overhead, so they will load and display faster than many of the other applets.

The slide show applets are designed to display a series of images with optional audio. Each slide show applet moves between images in a different way. Enjoy!

Common Settings for String Animation Applets

The first twelve applets in this chapter animate strings. Table 6–1 shows parameters that are common to these applets.

Table 6–1 Common Settings for String Animation Applets

Name	Description	Default
AppBGColor	The applet background color	Set by browser
AppBGImage	The applet background image	(none)
AppTile	If true, tile the background image	false
DelayBetweenChars	The delay (in milliseconds) between character movements	20
DelayBetweenRuns	The delay (in milliseconds) between strings	3000
XOffset	The horizontal distance (in pixels) from the left side of the applet to the text	0
YOffset	The vertical distance (in pixels) from the top of the applet to the baseline of the text	The height of the text
TextColor	The text color	Set by browser
HorizCenter	If true, the text is horizontal centered	false
VertCenter	If true, the text is vertical centered	false
Font	The font of the text: **TimesRoman, Helvetica, Courier, Dialog, DialogInput,** or **ZapfDingbats**	**Dialog**
Style	The style of the font: **Plain, Bold, Italic,** or **BoldItalic**	**Plain**
PointSize	The size of the font in points	10

Tracker

Highlights each character in a string from left to right

Displays multiple strings in succession

Description

The **Tracker** applet highlights each character in a string from left to right. You can select the color of the text and the color of the highlighting.

After a specified delay, the next string in the sequence, if any, is displayed in the same manner. There is no limit to the number of strings that can be displayed. After all of the strings have been displayed, the process starts again with the first string.

Interaction

The **Tracker** applet responds to the following keyboard input:

f	Highlighting speed 10% faster
s	Highlighting speed 10% slower
F	Delay between strings 10% shorter
S	Delay between strings 10% longer

Using Tracker in HTML Code

The following HTML code uses the **Tracker** applet to display the string *The Quick Brown Fox Jumps Over the Lazy Dog* as shown at the top of the page.

```
<applet
    codebase = Tracker
    code     = Tracker.class
    width    = 250
    height   = 35>
<param name=TextCount           value=3>
<param name=text1               value="The Quick Brown Fox">
<param name=text2               value="Jumps Over">
<param name=text3               value="the Lazy Dog">
<param name=DelayBetweenChars   value=50>
<param name=DelayBetweenRuns    value=2000>
<param name=HorizCenter         value=true>
```

```
<param name=VertCenter        value=true>
<param name=style             value=bold>
<param name=pointsize         value=20>
</applet>
```

Settings

See Table 6–1 on page 222 for common settings that apply to this applet. Three additional parameters specify the number of strings to display, the strings themselves, and the highlight color.

Table 6–2 Tracker Applet Settings

Name	Description	Default
TextCount	The number of strings to display (required)	0
TextN	The **N**th string of characters	(none)
HighlightColor	The highlight color	white

See Also

Related applets: **InOrder** on page 225
                        TrackFade on page 227

URL for **Tracker**:   http://www.vivids.com/ij2/assorted/Tracker.html

InOrder

Displays each character in a string from left to right

Displays multiple strings in succession

Description

The **InOrder** applet displays each character in a string from left to right.

After a specified delay, the next string in the sequence, if any, is displayed in the same manner. There is no limit to the number of strings that can be displayed. After all of the strings have been displayed, the process starts again with the first string.

Interaction

The **InOrder** applet responds to the following keyboard input:

f	Highlighting speed 10% faster
s	Highlighting speed 10% slower
F	Delay between strings 10% shorter
S	Delay between strings 10% longer

Using **InOrder** in HTML Code

The following HTML code uses the **InOrder** applet to display the string *No man of woman born, Coward or brave, can shun his destiny.* as shown at the top of the page.

```
<applet
    codebase = InOrder
    code     = InOrder.class
    width    = 300
    height   = 35>
<param name=Textcount value=3>
<param name=Text1    value="No man of woman born,">
<param name=Text2    value="Coward or brave,">
<param name=Text3    value="can shun his destiny.">
<param name=pointsize value=20>
<param name=style    value=bold>
</applet>
```

Settings

See Table 6–1 on page 222 for common settings that apply to this applet. Two additional parameters specify the number of strings to display, the strings themselves.

Table 6–3 InOrder Applet Settings

Name	Description	Default
TextCount	The number of strings to display (required)	0
TextN	The *N*th string of characters	(none)

See Also

Related applets: **Tracker** on page 223

URL for **InOrder**: `http://www.vivids.com/ij2/assorted/InOrder.html`

TrackFade

Highlights each character in a fading string from left to right

Displays multiple strings in succession

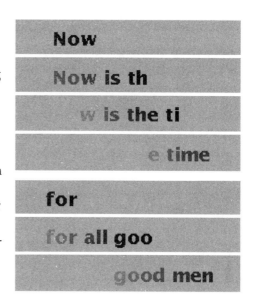

Description

The **TrackFade** applet displays each character in a string and then begins to fade that character as others are displayed. When the specified number of characters are displayed together, the leftmost character disappears entirely as each new character is added on the right. Characters in between are partially faded, depending on how far to the left they are. You can select the color of the text and the color of the highlighting.

After a specified delay, the next string in the sequence, if any, is displayed in the same manner. There is no limit to the number of strings that can be displayed. After all of the strings have been displayed, the process starts again with the first string.

Interaction

The **TrackFade** applet responds to the following keyboard input:

f	Highlighting speed 10% faster
s	Highlighting speed 10% slower
F	Delay between strings 10% shorter
S	Delay between strings 10% longer

Using **TrackFade** in HTML Code

The following HTML code uses the **TrackFade** to display the string *Now is the time for all good men to come to the aid of their country* as shown at the top of the page.

```
<applet
    codebase = TrackFade
    code     = TrackFade.class
    width    = 250
    height   = 35>
<param name=TextCount        value=4>
<param name=text1            value="Now is the time">
<param name=text2            value="for all good men">
```

```
<param name=text3          value="to come to the aid">
<param name=text4          value="of their country!">
<param name=FadeSize       value=12>
<param name=DelayBetweenChars value=50>
<param name=DelayBetweenRuns  value=1000>
<param name=HorizCenter    value=true>
<param name=VertCenter     value=true>
<param name=Style          value=bold>
<param name=Pointsize      value=20>
</applet>
```

Settings

See Table 6–1 on page 222 for common settings that apply to this applet. Four additional parameters specify the number of strings to display, the strings themselves, the color to which to fade, and the number of characters to display at once.

Table 6–4 TrackFade Applet Settings

Name	Description	Default
TextCount	The number of strings to display (required)	0
TextN	The **N**th string of characters	(none)
FadeToColor	The color to which the string fades	The background color
FadeSize	The number of characters to display simultaneously	10

The bigger the value of **FadeSize**, the more characters can be read together at any given time. Each displayed character will be a different color—some shade between **TextColor** and **FadeToColor**.

By default, **FadeToColor** is set to the background color of the applet. If you set **FadeToColor** to some other color, each character eventually appears drawn entirely in that color, rather than disappearing by fading to the background color.

See Also

Related applets: **Tracker** on page 223

URL for **TrackFade**:   http://www.vivids.com/ij2/assorted/TrackFade.html

Coalesce

Displays characters from a string at random positions

The string coalesces when the pointer enters the applet

Returns the characters to random positions when the pointer leaves the applet

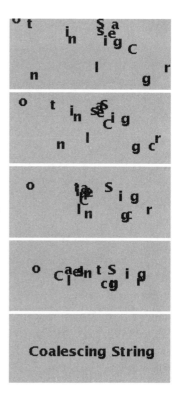

Coalescing String

Description

The **Coalesce** applet displays the characters in a string at random positions within the applet. When the pointer enters the applet, the characters begin to coalesce, until the specified string is displayed. When the pointer leaves the applet, the characters move to new random positions.

If the pointer enters or leaves the applet while the characters are moving, the direction of movement reverses. In other words, if the characters are coalescing and the pointer leaves the applet, the characters change direction—moving toward their random positions. If the characters are moving toward their random positions and the pointer enters the applet, the characters begin to coalesce.

Interaction

The **Coalesce** applet responds to the following keyboard input:

f   Character movement 10% faster

s   Character movement 10% slower

Using Coalesce in HTML Code

The following HTML code uses the **Coalesce** to display the string *Coalescing String* as shown at the top of the page.

```
<applet
    codebase = Coalesce
    code     = Coalesce.class
    width    = 250
    height   = 100>
<param name=text            value="Coalescing String">
<param name=AppBGImage      value=Coalesce/pattern.gif>
<param name=AppTile         value=true>
```

```
<param name=Steps              value=30>
<param name=DelayBetweenChars  value=50>
<param name=HorizCenter        value=true>
<param name=VertCenter         value=true>
<param name=style              value=bold>
<param name=pointsize          value=20>
</applet>
```

Settings

See Table 6–1 on page 222 for common settings that apply to this applet. Two additional parameters specify the string to display and the number of steps in the coalescing sequence.

Table 6–5 Coalesce Applet Settings

Name	Description	Default
Text	The string of characters to display	(none)
Steps	The number of steps in the coalescing sequence	50

The value of **Steps**, combined with the value of the **DelayBetweenChars** parameter, determines the speed with which the string coalesces.

See Also

URL for **Coalesce**:   `http://www.vivids.com/ij2/assorted/Coalesce.html`

Pages for source code: **Coalesce.java** on page 292

CoalesceContinuous

Displays characters from a string at random positions

The string coalesces and returns to random position continuously

Displays multiple strings in succession

Description

The **CoalesceContinuous** applet displays the characters in a string at random positions within the applet. Unlike the **Coalesce** applet, **CoalesceContinuous** operates independent of any user interaction. The characters move together, hold their position for the specified time period, then move to new random positions. The string of characters then changes to the next text string and the process repeats itself.

The characters displayed in the text strings may also be individually colored using the **Colors** parameter. If the **Colors** parameter is not specified then all characters will display in the color specified by **TxColor**. If the **Colors** parameter is used, its value may be set to one or more colors that are used to color successive characters. For example, to color the characters red, yellow, and blue, use the following parameter:

```
<param name=Colors value="red yellow blue">
```

If you specify a value for the **DelayBetweenColors** parameter, the displayed colors will alternate between characters.

Interaction

The **CoalesceContinuous** applet responds to the following keyboard input:

f	Character movement 10% faster
s	Character movement 10% slower
F	Delay between strings 10% shorter
S	Delay between strings 10% longer
c	Delay between colors changes 10% shorter
C	Delay between color changes 10% longer

Using CoalesceContinuous in HTML Code

The following HTML code uses the **CoalesceContinuous** to display the string *Ye seek for happiness–alas the day!* as shown in the "Description" graphic.

```
<applet
    codebase = CoalesceContinuous
    code     = CoalesceContinuous.class
    width    = 650
    height   = 100>
<param name=TextCount          value=2>
<param name=text1              value="Ye seek for happiness">
<param name=text2              value="-alas the day!,">
<param name=AppBGColor         value=#ffffff>
<param name=Steps              value=20>
<param name=DelayBetweenChars  value=20>
<param name=DelayBetweenRuns   value=3000>
<param name=HorizCenter        value=true>
<param name=VertCenter         value=true>
<param name=style              value=bold>
<param name=pointsize          value=20>
</applet>
```

Settings

See Table 6–1 on page 222 for common settings that apply to this applet. Five additional parameters specify the number of strings to display, the strings themselves, the number of steps in the coalescing sequence, the colors of the characters, and the delay between color changes.

Table 6–6 CoalesceContinuous Applet Settings

Name	Description	Default
TextCount	The number of strings to display (required)	0
Text*N*	The *N*th string of characters	(none)
Steps	The number of steps in the coalescing sequence	50
Colors	The colors to use for the characters	black
DelayBetweenColors	The delay (in milliseconds) between color changes	0 (no change)

The value of **Steps**, combined with the value of the **DelayBetweenChars** parameter, determines the speed with which the string coalesces.

See Also

URL for **CoalesceContinuous**

        hhttp://www.vivids.com/ij2/assorted/CoalesceContinuous.html

MoveLeft

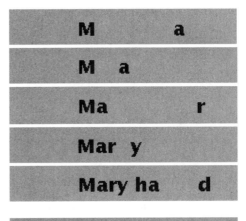

Each character in a string moves left to takes its position

Displays multiple strings in succession

Description

The **MoveLeft** applet displays each character as it moves left into its position in the string.

After a specified delay, the next string in the sequence, if any, is displayed in the same manner. There is no limit to the number of strings that can be displayed. After all of the strings have been displayed, the process starts again with the first string.

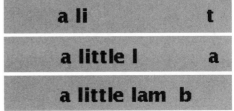

Interaction

The **MoveLeft** applet responds to the following keyboard input:

f	Character movement 10% faster
s	Character movement 10% slower
F	Delay between strings 10% shorter
S	Delay between strings 10% longer

Using **MoveLeft** in HTML Code

The following HTML code uses the **MoveLeft** to display the string *Mary had a little lamb* as shown at the top of the page.

```
<applet
    codebase = MoveLeft
    code     = MoveLeft.class
    width    = 250
    height   = 35>
<param name=AppBGImage       value=MoveLeft/pattern3.gif>
<param name=AppTile          value=true>
<param name=TextCount        value=2>
<param name=text1            value="Mary had">
<param name=text2            value="a little lamb">
<param name=DelayBetweenChars value=50>
<param name=DelayBetweenRuns  value=1000>
```

```
<param name=Continuous          value=true>
<param name=HorizCenter         value=true>
<param name=VertCenter          value=true>
<param name=Style               value=bold>
<param name=Pointsize           value=20>
</applet>
```

Settings

See Table 6–1 on page 222 for common settings that apply to this applet. Two additional parameters specify the number of strings to display, and the strings themselves.

Table 6–7 MoveLeft Applet Settings

Name	Description	Default
TextCount	The number of strings to display (required)	0
Text*N*	The *N*th string of characters	(none)

See Also

Related applets:

MoveUp on page 235
UpAndOver on page 237

URL for **MoveLeft**:

`http://www.vivids.com/ij2/assorted/MoveLeft.html`

MoveUp

Each character in a string moves up to takes its position in the string

Displays multiple strings in succession

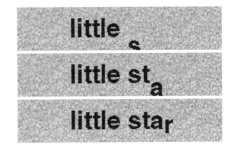

Description

The **MoveUp** applet displays each character as it moves up into its position in the string.

After a specified delay, the next string in the sequence, if any, is displayed in the same manner. There is no limit to the number of strings that can be displayed. After all of the strings have been displayed, the process starts again with the first string.

Interaction

The **MoveUp** applet responds to the following keyboard input:

f	Character movement 10% faster
s	Character movement 10% slower
F	Delay between strings 10% shorter
S	Delay between strings 10% longer

Using **MoveUp** in HTML Code

The following HTML code uses the **MoveUp** to display the string *Twinkle, twinkle little star* as shown at the top of the page.

```
<applet
    codebase = MoveUp
    code     = MoveUp.class
    width    = 250
    height   = 50>
<param name=TextCount          value=2>
<param name=text1              value="Twinkle, twinkle">
<param name=text2              value="little star">
<param name=AppBGImage         value=MoveUp/pattern.gif>
<param name=AppTile            value=true>
<param name=DelayBetweenChars  value=50>
<param name=DelayBetweenRuns   value=2000>
```

```
<param name=HorizCenter        value=true>
<param name=VertCenter         value=true>
<param name=Font               value=Helvetica>
<param name=Style              value=bold>
<param name=Pointsize          value=30>
</applet>
```

Settings

See Table 6–1 on page 222 for common settings that apply to this applet. Two additional parameters specify the number of strings to display, and the strings themselves.

Table 6–8 MoveUp Applet Settings

Name	Description	Default
TextCount	The number of strings to display (required)	0
TextN	The *N*th string of characters	(none)

See Also

Related applets: **MoveLeft** on page 233
UpAndOver on page 237

URL for **MoveUp**:   http://www.vivids.com/ij2/assorted/MoveUp.html

UpAndOver

Each character in a string moves up to takes its position

The string moves left out of view

Displays multiple strings in succession

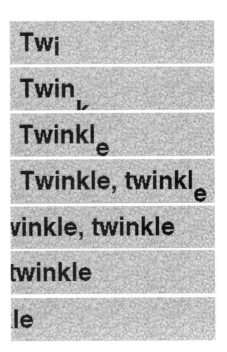

Description

The **UpAndOver** applet displays each character as it moves up into its position in the string.

After a specified delay, the string moves out of view to the left and the next string in the sequence, if any, is displayed in the same manner. There is no limit to the number of strings that can be displayed. After all of the strings have been displayed, the process starts again with the first string.

Interaction

The **UpAndOver** applet responds to the following keyboard input:

f	Character movement 10% faster
s	Character movement 10% slower
F	Delay between strings 10% shorter
S	Delay between strings 10% longer

Using UpAndOver in HTML Code

The following HTML code uses the **UpAndOver** to display the string *Twinkle, twinkle little star* as shown at the top of the page.

```
<applet
    codebase = UpAndOver
    code     = UpAndOver.class
    width    = 450
    height   = 50>
<param name=TextCount value=4>
<param name=text1      value="Then gently scan your brother man,">
<param name=text2      value="Still gentler sister woman;">
<param name=text3      value="Tho' they may gang a kennin wrang,">
<param name=text4      value="To step aside is human.">
```

```
<param name=Style      value=bold>
<param name=Pointsize value=30>
</applet>
```

Settings

See Table 6–1 on page 222 for common settings that apply to this applet. Three additional parameters specify the number of strings to display, the strings themselves, and the distance to move the string each time during exit.

Table 6–9 UpAndOver Applet Settings

Name	Description	Default
TextCount	The number of strings to display (required)	0
Text*N*	The text for the *N*th string of characters	(none)
MoveLeftDist	The distance (in pixels) to move the string left each time during exit from the applet	10

The speed of the text as it moves out of view is controlled by two parameters: **DelayBetweenChars** and **MoveLeftDist**. Smaller values of **MoveLeftDist** will make the movement smoother but slower because it will be moving a few number of pixels each time. Smaller values of **DelayBetweenChars** will speed the movement, but values that are too small will result in applets that do no run on slower machines.

See Also

Related applets: **MoveLeft** on page 233
MoveUp on page 235

URL for **UpAndOver**:   http://www.vivids.com/ij2/assorted/UpAndOver.html

CenterExpand

Displays a string of characters that expand from the center to their final positions

Displays multiple strings in succession

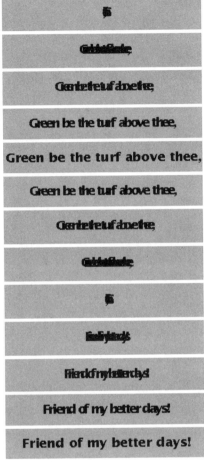

Descripti on

The **CenterExpand** lapplet displays a string of characters whose initial position is at the center for all characters. Each character then moves into its normal position in the string. The effect is similar to that of the **Coalesce** applet except that rather than the position of the characters being initially random, the characters in **CenterExpand** are all position together at the center of the applet.

The characters displayed in the text strings may also be individually colored using the **Colors** parameter. If the **Colors** parameter is not specified then all characters will display in the color specified by **TxColor**. If the **Colors** parameter is used, its value may be set to one or more colors that are used to color successive characters. For example, to color the characters red, yellow, and blue, use the following parameter:

```
<param name=Colors value="red yellow blue">
```

If you specify a value for the **DelayBetweenColors** parameter, the displayed colors will alternate between characters.

After a specified delay, the next string in the sequence, if any, is displayed in the same manner. There is no limit to the number of strings that can be displayed. After all of the strings have been displayed, the process starts again with the first string.

Interaction

The **CenterExpand** applet responds to the following keyboard input:

f	Character movement 10% faster
s	Character movement 10% slower
F	Delay between strings 10% shorter
S	Delay between strings 10% longer

c	Delay between colors changes 10% shorter
C	Delay between color changes 10% longer

Using CenterExpand in HTML Code

The following HTML code uses the **CenterExpand** to display *Green be the turf above thee, Friend of my better days!* as shown at the top of the page.

```
<applet
    codebase = CenterExpand
    code     = CenterExpand.class
    width    = 450
    height   = 35>
<param name=TextCount   value=4>
<param name=text1       value="Green be the turf above thee,">
<param name=text2       value="Friend of my better days!">
<param name=text3       value="None knew thee but to love thee,">
<param name=text4       value="Nor named thee but to praise.">
<param name=HorizCenter value=true>
<param name=VertCenter  value=true>
<param name=style       value=bold>
<param name=pointsize   value=20>
</applet>
```

Settings

See Table 6–1 on page 222 for common settings that apply to this applet. Five additional parameters specify the number of strings to display, the strings themselves, the number of steps in the expanding sequence, the colors of the characters, and the delay between color changes.

Table 6–10 CenterExpand Applet Settings

Name	Description	Default
TextCount	The number of strings to display (required)	0
Text*N*	The *N*th string of characters	(none)
Steps	The number of steps in the expanding sequence	50
Colors	The colors to use for the characters	black
DelayBetweenColors	The delay (in milliseconds) between color changes	0 (no change)

The value of **Steps**, combined with the value of the **DelayBetweenChars** parameter, determines the speed with which the string coalesces.

See Also

URL for **CenterExpand**:

`http://www.vivids.com/ij2/assorted/CenterExpand.html`

EveryOther

Alternate characters in a string move into position from opposite sides of the applet

Displays multiple strings in succession

i d s	L v s
a l e i d s	L v s f r a
t e a l e L d ss f r a m n	
ɔ g e L ves afl e ai ʍɪ ɪɪs I r m	
Lives of great men all remind us	
ɔ g e L ves afl e ai ʍɪ ɪɪs I r m	
t e a l e L d ss f r a m n	
a l e i d s	L v s f r a
i d s	L v s
b i e	W c r
i e s b i e	W c n a e
o r i e s ᴎʍi e n a e u l	
m k ʍ ɪc ɪne æ ɕb iu eɪ v s u	
We can make our lives sublime,	

Description

The **EveryOther** applet scrolls alternate characters from a string of characters from different directions. The characters at even numbered positions scroll from the left, characters at odd numbered positions scroll from the right. The characters meet in the middle to form the readable string.

The characters displayed in the text strings may also be individually colored using the **Colors** parameter. If the **Colors** parameter is not specified then all characters will display in the color specified by **TxColor**. If the **Colors** parameter is used, its value may be set to one or more colors that are used to color successive characters. For example, to color the characters red, yellow, and blue, use the following parameter:

```
<param name=Colors value="red yellow blue">
```

If you specify a value for the **DelayBetweenColors** parameter, the displayed colors will alternate between characters.

After a specified delay, the next string in the sequence, if any, is displayed in the same manner. There is no limit to the number of strings that can be displayed. After all of the strings have been displayed, the process starts again with the first string.

Interaction

The **EveryOther** applet responds to the following keyboard input:

f	Character movement 10% faster
s	Character movement 10% slower
F	Delay between strings 10% shorter
S	Delay between strings 10% longer
c	Delay between colors changes 10% shorter
C	Delay between color changes 10% longer

Using EveryOther in HTML Code

The following HTML code uses the **EveryOther** to display *Welcome to the Instant Java Home Page* as shown at the top of the page.

```
<applet
    codebase = EveryOther
    code     = EveryOther.class
    width    = 400
    height   = 35>
<param name=TextCount    value=4>
<param name=AppBGColor   value=white>
<param name=text1        value="Lives of great men all remind us">
<param name=text2        value="We can make our lives sublime,">
<param name=text3        value="And, departing, leave behind us">
<param name=text4        value="Footprints on the sands of time.">
<param name=HorizCenter  value=true>
<param name=VertCenter   value=true>
<param name=style        value=bold>
<param name=pointsize    value=20>
</applet>
```

Settings

See Table 6–1 on page 222 for common settings that apply to this applet. Five additional parameters specify the number of strings to display, the strings themselves, the number of steps in the character moving sequence, the colors of the characters, and the delay between color changes.

Table 6–11 EveryOther Applet Settings

Name	Description	Default
TextCount	The number of strings to display (required)	0
Text*N*	The *N*th string of characters	(none)
Steps	The number of steps in the character moving sequence	50
Colors	The colors to use for the characters	black
DelayBetweenColors	The delay (in milliseconds) between color changes	0 (no change)

See Also

URL for **EveryOther**:   `http://www.vivids.com/ij2/assorted/EveryOther.html`

Ticker

Displays a scrolling string of characters

Displays multiple strings in succession

Description

The **Ticker** applet scrolls a string of characters from right to left across the applet. The effect is similar to that of a scrolling electronic display.

After a specified delay, the next string in the sequence, if any, is displayed in the same manner. There is no limit to the number of strings that can be displayed. After all of the strings have been displayed, the process starts again with the first string.

Interaction

The **Ticker** applet responds to the following mouse input:

Button Press	The text stops scrolling. Press again and it restarts
Shift Button Press	The text scrolls in the reverse direction

The **Ticker** applet also responds to the following keyboard input:

f	Character movement 10% faster
s	Character movement 10% slower
F	Delay between strings 10% shorter
S	Delay between strings 10% longer
m	Increase the move distance by one pixel
l	Decrease the move distance by one pixel

Using Ticker in HTML Code

The following HTML code uses the **Ticker** to display *Welcome to the Instant Java Home Page* as shown at the top of the page.

```
<applet
    codebase = Ticker
    code     = Ticker.class
    width    = 450
```

```
       height    = 50>
<param name=TextCount      value=2>
<param name=text1          value="Welcome to the Instant Java Home Page">
<param name=text2          value="Brought to you by Vivid Solutions">
<param name=AppBGImage     value=Ticker/pattern.gif>
<param name=AppTile        value=true>
<param name=DelayBetweenChars value=30>
<param name=DelayBetweenRuns  value=30>
<param name=VertCenter     value=true>
<param name=Font           value=Helvetica>
<param name=Style          value=BoldItalic>
<param name=Pointsize      value=36>
</applet>
```

Settings

See Table 6–1 on page 222 for common settings that apply to this applet. Four additional parameters specify the number of strings to display, the strings themselves, the distance to move the string each time, and the initial direction of movement.

Table 6–12 Ticker Applet Settings

Name	Description	Default
TextCount	The number of strings to display (required)	0
Text*N*	The *N*th string of characters	(none)
MoveDist	The distance (in pixels) to move the string each time	20
Reverse	If true, the initial direction of the moving text is from left to right	false

The speed of the moving text is controlled by two parameters: **DelayBetweenChars** and **MoveDist**. Smaller values of **MoveDist** will make the movement smoother but slower because it will be moving a few number of pixels each time. Smaller values of **DelayBetweenChars** will speed the movement, but values that are too small will result in applets that do not run on slower machines.

The **VertCenter** parameter is not used in this applet.

See Also

URL for **Ticker:**   `http://www.vivids.com/ij2/assorted/Ticker.html`

VerticalTicker

Displays a scrolling string of characters

Displays multiple strings in succession

An expert is one who knows
An expert is one who knows
An expert is one who knows

more and more
more and more
more and more
more and more

Description

The **VerticalTicker** applet scrolls a string of characters vertically. The effect is similar to that of a scrolling electronic display.

After a specified delay, the next string in the sequence, if any, is displayed in the same manner. There is no limit to the number of strings that can be displayed. After all of the strings have been displayed, the process starts again with the first string.

Interaction

The **VerticalTicker** applet responds to the following mouse input:

Button Press	The text stops scrolling. Press again and it restarts
Shift Button Press	The text scrolls in the reverse direction

The **VerticalTicker** applet also responds to the following keyboard input:

f	Character movement 10% faster
s	Character movement 10% slower
F	Delay between strings 10% shorter
S	Delay between strings 10% longer
m	Increase the move distance by one pixel
l	Decrease the move distance by one pixel

Using **VerticalTicker** in HTML Code

The following HTML code uses the **VerticalTicker** to display *An expert is one who know more and more* as shown at the top of the page.

```
<applet
    codebase = VerticalTicker
    code     = VerticalTicker.class
    width    = 550
    height   = 50>
<param name=TextCount       value=4>
<param name=text1           value="An expert is one who knows">
<param name=text2           value="more and more">
```

```
<param name=text3          value="about less and less.">
<param name=text4          value="                -Nicholas M. Butler">
<param name=AppBGImage     value=VerticalTicker/pattern.gif>
<param name=AppTile        value=true>
<param name=XOffset        value=10>
<param name=DelayBetweenChars value=30>
<param name=DelayBetweenRuns  value=2000>
<param name=MoveDist       value=5>
<param name=Font           value=TimesRoman>
<param name=Style          value=Bold>
<param name=Pointsize      value=36>
</applet>
```

Settings

See Table 6–1 on page 222 for common settings that apply to this applet. Four additional parameters specify the number of strings to display, the strings themselves, the distance to move the string each time, and the initial direction of movement.

Table 6–13 VerticalTicker Applet Settings

Name	Description	Default
TextCount	The number of strings to display (required)	0
Text*N*	The *N*th string of characters	(none)
MoveDist	The distance (in pixels) to move the string each time	20
Reverse	If true, the initial direction of the moving text is from left to right	false

The speed of the moving text is controlled by two parameters: **DelayBetweenChars** and **MoveDist**. Smaller values of **MoveDist** will make the movement smoother but slower because it will be moving a few number of pixels each time. Smaller values of **DelayBetweenChars** will speed the movement, but values that are too small will result in applets that do not run on slower machines.

The **HorizCenter** parameter is not used in this applet.

See Also

URL for **VerticalTicker**: http://www.vivids.com/ij2/assorted/VerticalTicker.html

Slide Show Applets

The following six applets are slide show applets. Each displays a series of images in sequence. What makes each applet unique is the way in which it moves from one image to the next.

The slide show applets all share some common features. Each can operate automatically (the image changes without user interaction), or they can be manually operated by the user. Parameters allow you to specify automatic or manual play.

Table 6–12 includes parameters that are common to all six slide show applets.

Table 6–14 Common Settings for Slide Show Applets

Name	Description	Default
NumImages	The number of images to display (required)	0
ImageN	The Nth image	(none)
SoundN	The sound file played when the Nth image is displayed	(none)
BGSound	The sound file played throughout the slide show	(none)
Controls	If true, the slide show includes Next and Previous buttons and an Audio checkbox	false
AutoPlay	If true, the images are displayed in sequence without user interaction (overrides **Controls**)	false
DelayBetweenImages	The delay (in seconds) between images (**AutoPlay** only)	5
AppBGColor	The applet background color	Set by browser

The slide show applets were originally designed to display images of the same size. However, you may use images of different sizes. The dimensions of the largest image determine the size of the image area. Smaller images are displayed within a rectangular region the width and height of the largest image.

If you set the **Controls** parameter to true (and do not set **AutoPlay** to true) then the slide show applets include *Next* and *Previous* buttons and the *Audio* checkbox, as shown below:

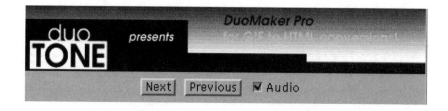

If you specify neither **AutoPlay** nor **Controls**, the images are displayed manually without controls. To change images you must use the mouse. With the pointer over the applet, press any mouse button to advance to the next image. Hold down the Shift key and press any mouse button to move to the previous image. To toggle the audio between on and off, press **a**.

SlideShow

Displays a series of images in sequence with optional audio and controls

Description

The **SlideShow** applet displays a series of images in sequence.

It can optionally include controls for displaying the next or previous image in the sequence. If the **AutoPlay** parameter is true, the images in the sequence automatically change every **DelayBetweenImages** seconds.

Interaction

The **SlideShow** applet responds to the following mouse input:

Button Press   Advance to next slide (if **AutoPlay** is false)

Shift Button Press   View slides in reverse order

The **SlideShow** applet also responds to the following keyboard input:

F   Interval between images 10% shorter (if **AutoPlay** is true)

S   Interval between images 10% longer (if **AutoPlay** is true)

a   Toggle audio

Using SlideShow in HTML Code

The following HTML code uses **SlideShow** to display three images in sequence as shown at the top of the page. Each image has an associated audio file, **AutoPlay** is true, and the delay between images is 7 seconds.

```
<applet
    archive  = SlideShow.zip
    codebase = SlideShow
    code     = SlideShow.class
    width    = 432
    height   = 72>
<param name=NumImages          value=3>
<param name=Image1             value=SlideShow/duotone.gif>
<param name=Image2             value=SlideShow/machine.gif>
<param name=Image3             value=SlideShow/powertr.gif>
<param name=Sound1             value=SlideShow/duotone.au>
<param name=Sound2             value=SlideShow/machine.au>
<param name=Sound3             value=SlideShow/powertr.au>
<param name=AutoPlay           value=true>
<param name=DelayBetweenImages value=7>
</applet>
```

Settings

See Table 6–14 on page 248 for common settings that apply to this applet.

See Also

URL for **SlideShow**:   `http://www.vivids.com/ij2/assorted/SlideShow.html`

Related applets: **SlideShowPush** on page 252
SlideShowSlide on page 254
SlideShowSplit on page 256
SlideShowSwap on page 258
SlideShowFade on page 260

SlideShowPush

Displays a series of images in sequence with optional audio and controls

Transition between images is by pushing

Description

The **SlideShowPush** applet displays a series of images in sequence. The transition from one image to the next is by pushing; the new image pushes the old image out of view to the right.

SlideShowPush can optionally include controls for displaying the next or previous image in the sequence. If the **AutoPlay** parameter is true, the images in the sequence automatically change every **DelayBetweenImages** seconds.

Interaction

The **SlideShowPush** applet responds to the following mouse input:

Button Press	Advance to next slide (if **AutoPlay** is false)
Shift Button Press	View slides in reverse order

The **SlideShowPush** applet also responds to the following keyboard input:

f	Interval between image movements 10% shorter
s	Interval between image movements 10% longer
F	Interval between images 10% shorter (if **AutoPlay** is true)
S	Interval between images 10% longer (if **AutoPlay** is true)
m	Increase image movement by one pixel per movement
l	Decrease image movement by one pixel per movement
a	Toggle audio

Using **SlideShowPush** in HTML Code

The following HTML code uses **SlideShowPush** to display three images in sequence as shown at the top of the page. Each image has an associated audio file, **Controls** is true—which adds the *Next*, *Previous*, and *Audio* buttons—and the delay between images is 2 seconds.

```
<applet
    archive  = SlideShowPush.zip
    codebase = SlideShowPush
    code     = SlideShowPush.class
```

```
    width    = 432
    height   = 72>
<param name=NumImages         value=3>
<param name=Image1            value=SlideShowPush/duotone.gif>
<param name=Image2            value=SlideShowPush/machine.gif>
<param name=Image3            value=SlideShowPush/powertr.gif>
<param name=Sound1            value=SlideShowPush/duotone.au>
<param name=Sound2            value=SlideShowPush/machine.au>
<param name=Sound3            value=SlideShowPush/powertr.au>
<param name=AutoPlay          value=true>
<param name=DelayBetweenMoves value=25>
<param name=DelayBetweenImages value=2>
<param name=BGSound           value=SlideShowPush/mozart.au>
</applet>
```

Settings

See Table 6–14 on page 248 for common settings that apply to this applet. Two additional parameters specify the transition speed and movement.

Table 6–15 SlideShowPush Applet Settings

Name	Description	Default
DelayBetweenMoves	The delay (in milliseconds) between image movements	20
MoveSize	The distance (in pixels) of each image movement	5

See Also

URL for **SlideShowPush**:   http://www.vivids.com/ij2/assorted/SlideShowPush.html

Related applets:
SlideShow on page 250
SlideShowSlide on page 254
SlideShowSplit on page 256
SlideShowSwap on page 258
SlideShowFade on page 260

SlideShowSlide

Displays a series of images in sequence with optional audio and controls

Transition between images is by sliding the older image out of view

Description

The **SlideShowSlide** applet displays a series of images in sequence. The transition from one image to the next is by sliding the older image out of view to the right.

SlideShowSlide can optionally include controls for displaying the next or previous image in the sequence. If the **AutoPlay** parameter is true, the images in the sequence automatically change every **DelayBetweenImages** seconds. The speed of the transition is controlled by the **DelayBetweenMoves** and **MoveSize** parameters.

Interaction

The **SlideShowSlide** applet responds to the following mouse input:

Button Press	Advance to next slide (if **AutoPlay** is false)
Shift Button Press	View slides in reverse order

The **SlideShowSlide** applet also responds to the following keyboard input:

f	Interval between image movements 10% shorter
s	Interval between image movements 10% longer
F	Interval between images 10% shorter (if **AutoPlay** is true)
S	Interval between images 10% longer (if **AutoPlay** is true)
m	Increase image movement by one pixel per movement
l	Decrease image movement by one pixel per movement
a	Toggle audio

Using **SlideShowSlide** in HTML Code

The following HTML code uses **SlideShowSlide** to display three images in sequence, as shown at the top of the page. The first image has an associated audio file, **AutoPlay** is true, and the delay between images is 3 seconds.

```
<applet
    archive  = SlideShowSlide.zip
    codebase = SlideShowSlide
    code     = SlideShowSlide.class
```

```
     width       = 432
     height      = 72>
<param name=NumImages               value=3>
<param name=Image1                  value=SlideShowSlide/duotone.gif>
<param name=Image2                  value=SlideShowSlide/machine.gif>
<param name=Image3                  value=SlideShowSlide/powertr.gif>
<param name=Sound1                  value=SlideShowSlide/duotone.au>
<param name=Sound2                  value=SlideShowSlide/machine.au>
<param name=Sound3                  value=SlideShowSlide/powertr.au>
<param name=AutoPlay                value=true>
<param name=DelayBetweenMoves  value=20>
<param name=DelayBetweenImages value=3>
</applet>
```

Settings

See Table 6–14 on page 248 for common settings that apply to this applet. Two additional parameters specify the transition speed and movement.

Table 6–16 SlideShowSlide Applet Settings

Name	Description	Default
DelayBetweenMoves	The delay (in milliseconds) between image movements	20
MoveSize	The distance (in pixels) of each image movement	5

See Also

URL for **SlideShowSlide**:   http://www.vivids.com/ij2/assorted/SlideShowSlide.html

Related applets: **SlideShow** on page 250
                        SlideShowPush on page 252
                        SlideShowSplit on page 256
                        SlideShowSwap on page 258
                        SlideShowFade on page 260

SlideShowSplit

Displays a series of images in sequence with optional audio and controls

Transition between images is by splitting the current image down the middle

Description

The **SlideShowSplit** applet displays a series of images in sequence. The transition from one image to the next is by splitting the current image in half and sliding each half out of view, one to the right and one to the left.

SlideShowSplit can optionally include controls for displaying the next or previous image in the sequence. If the **AutoPlay** parameter is true, the images in the sequence automatically change every **DelayBetweenImages** seconds. The speed of the transition is controlled by the **DelayBetweenMoves** and **MoveSize** parameters.

Interaction

The **SlideShowSplit** applet responds to the following mouse input:

Button Press	Advance to next slide (if **AutoPlay** is false)
Shift Button Press	View slides in reverse order

The **SlideShowSplit** applet also responds to the following keyboard input:

f	Interval between image movements 10% shorter
s	Interval between image movements 10% longer
F	Interval between images 10% shorter (if **AutoPlay** is true)
S	Interval between images 10% longer (if **AutoPlay** is true)
m	Increase image movement by one pixel per movement
l	Decrease image movement by one pixel per movement
a	Toggle audio

Using SlideShowSplit in HTML Code

The following HTML code uses **SlideShowSplit** to display three images in sequence as shown at the top of the page. Each image has an associated audio file, **Controls** is true—which adds the *Next*, *Previous*, and *Audio* buttons—and the delay between images is 5 seconds.

```
<applet
    archive = SlideShowSplit.zip
```

```
        codebase = SlideShowSplit
        code     = SlideShowSplit.class
        width    = 432
        height   = 106>
<param name=NumImages              value=3>
<param name=Controls               value=true>
<param name=Image1                 value=SlideShowSplit/duotone.gif>
<param name=Image2                 value=SlideShowSplit/powertr.gif>
<param name=Image3                 value=SlideShowSplit/machine.gif>
<param name=Sound1                 value=SlideShowSplit/duotone.au>
<param name=Sound2                 value=SlideShowSplit/powertr.au>
<param name=Sound3                 value=SlideShowSplit/machine.au>
<param name=DelayBetweenMoves  value=5>
<param name=DelayBetweenImages value=2>
<param name=MoveSize               value=2>
</applet>
```

Settings

See Table 6–14 on page 248 for common settings that apply to this applet. Two additional parameters specify the transition speed and movement.

Table 6–17 SlideShowSplit Applet Settings

Name	Description	Default
DelayBetweenMoves	The delay (in milliseconds) between image movements	20
MoveSize	The distance (in pixels) of each image movement	5

See Also

URL for **SlideShowSplit**:

```
        http://www.vivids.com/ij2/assorted/SlideShowSplit.html
```

Related applets:

SlideShow on page 250
SlideShowPush on page 252
SlideShowSlide on page 254
SlideShowSwap on page 258
SlideShowFade on page 260

SlideShowSwap

Displays a series of images in sequence with optional audio and controls

Transition between images is by swapping

Description

The **SlideShowSwap** applet displays a series of images in sequence. The transition from one image to the next is by swapping. First one image moves to the right and the other to the left until the half-way point is reached. Then the images swap positions: the one that was behind comes to the front, the one that was in front goes to the back, and the direction each is travelling reverses. The effect is similar to automated shuffling of a stack of pictures.

SlideShowSwap can optionally include controls for displaying the next or previous image in the sequence. If the **AutoPlay** parameter is true, the images in the sequence automatically change every **DelayBetweenImages** seconds. The speed of the transition is controlled by the **DelayBetweenMoves** and **MoveSize** parameters.

Interaction

The **SlideShowSwap** applet responds to the following mouse input:

Button Press	Advance to next slide (if **AutoPlay** is false)
Shift Button Press	View slides in reverse order

The page 258 applet also responds to the following keyboard input:

f	Interval between image movements 10% shorter
s	Interval between image movements 10% longer
F	Interval between images 10% shorter (if **AutoPlay** is true)
S	Interval between images 10% longer (if **AutoPlay** is true)
m	Increase image movement by one pixel per movement
l	Decrease image movement by one pixel per movement
a	Toggle audio

Using **SlideShowSwap** in HTML Code

The following HTML code uses **SlideShowSwap** to display three images in sequence, as shown at the top of the page. Each image has an associated audio file, **AutoPlay** is true, and the delay between images defaults to 5 seconds.

```
<applet
    archive  = SlideShowSwap.zip
    codebase = SlideShowSwap
    code     = SlideShowSwap.class
    width    = 432
    height   = 72>
<param name=NumImages value=3>
<param name=Controls  value=true>
<param name=Image1    value=SlideShowSwap/duotone.gif>
<param name=Image2    value=SlideShowSwap/powertr.gif>
<param name=Image3    value=SlideShowSwap/machine.gif>
<param name=Sound1    value=SlideShowSwap/duotone.au>
<param name=Sound2    value=SlideShowSwap/powertr.au>
<param name=Sound3    value=SlideShowSwap/machine.au>
<param name=AutoPlay  value=true>
</applet>
```

Settings

See Table 6–14 on page 248 for common settings that apply to this applet. Two additional parameters specify the transition speed and movement.

Table 6–18 SlideShowSwap Applet Settings

Name	Description	Default
DelayBetweenMoves	The delay (in milliseconds) between image movements	20
MoveSize	The distance (in pixels) of each image movement	5

See Also

URL for **SlideShowSwap**:

http://www.vivids.com/ij2/assorted/SlideShowSwap.html

Related applets:

SlideShow on page 250
SlideShowPush on page 252
SlideShowSlide on page 254
SlideShowSplit on page 256
SlideShowFade on page 260

SlideShowFade

Displays a series of images in sequence with optional audio and controls

Transition between images is by fading to the background color

Description

The **SlideShowFade** applet displays a series of images in sequence. The transition from one image to the next is by fading. First the older image fades to the background color, then the next image fades in from the background color.

SlideShowFade can optionally include controls for displaying the next or previous image in the sequence. If the **AutoPlay** parameter is true, the images in the sequence automatically change every **DelayBetweenImages** seconds. The speed of the transition is controlled by the **DelayBetweenMoves** and **MoveSize** parameters.

Interaction

The **SlideShowFade** applet responds to the following mouse input:

Button Press	Advance to next slide (if **AutoPlay** is false)
Shift Button Press	View slides in reverse order

The **SlideShowSplit** applet also responds to the following keyboard input:

f	Interval between image movements 10% shorter
s	Interval between image movements 10% longer
F	Interval between images 10% shorter (if **AutoPlay** is true)
S	Interval between images 10% longer (if **AutoPlay** is true)
a	Toggle audio

Using SlideShowFade in HTML Code

The following HTML code uses **SlideShowFade** to display three images in sequence, as shown at the top of the page. Each image has an associated audio file, **AutoPlay** is true, the delay between images is 7 seconds, and the delay between transitional faded images is 150 milliseconds.

```
<applet
    archive = SlideShowFade.zip
```

```
     codebase = SlideShowFade
     code     = SlideShowFade.class
     width    = 432
     height   = 72>
<param name=NumImages           value=3>
<param name=FadeSize            value=8>
<param name=DelayBetweenFades   value=150>
<param name=DelayBetweenImages  value=7>
<param name=Controls            value=true>
<param name=Image1              value=SlideShowFade/duotone.gif>
<param name=Image2              value=SlideShowFade/powertr.gif>
<param name=Image3              value=SlideShowFade/machine.gif>
<param name=AutoPlay            value=true>
<param name=Sound1              value=SlideShowFade/duotone.au>
<param name=Sound2              value=SlideShowFade/powertr.au>
<param name=Sound3              value=SlideShowFade/machine.au>
</applet>
```

Settings

See Table 6–14 on page 248 for common settings that apply to this applet. Two additional parameters specify the transition speed and number of transitional images in the fade effect.

Table 6–19 SlideShowFade Applet Settings

Name	Description	Default
DelayBetweenFades	The delay (in milliseconds) between transitional images	20
FadeSize	The number of transitional images to use to create fade effect	10

See Also

URL for **SlideShowFade**:

```
        http://www.vivids.com/ij2/assorted/SlideShowFade.html
```

Related applets:
SlideShow on page 250
SlideShowPush on page 252
SlideShowSlide on page 254
SlideShowSplit on page 256
SlideShowSwap on page 258

CHAPTER

7

Bonus Animation Examples

This chapter contains 60 animation examples using the animation applets from Chapter 5 to create new and interesting animations. This chapter is intended to provide you with samples that will spark your imagination and suggest ways that you can use the animation applets for your own purposes.

Each example includes a brief description, the HTML code for the example, screen shots of the animation, a list of related applets, and a URL. The screen shots do not exactly match the example code in all cases. For instance, example Six contains 75 images in the animation sequence. Rather than fill up page after page with all 75 images, a few samples are provided to give you the idea of what the animation looks like.

Some of the animation examples alter colors in the image. Because this book in printed without color, the screen shots may not convey the full impact of the example. For instance, applet FiftyNine initially displays a black and white image that is displayed in color when the user presses a mouse button over the image. In order to do these examples justice view the applet by either using the CD-ROM provided with the book, or connect to the specified URL.

One

Pulsating Gradient Background

Description

Example **One** uses the **AnimateTwoWay** applet. An image containing a gradient pattern of colors from black to white is displayed using the **Negative** applet on page 137. The **Sub-From** parameter is altered to create a series of images that give a pulsating effect. Text is also displayed in the center of the pulsating image.

The HTML Code for Example One

```
<applet
    archive  = One.zip
    codebase = One
    code     = AnimateTwoWay.class
    width    = 72
    height   = 72>

<param name=ImgDelayBetweenRuns    value=50>
<param name=ImgDelayBetweenImages  value=50>
<param name=WaitForEverything      value=true>

<param name=ImgNumImages           value=11>
<param name=ImgHorizCenter         value=true>
<param name=ImgVertCenter          value=true>
<param name=Image1                 value=One/gradient2.gif>
<param name=ImgFilter1             value="negative 0">
<param name=ImgFilter2             value="negative 25">
<param name=ImgFilter3             value="negative 50">
<param name=ImgFilter4             value="negative 75">
<param name=ImgFilter5             value="negative 100">
<param name=ImgFilter6             value="negative 125">
<param name=ImgFilter7             value="negative 150">
<param name=ImgFilter8             value="negative 175">
<param name=ImgFilter9             value="negative 200">
<param name=ImgFilter10            value="negative 225">
<param name=ImgFilter11            value="negative 250">

<param name=TxNumImages            value=1>
<param name=TxHorizCenter          value=true>
<param name=TxVertCenter           value=true>
<param name=TxFont                 value="TimesRoman">
<param name=TxStyle                value="Bold">
<param name=TxColor                value=white>
```

```
<param name=TxPointSize          value="14">
<param name=TxFilter1            value="text">
<param name=Text                 value="Pulsate">

<param name=ImgFrameThickness    value=4>
<param name=ImgFrameType         value=ShadowEtchedIn>
</applet>
```

Animation Display for Example One

See Also

Related applets: **AnimateTwoWay** on page 191
                      Negative on page 137

URL for **One**:   http://www.vivids.com/ij2/bonus/One.html

Two

Pulsating Gradient Background Variation 1

Description

Example **Two** uses the **AnimateTwoWay** applet. An image containing a gradient pattern of colors from black to white is displayed using the **Negative** applet on page 137. The **Sub-From** parameter is altered to create a series of images that give a pulsating effect. This time the negative values are increased up to 575. Text is also displayed in the center of the pulsating image and is rotated 180 degrees.

The HTML Code for Example Two

```
<applet
    archive  = Two.zip
    codebase = Two
    code     = AnimateTwoWay.class
    width    = 72
    height   = 72>

<param name=ImgDelayBetweenRuns    value=50>
<param name=ImgDelayBetweenImages  value=50>
<param name=WaitForEverything      value=true>

<param name=ImgNumImages           value=21>
<param name=ImgHorizCenter         value=true>
<param name=ImgVertCenter          value=true>
<param name=Image1                 value=Two/gradient2.gif>
<param name=ImgFilter1             value="negative 0">
<param name=ImgFilter2             value="negative 25">
<param name=ImgFilter3             value="negative 50">
<param name=ImgFilter4             value="negative 75">
<param name=ImgFilter5             value="negative 100">
<param name=ImgFilter6             value="negative 125">
<param name=ImgFilter7             value="negative 150">
<param name=ImgFilter8             value="negative 175">
<param name=ImgFilter9             value="negative 200">
<param name=ImgFilter10            value="negative 225">
<param name=ImgFilter11            value="negative 250">
<param name=ImgFilter12            value="negative 275">
<param name=ImgFilter13            value="negative 300">
<param name=ImgFilter14            value="negative 325">
<param name=ImgFilter15            value="negative 350">
<param name=ImgFilter16            value="negative 375">
<param name=ImgFilter17            value="negative 400">
<param name=ImgFilter18            value="negative 425">
```

```
<param name=ImgFilter19          value="negative 450">
<param name=ImgFilter20          value="negative 475">
<param name=ImgFilter21          value="negative 500">
<param name=ImgFilter22          value="negative 525">
<param name=ImgFilter23          value="negative 550">
<param name=ImgFilter24          value="negative 575">

<param name=TxNumImages          value=1>
<param name=TxHorizCenter        value=true>
<param name=TxVertCenter         value=true>
<param name=TxFont               value="TimesRoman">
<param name=TxStyle              value="Bold">
<param name=TxColor              value=white>
<param name=TxPointSize          value="14">
<param name=TxFilter1            value="text|rotate 180">
<param name=Text                 value="Variation">
</applet>
Animation Display for Example Two
```

See Also

Related applets: **AnimateTwoWay** on page 191
                          Negative on page 137
                          Rotate on page 112

URL for **Two**:   http://www.vivids.com/ij2/bonus/Two.html

Three

Pulsating Gradient Background Variation 2

Description

Example **Three** uses the **AnimateTwoWay** applet. It is similar to example **Two** except that the text displayed in the center of the image is changing.

The HTML Code for Example Three

```
<applet
    archive  = Three.zip
    codebase = Three
    code     = AnimateContinuous.class
    width    = 72
    height   = 72>

<param name=ImgDelayBetweenRuns      value=100>
<param name=ImgDelayBetweenImages    value=100>
<param name=WaitForEverything        value=true>

<param name=ImgNumImages             value=10>
<param name=ImgHorizCenter           value=true>
<param name=ImgVertCenter            value=true>
<param name=Image1                   value=Three/gradient2.gif>
<param name=ImgFilter1               value="negative 250">
<param name=ImgFilter2               value="negative 275">
<param name=ImgFilter3               value="negative 300">
<param name=ImgFilter4               value="negative 325">
<param name=ImgFilter5               value="negative 350">
<param name=ImgFilter6               value="negative 375">
<param name=ImgFilter7               value="negative 400">
<param name=ImgFilter8               value="negative 425">
<param name=ImgFilter9               value="negative 450">
<param name=ImgFilter10              value="negative 475">

<param name=TxNumImages              value=2>
<param name=TxDelayBetweenRuns       value=800>
<param name=TxDelayBetweenImages     value=800>
<param name=TxHorizCenter            value=true>
<param name=TxVertCenter             value=true>
<param name=TxFont                   value="TimesRoman">
<param name=TxStyle                  value="Bold">
<param name=TxColor                  value=yellow>
<param name=TxPointSize              value="14">
<param name=TxFilter1                value="text">
```

```
<param name=Text1                    value="Another">
<param name=Text2                    value="Variation">
</applet>
```

Animation Display for Example Three

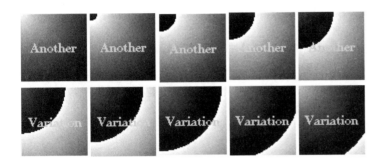

See Also

Related applets: **AnimateContinuous** on page 189
                          Negative on page 137

URL for **Three**:   http://www.vivids.com/ij2/bonus/Three.html

Four

Flashing DepthShade

Description

Example **Four** uses the **AnimateTwoWay** applet. The string *DepthShade* is displayed in a variety of colors using the **DepthShade** applet on page 77.

The HTML Code for Example **Four**

```
<applet
    archive  = Four.zip
    codebase = Four
    code     = AnimateTwoWay.class
    width    = 500
    height   = 100>

<param name=AppBGColor               value=black>
<param name=TxColor                  value=white>
<param name=TxNumImages              value=7>
<param name=TxHorizCenter            value=true>
<param name=TxVertCenter             value=true>
<param name=TxFont                   value="TimesRoman">
<param name=TxPointSize              value="60">
<param name=TxDelayBetweenRuns     value=200>
<param name=TxDelayBetweenImages value=200>
<param name=Text           value="DepthShade">
<param name=TxFilter1   value="depthshade -20 -20 red black">
<param name=TxFilter2   value="depthshade -20 -20 blue black">
<param name=TxFilter3   value="depthshade -20 -20 yellow black">
<param name=TxFilter4   value="depthshade -20 -20 black black">
<param name=TxFilter5   value="depthshade -20 -20 pink black">
<param name=TxFilter6   value="depthshade -20 -20 purple black">
<param name=TxFilter7   value="depthshade -20 -20 green black">
</applet>
```

Animation Display for Example Four

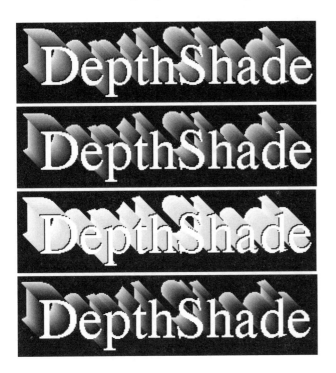

See Also

Related applets: **AnimateTwoWay** on page 191
                                      DepthShade on page 77

URL for **Four**:   `http://www.vivids.com/ij2/bonus/Four.html`

Five

Don't Press Here

Description

Example **Five** uses the **AnimateOnPressRelease** applet. The string *Don't Press Here* appears initially when the applet is loaded. When the user press the mouse button over the applet the phrase *I told you not to press!* is displayed one word at a time. The **Shadow** applet on page 64 and the **Text** applet on page 63 are used as a filters for generating the text.

The HTML Code for Example Five

```
<applet
    archive  = Five.zip
    codebase = Five
    code     = AnimateOnPressRelease.class
    width    = 500
    height   = 100>

<param name=AppBGColor          value=white>
<param name=TxNumImages         value=7>
<param name=TxFont              value="TimesRoman">
<param name=TxPointSize         value="30">
<param name=TxDelayBetweenRuns  value=300>
<param name=TxDelayBetweenImages value=300>
<param name=Text1               value="Don't Press Here">
<param name=Text2               value="I">
<param name=Text3               value="I told">
<param name=Text4               value="I told you">
<param name=Text5               value="I told you not">
<param name=Text6               value="I told you not to">
<param name=Text7               value="I told you not to press!">
<param name=TxFilter1           value="shadow 3 3 #dddddd">
<param name=TxFilter2           value="text">
<param name=TxFilter3           value="text">
<param name=TxFilter4           value="text">
<param name=TxFilter5           value="text">
<param name=TxFilter6           value="text">
<param name=TxFilter7           value="text">
<param name=TxXOffset1          value=0>
<param name=TxXOffset2          value=3>
<param name=TxYOffset1          value=0>
<param name=TxYOffset2          value=3>
</applet>
```

Animation Display for Example Five

Initial Display

Don't Press Here

Button Press	Button Release
I	I told you not to press!
I told	I told you not to
I told you	I told you not
I told you not	I told you
I told you not to	I told
I told you not to press!	I

See Also

Related applets:

AnimateOnPressRelease on page 206
Text on page 63
Shadow on page 64

URL for **Five**:

`http://www.vivids.com/ij2/bonus/Five.html`

Six

Astronaut Flying Through Space

Description

Example **Six** uses the **AnimateContinuous** applet. An image of an astronaut is shown flying through space. The image simply moves from one point to another against a background of stars.

The HTML Code for Example Six

```
<applet
    archive  = Six.zip
    codebase = Six
    code     = AnimateContinuous.class
    width    = 300
    height   = 120>

<param name=AppBGImage            value=Six/starfill.gif>
<param name=AppTile               value=true>
<param name=ImgNumImages          value=75>
<param name=ImgDelayBetweenRuns   value=1000>
<param name=ImgDelayBetweenImages value=40>
<param name=Image1                value=Six/astronaut.gif>
<param name=ImgAutoMove           value=true>
<param name=ImgYOffset1           value=10>
<param name=ImgXOffset1           value=300>
<param name=ImgXOffset75          value=-70>
</applet>
```

Animation Display for Example Six

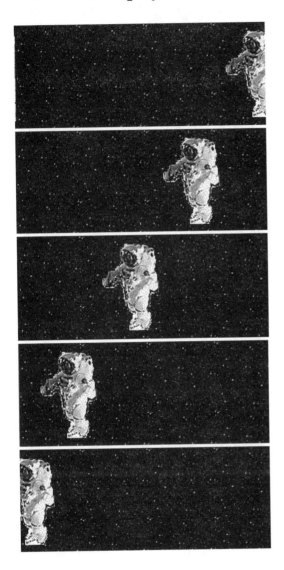

See Also

Related applets: **AnimateContinuous** on page 189

URL for **Six**:   http://www.vivids.com/ij2/bonus/Six.html

Seven

Astronaut Flying Through Space Both Ways

Description

Example **Seven** uses the **AnimateContinuous** applet. An image of an astronaut is shown flying through space. The astronaut then flies back the other direction. Each image simply moves from one point to another against a background of stars.

The HTML Code for Example Seven

```
<applet
    archive  = Seven.zip
    codebase = Seven
    code     = AnimateContinuous.class
    width    = 300
    height   = 120>

<param name=AppBGImage               value=Seven/starfill.gif>
<param name=AppTile                  value=true>
<param name=ImgNumImages             value=149>
<param name=ImgDelayBetweenRuns      value=1000>
<param name=ImgDelayBetweenImages value=40>
<param name=Image1                   value=Seven/astronaut.gif>
<param name=Image76                  value=Seven/astronautflip.gif>
<param name=ImgAutoMove              value=true>
<param name=ImgYOffset1              value=10>
<param name=ImgXOffset1              value=300>
<param name=ImgXOffset75             value=-70>
<param name=ImgXOffset149            value=300>

</applet>
```

Animation Display for Example Seven

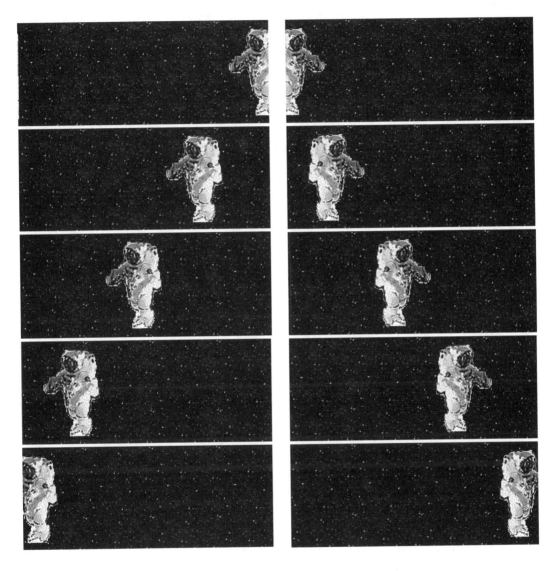

See Also

Related applets:	**AnimateContinuous** on page 189
URL for **Seven**:	http://www.vivids.com/ij2/bonus/Seven.html

Eight

Astronaut Rocking Through Space

Description

Example **Eight** uses the **AnimateContinuous** applet. The astronaut image flies through space while rocking back and forth. The **Rotate** applet on page 112 is used to create the rocking effect.

The HTML Code for Example Eight

```
<applet
    archive  = Eight.zip
    codebase = Eight
    code     = AnimateContinuous.class
    width    = 300
    height   = 120>

<param name=AppBGImage              value=Eight/starfill.gif>
<param name=AppTile                 value=true>
<param name=ImgNumImages            value=90>
<param name=ImgDelayBetweenRuns     value=1000>
<param name=ImgDelayBetweenImages   value=40>
<param name=Image1                  value=Eight/astronaut.gif>
<param name=ImgInitialImage         value=11>
<param name=ImgFilter1              value="rotate 15">
<param name=ImgFilter2              value="rotate 10">
<param name=ImgFilter3              value="rotate 5">
<param name=ImgFilter4              value="rotate 0">
<param name=ImgFilter5              value="rotate -5">
<param name=ImgFilter6              value="rotate -10">
<param name=ImgFilter7              value="rotate -15">
<param name=ImgFilter8              value="rotate -20">
<param name=ImgFilter9              value="rotate -25">
<param name=ImgFilter10             value="rotate -30">
<param name=ImgVertCenter           value=true>
<param name=ImgAutoMove             value=true>
<param name=ImgXOffset11            value=300>
<param name=ImgXOffset90            value=-90>

<param name=ImgFilter11             value=$1>
<param name=ImgFilter12             value=$2>
<param name=ImgFilter13             value=$3>
<param name=ImgFilter14             value=$4>
<param name=ImgFilter15             value=$5>
<param name=ImgFilter16             value=$6>
```

```
<param name=ImgFilter17          value=$7>
<param name=ImgFilter18          value=$8>
<param name=ImgFilter19          value=$9>
<param name=ImgFilter20          value=$8>
<param name=ImgFilter21          value=$7>
<param name=ImgFilter22          value=$6>
<param name=ImgFilter23          value=$5>
<param name=ImgFilter24          value=$4>
<param name=ImgFilter25          value=$3>
<param name=ImgFilter26          value=$2>
<param name=ImgFilter27          value=$1>
<param name=ImgFilter28          value=$2>
<param name=ImgFilter29          value=$3>
<param name=ImgFilter30          value=$4>
<param name=ImgFilter31          value=$5>
<param name=ImgFilter32          value=$6>
<param name=ImgFilter33          value=$7>
<param name=ImgFilter34          value=$8>
<param name=ImgFilter35          value=$9>
<param name=ImgFilter36          value=$8>
<param name=ImgFilter37          value=$7>
<param name=ImgFilter38          value=$6>
<param name=ImgFilter39          value=$5>
<param name=ImgFilter40          value=$4>
<param name=ImgFilter41          value=$3>
<param name=ImgFilter42          value=$2>
<param name=ImgFilter43          value=$1>
<param name=ImgFilter44          value=$2>
<param name=ImgFilter45          value=$3>
<param name=ImgFilter46          value=$4>
<param name=ImgFilter47          value=$5>
<param name=ImgFilter48          value=$6>
<param name=ImgFilter49          value=$7>
<param name=ImgFilter50          value=$8>
<param name=ImgFilter51          value=$9>
<param name=ImgFilter52          value=$8>
<param name=ImgFilter53          value=$7>
<param name=ImgFilter54          value=$6>
<param name=ImgFilter55          value=$5>
<param name=ImgFilter56          value=$4>
<param name=ImgFilter57          value=$3>
<param name=ImgFilter58          value=$2>
<param name=ImgFilter59          value=$1>
<param name=ImgFilter60          value=$2>
<param name=ImgFilter61          value=$3>
<param name=ImgFilter62          value=$4>
<param name=ImgFilter63          value=$5>
<param name=ImgFilter64          value=$6>
```

```
<param name=ImgFilter65          value=$7>
<param name=ImgFilter66          value=$8>
<param name=ImgFilter67          value=$9>
<param name=ImgFilter68          value=$8>
<param name=ImgFilter69          value=$7>
<param name=ImgFilter70          value=$6>
<param name=ImgFilter71          value=$5>
<param name=ImgFilter72          value=$4>
<param name=ImgFilter73          value=$3>
<param name=ImgFilter74          value=$2>
<param name=ImgFilter75          value=$1>
<param name=ImgFilter76          value=$2>
<param name=ImgFilter77          value=$3>
<param name=ImgFilter78          value=$4>
<param name=ImgFilter79          value=$5>
<param name=ImgFilter80          value=$6>
<param name=ImgFilter81          value=$7>
<param name=ImgFilter82          value=$8>
<param name=ImgFilter83          value=$9>
<param name=ImgFilter84          value=$8>
<param name=ImgFilter85          value=$7>
</applet>
```

Animation Display for Example **Eight**

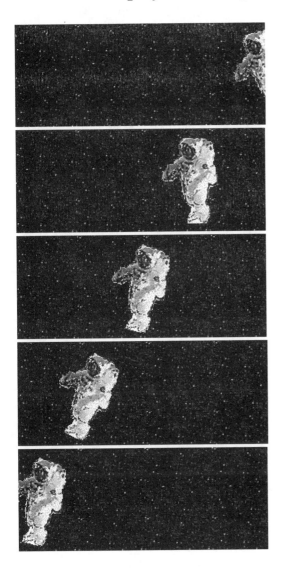

See Also

Related applets:	**AnimateContinuous** on page 189
	Rotate on page 112
URL for **Eight**:	http://www.vivids.com/ij2/bonus/Eight.html

Nine

Blurring Image On Button Press

Description

Example **Nine** uses the **AnimateOnPressRelease** applet. An image is displayed and labeled *Press the image*. When the mouse button is pressed, the image blurs. The **Blur** applet on page 130 is used to create the blurring effect. If the mouse button is pressed and released while over the image, the page specified by the URL is loaded.

The HTML Code for Example Nine

```
<applet
    archive   = Nine.zip
    codebase  = Nine
    code      = AnimateOnPressRelease.class
    width     = 250
    height    = 130>

<param name=WaitForEverything value=true>
<param name=AppBGColor        value=white>

<param name=ImgNumImages      value=2>
<param name=Image1            value=Nine/IJ_logo.jpg>
<param name=ImgHorizCenter    value=true>
<param name=ImgYOffset        value=10>
<param name=ImgFilter1        value="noop">
<param name=ImgFilter2        value="blur">
<param name=ImgURL            value="http://www.vivids.com/ij2">

<param name=TxNumImages       value=3>
<param name=Text1             value="Press the image">
<param name=TxHorizCenter     value=true>
<param name=TxFont            value=TimesRoman>
<param name=TxPointSize       value=20>
<param name=TxYOffset1        value=100>
<param name=TxAudio           value=Nine/press_image.au>
</applet>
```

Animation Display for Example Nine

Initial Display

Press the image

Button Press

Press the image

Button Release

Press the image

http://...

See Also

Related applets:

AnimateOnPressRelease on page 206
Blur on page 130

URL for **Nine**:

http://www.vivids.com/ij2/bonus/Nine.html

Ten

Mirror On Entry

Description

Example **Ten** uses the **AnimateOnEntryTwoWay** applet. The FontMaker image is displayed initially. When the pointer enters the area, the image flips and an audio file plays. The **Mirror** applet on page 113 is used as a filter for generating the mirrored images.

The HTML Code for Example Ten

```
<applet
    archive   = Ten.zip
    codebase = Ten
    code      = AnimateOnEntryTwoWay.class
    width     = 184
    height    = 218>

<param name=ImgNumImages      value=2>
<param name=Image1            value=Ten/fmaker.gif>
<param name=ImgHorizCenter    value=true>
<param name=ImgVertCenter     value=true>
<param name=ImgFilter1        value="noop">
<param name=ImgFilter2        value="mirror">
<param name=ImgFrameThickness value=4>
<param name=ImgFrameType      value=ShadowEtchedOut>
<param name=ImgURL            value=http://www.vivids.com/fontmaker>
<param name=ImgAudio          value=Ten/learnmore.au>
</applet>
```

Animation Display for Example Ten

Initial Display   Mirror on Pointer Entry   Load URL on button press

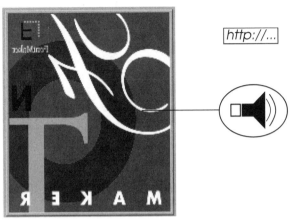

See Also

Related applets: **AnimateOnEntryTwoWay** on page 203
                          Mirror on page 113

URL for **Ten**:   `http://www.vivids.com/ij2/bonus/Ten.html`

Eleven

Rotate On Entry

Description

Example **Eleven** uses the **AnimateOnEntry** applet. The FontMaker image is displayed initially. When the pointer enters the area, the image begins rotating 90 degrees and an audio file plays. The **Rotate** applet on page 112 is used as a filter for generating the rotated images.

The HTML Code for Example Eleven

```
<applet
    archive  = Eleven.zip
    codebase = Eleven
    code     = AnimateOnEntry.class
    width    = 218
    height   = 218>

<param name=ImgNumImages            value=4>
<param name=Image1                  value=Eleven/fmaker.gif>
<param name=ImgDelayBetweenImages value=800>
<param name=ImgDelayBetweenRuns   value=800>
<param name=ImgHorizCenter          value=true>
<param name=ImgVertCenter           value=true>
<param name=ImgFilter1              value="noop">
<param name=ImgFilter2              value="rotate 90">
<param name=ImgFilter3              value="rotate 180">
<param name=ImgFilter4              value="rotate 270">
<param name=ImgFrameThickness       value=4>
<param name=ImgFrameType            value=ShadowEtchedOut>
<param name=ImgURL             value=http://www.vivids.com/fontmaker>
<param name=ImgAudio                value=Eleven/learnmore.au>
</applet>
```

Animation Display for Example **Eleven**

Initial Display

Load URL on button press

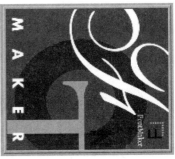

Rotation begins on Pointer Entry

See Also

Related applets: **AnimateOnEntry** on page 200
Rotate on page 112

URL for **Eleven**:   `http://www.vivids.com/ij2/bonus/Eleven.html`

Twelve

Moving Text

Description

Example **Twelve** uses the **AnimateMultiple** applet. Two text strings are displayed. The *Let's go to...* string moves across the screen. The *California* string is stationary but changes color.

The HTML Code for Example **Twelve**

```
<applet
    archive  = Twelve.zip
    codebase = Twelve
    code     = AnimateMultiple.class
    width    = 300
    height   = 100>

<param name=TxCount                value=2>
<param name=AppBGColor             value=white>
<param name=WaitForEverything      value=true>

<param name=Text1                  value="Let's go to...">
<param name=Tx1DelayBetweenImages value=80>
<param name=Tx1DelayBetweenRuns   value=2000>
<param name=Tx1AnimationType       value=Continuous>
<param name=Tx1NumImages           value=49>
<param name=Tx1Filter1             value="text">
<param name=Tx1AutoMove            value=true>
<param name=Tx1XOffset1            value=300>
<param name=Tx1XOffset49           value=-180>
<param name=Tx1Font1               value=Helvetica>
<param name=Tx1Style1              value=BoldItalic>
<param name=Tx1PointSize           value=24>
<param name=Tx1Color               value=hotpink>

<param name=Text2                  value="California">
<param name=Tx2DelayBetweenImages value=1000>
<param name=Tx2DelayBetweenRuns   value=1000>
<param name=Tx2AnimationType       value=Continuous>
<param name=Tx2PointSize           value=60>
<param name=Tx2Font                value=TimesRoman>
<param name=Tx2Style               value=BoldItalic>
<param name=Tx2NumImages           value=4>
<param name=Tx2Color1              value=deepskyblue>
<param name=Tx2Color2              value=olivedrab>
```

```
<param name=Tx2Color3          value=navyblue>
<param name=Tx2Color4          value=sienna>

</applet>
```

Animation Display for Example Twelve

California •Let's g

California Let's go to...

California Let's go to... •

California 't's go to...•

California 'o to...

See Also

Related applets: **AnimateMultiple** on page 209

URL for **Twelve**:   `http://www.vivids.com/ij2/bonus/Twelve.html`

Thirteen

Multiple Moving Text

Description

Example **Thirteen** uses the **AnimateMultiple** applet. Three text strings are displayed. The *Follow me to...* string moves across the screen from right to left. The *...Don't Forget* string moves across the screen from left to right. The *California* string is stationary but changes color. The **SmoothText** applet on page 68 is used to generate the smooth text for the *California* string.

The HTML Code for Example Thirteen

```
<applet
    archive  = Thirteen.zip
    codebase = Thirteen
    code     = AnimateMultiple.class
    width    = 300
    height   = 100>

<param name=TxCount                    value=3>
<param name=AppBGColor                 value=white>
<param name=WaitForEverything          value=true>

<param name=Text1                      value="Follow me to...">
<param name=Tx1DelayBetweenImages value=80>
<param name=Tx1DelayBetweenRuns   value=2000>
<param name=Tx1AnimationType           value=Continuous>
<param name=Tx1NumImages               value=49>
<param name=Tx1AutoMove                value=true>
<param name=Tx1XOffset1                value=300>
<param name=Tx1XOffset49               value=-180>
<param name=Tx1Font1                   value=TimesRoman>
<param name=Tx1Style1                  value=BoldItalic>
<param name=Tx1PointSize               value=24>
<param name=Tx1Color                   value=hotpink>

<param name=Text2                      value="California">
<param name=Tx2DelayBetweenImages value=1000>
<param name=Tx2DelayBetweenRuns   value=1000>
<param name=Tx2Filter1                 value="smoothtext">
<param name=Tx2Filter2                 value="smoothtext">
<param name=Tx2Filter3                 value="smoothtext">
<param name=Tx2AnimationType           value=Continuous>
<param name=Tx2PointSize               value=60>
<param name=Tx2Font                    value=TimesRoman>
```

```
<param name=Tx2Style              value=BoldItalic>
<param name=Tx2NumImages          value=3>
<param name=Tx2Color1             value=red>
<param name=Tx2Color2             value=yellow>
<param name=Tx2Color3             value=blue>

<param name=Text3                 value="...Don't forget!">
<param name=Tx3DelayBetweenImages value=90>
<param name=Tx3DelayBetweenRuns   value=1800>
<param name=Tx3AnimationType      value=Continuous>
<param name=Tx3YOffset1           value=50>
<param name=Tx3NumImages          value=49>
<param name=Tx3AutoMove           value=true>
<param name=Tx3XOffset1           value=-180>
<param name=Tx3XOffset49          value=300>
<param name=Tx3Font1              value=TimesRoman>
<param name=Tx3Style1             value=BoldItalic>
<param name=Tx3PointSize          value=18>
<param name=Tx3Color              value=orange>

</applet>
```
Animation Display for Example **Thirteen**

See Also

Related applets: **AnimateMultiple** on page 209
                         SmoothText on page 68

URL for **Thirteen**:   http://www.vivids.com/ij2/bonus/Thirteen.html

Fourteen

Oscillating Softshadow

Description

Example **Fourteen** uses the **AnimateTwoWay** applet. The string *Sale!* is displayed using the **SoftShadow** applet on page 66 with varying settings for the **SoftThickness** parameter.

The HTML Code for Example Fourteen

```
<applet
    archive  = Fourteen.zip
    codebase = Fourteen
    code     = AnimateTwoWay.class
    width    = 200
    height   = 100>

<param name=AppBGColor              value=white>
<param name=TxNumImages             value=10>
<param name=Text                    value=Sale!>
<param name=TxPointSize             value=48>
<param name=TxStyle                 value=bold>
<param name=TxFont                  value=TimesRoman>
<param name=TxDelayBetweenImages value=130>
<param name=TxDelayBetweenRuns   value=130>
<param name=TxColor                 value=white>
<param name=TxHorizCenter           value=true>
<param name=TxVertCenter            value=true>
<param name=TxFilter1               value="softshadow 0 0 #646464 0">
<param name=TxFilter2               value="softshadow 0 0 #646464 1">
<param name=TxFilter3               value="softshadow 0 0 #646464 2">
<param name=TxFilter4               value="softshadow 0 0 #646464 3">
<param name=TxFilter5               value="softshadow 0 0 #646464 4">
<param name=TxFilter6               value="softshadow 0 0 #646464 6">
<param name=TxFilter7               value="softshadow 0 0 #646464 7">
<param name=TxFilter8               value="softshadow 0 0 #646464 8">
<param name=TxFilter9               value="softshadow 0 0 #646464 9">
<param name=TxFilter10              value="softshadow 0 0 #646464 10">
</applet>
```

Animation Display for Example Fourteen

See Also

Related applets: **AnimateTwoWay** on page 191
                                    SoftShadow on page 66

URL for **Fourteen**:   `http://www.vivids.com/ij2/bonus/Fourteen.html`

Fifteen

Oscillating Softshadow With Multiple Text Strings

Description

Example **Fifteen** uses the **AnimateContinuous** applet. Two strings, *Don't miss* and *the BIG event!* are displayed using the **SoftShadow** applet on page 66 with varying settings for the **SoftThickness** parameter.

The HTML Code for Example Fifteen

```
<applet
    archive  = Fifteen.zip
    codebase = Fifteen
    code     = AnimateContinuous.class
    width    = 400
    height   = 100>

<param name=AppBGColor             value=white>
<param name=TxNumImages            value=22>
<param name=Text1                  value="Don't miss">
<param name=Text12                 value="the BIG event!">
<param name=TxPointSize            value=48>
<param name=TxStyle                value=bold>
<param name=TxFont                 value=TimesRoman>
<param name=TxDelayBetweenImages   value=170>
<param name=TxDelayBetweenRuns     value=2000>
<param name=TxColor                value=white>
<param name=TxHorizCenter          value=true>
<param name=TxVertCenter           value=true>
<param name=TxFilter1              value="softshadow 0 0 #646464 0">
<param name=TxFilter2              value="softshadow 0 0 #646464 1">
<param name=TxFilter3              value="softshadow 0 0 #646464 2">
<param name=TxFilter4              value="softshadow 0 0 #646464 3">
<param name=TxFilter5              value="softshadow 0 0 #646464 4">
<param name=TxFilter6              value="softshadow 0 0 #646464 5">
<param name=TxFilter7              value="$5">
<param name=TxFilter8              value="$4">
<param name=TxFilter9              value="$3">
<param name=TxFilter10             value="$2">
<param name=TxFilter11             value="$1">

<param name=TxFilter12             value="softshadow 0 0 #646464 0">
<param name=TxFilter13             value="softshadow 0 0 #646464 1">
<param name=TxFilter14             value="softshadow 0 0 #646464 2">
<param name=TxFilter15             value="softshadow 0 0 #646464 3">
```

```
<param name=TxFilter16        value="softshadow 0 0 #646464 4">
<param name=TxFilter17        value="softshadow 0 0 #646464 5">
<param name=TxFilter18        value="$16">
<param name=TxFilter19        value="$15">
<param name=TxFilter20        value="$14">
<param name=TxFilter21        value="$13">
<param name=TxFilter22        value="$12">
</applet>
```

Animation Display for Example **Fifteen**

See Also

Related applets: **AnimateContinuous** on page 189
                    SoftShadow on page 66

URL for **Fifteen**:   http://www.vivids.com/ij2/bonus/Fifteen.html

Sixteen

Oscillating Softshadow With Multiple Text String And Colors

Description

Example **Sixteen** uses the **AnimateContinuous** applet. Two strings, *Welcome* and *To My Home Page*, are displayed using the **SoftShadow** applet on page 66. The strings are displayed in yellow and cyan against a black background with varying settings for the **Soft-Thickness** parameter.

The HTML Code for Example Sixteen

```
<applet
    archive  = Sixteen.zip
    codebase = Sixteen
    code     = AnimateContinuous.class
    width    = 400
    height   = 100>

<param name=AppBGColor               value=black>
<param name=TxNumImages              value=27>
<param name=Text1                    value="Welcome">
<param name=Text14                   value="To My Home Page">
<param name=TxPointSize              value=48>
<param name=TxFont                   value=TimesRoman>
<param name=TxStyle                  value=bolditalic>
<param name=TxDelayBetweenImages value=130>
<param name=TxDelayBetweenRuns       value=800>
<param name=TxColor                  value=black>
<param name=TxHorizCenter            value=true>
<param name=TxVertCenter             value=true>
<param name=TxFilter1                value="softshadow 0 0 yellow 0">
<param name=TxFilter2                value="softshadow 0 0 yellow 1">
<param name=TxFilter3                value="softshadow 0 0 yellow 2">
<param name=TxFilter4                value="softshadow 0 0 yellow 3">
<param name=TxFilter5                value="softshadow 0 0 yellow 4">
<param name=TxFilter6                value="softshadow 0 0 yellow 6">
<param name=TxFilter7                value="$6">
<param name=TxFilter6                value="$5">
<param name=TxFilter7                value="$4">
<param name=TxFilter8                value="$3">
<param name=TxFilter9                value="$2">
<param name=TxFilter10               value="$1">
<param name=TxFilter11               value="$1">
<param name=TxFilter12               value="$1">
<param name=TxFilter13               value="$1">
```

```
<param name=TxFilter14          value="softshadow 0 0 cyan 0">
<param name=TxFilter15          value="softshadow 0 0 cyan 1">
<param name=TxFilter16          value="softshadow 0 0 cyan 2">
<param name=TxFilter17          value="softshadow 0 0 cyan 3">
<param name=TxFilter18          value="softshadow 0 0 cyan 4">
<param name=TxFilter19          value="softshadow 0 0 cyan 6">
<param name=TxFilter20          value="$18">
<param name=TxFilter21          value="$17">
<param name=TxFilter22          value="$16">
<param name=TxFilter23          value="$15">
<param name=TxFilter24          value="$14">
<param name=TxFilter25          value="$14">
<param name=TxFilter26          value="$14">
<param name=TxFilter27          value="$14">
</applet>
```

Animation Display for Example Sixteen

(animation frames showing "Welcome" and "To My Home Page" text)

See Also

Related applets: **AnimateContinuous** on page 189
                 SoftShadow on page 66

URL for **Sixteen**: `http://www.vivids.com/ij2/bonus/Sixteen.html`

Seventeen

Text Moving Out Of Screen

Description

Example **Seventeen** uses the **AnimateTwoWay** applet. The string *This is the place* is displayed using the **SoftShadow** applet on page 66. The shadow's X offset, Y offset, and shadow color are altered to create the appearance of the text coming out of the screen.

The HTML Code for Example Seventeen

```
<applet
    archive   = Seventeen.zip
    codebase  = Seventeen
    code      = AnimateTwoWay.class
    width     = 360
    height    = 80>

<param name=AppBGColor              value=white>
<param name=TxNumImages             value=10>
<param name=Text                    value="This is the place">
<param name=TxFont                  value=TimesRoman>
<param name=TxPointSize             value=48>
<param name=TxStyle                 value=bold>
<param name=TxDelayBetweenImages    value=130>
<param name=TxDelayBetweenRuns      value=130>
<param name=TxColor                 value=black>
<param name=TxHorizCenter           value=true>
<param name=TxVertCenter            value=true>
<param name=TxFilter1               value="softshadow 0 0 #444444 2">
<param name=TxFilter2               value="softshadow 2 2 #666666 2">
<param name=TxFilter3               value="softshadow 4 4 #777777 2">
<param name=TxFilter4               value="softshadow 6 6 #888888 2">
<param name=TxFilter5               value="softshadow 8 8 #999999 2">
<param name=TxFilter6               value="softshadow 10 10 #aaaaaa 2">
<param name=TxFilter7               value="softshadow 12 12 #bbbbbb 2">
<param name=TxFilter8               value="softshadow 14 14 #bbbbbb 2">
<param name=TxFilter9               value="softshadow 16 16 #bbbbbb 2">
<param name=TxFilter10              value="softshadow 18 18 #bbbbbb 2">
</applet>
```

Animation Display for Example Seventeen

This is the place

This is the place

This is the place

This is the place

This is the place

This is the place

This is the place

See Also

Related applets:

AnimateTwoWay on page 191
SoftShadow on page 66

URL for **Seventeen**:

http://www.vivids.com/ij2/bonus/Seventeen.html

Eighteen

Waving Text

Description

Example **Eighteen** uses the **AnimateTwoWay** applet. The string *Life has its little ups and down, doesn't it?* is displayed using the **WaveText** applet on page 70. A selected portion of the text waves by altering the **Amplitude** parameter.

The HTML Code for Example Eighteen

```
<applet
    archive  = Eighteen.zip
    codebase = Eighteen
    code     = AnimateTwoWay.class
    width    = 330
    height   = 75>

<param name=AppBGColor          value=white>
<param name=TxNumImages         value=11>
<param name=Text                value="Life has its little ups and downs,
doesn't it?">
<param name=TxPointSize          value=18>
<param name=TxFont               value=TimesRoman>
<param name=TxDelayBetweenImages value=130>
<param name=TxDelayBetweenRuns   value=130>
<param name=TxColor              value=black>
<param name=TxHorizCenter        value=true>
<param name=TxVertCenter         value=true>
<param name=TxFilter1            value="wavetext  25 20   30 0 15 31">
<param name=TxFilter2            value="wavetext  20 20   30 0 15 31">
<param name=TxFilter3            value="wavetext  15 20   30 0 15 31">
<param name=TxFilter4            value="wavetext  10 20   30 0 15 31">
<param name=TxFilter5            value="wavetext   5 20   30 0 15 31">
<param name=TxFilter6            value="wavetext   0 20   30 0 15 31">
<param name=TxFilter7            value="wavetext   5 20   95 0 15 31">
<param name=TxFilter8            value="wavetext  10 20   95 0 15 31">
<param name=TxFilter9            value="wavetext  15 20   95 0 15 31">
<param name=TxFilter10           value="wavetext 20 20   95 0 15 31">
<param name=TxFilter11           value="wavetext 25 20   95 0 15 31">
</applet>
```

Animation Display for Example Eighteen

Life has its li$t^{tle\ ups}_{a}{}_{nd\ do}{}^{w}ns$, doesn't it?

Life has its li$t^{tle\ ups}_{a}{}_{nd\ do}{}^{w}ns$, doesn't it?

Life has its lit$^{tle\ ups}a_{nd\ do}{}^{w}ns$, doesn't it?

Life has its litt$^{le\ ups}$ an$_d$ do$_{w}$ns, doesn't it?

Life has its litt$_{le}$ ups and do$_{w}$ns, doesn't it?

Life has its litt$_{le}$ ups and ^{do}wns, doesn't it?

Life has its lit$_{tle}$ ups an$^d\ do$wns, doesn't it?

Life has its lit$_{t_{le}}$ up^s an$^{d\ do}{}_{w}$ns, doesn't it?

Life has its lit$_{t_{le}}$ up^s a$^{nd\ do}{}_{w}$ns, doesn't it?

Life has its li$_{t_{t_{le}\ up}{}^{s}}$ a$^{nd\ do}{}_{w}$ns, doesn't it?

See Also

Related applets: **AnimateTwoWay** on page 191
WaveText on page 70

URL for **Eighteen**:   http://www.vivids.com/ij2/bonus/Eighteen.html

Nineteen

Waving Depthshade

Description

Example **Nineteen** uses the **AnimateTwoWay** applet. The string *WOW!!* is displayed using the **DepthShade** applet on page 77 and the **WaveImage** applet on page 128. The **Amplitude** and **XTranslate** parameters of the **WaveImage** applet are altered to create the gradually decreasing wavy text.

The HTML Code for Example **Nineteen**

```
<applet
    archive  = Nineteen.zip
    codebase = Nineteen
    code     = AnimateTwoWay.class
    width    = 130
    height   = 90>

<param name=AppBGColor            value=black>
<param name=TxNumImages           value=11>
<param name=Text                  value="WOW!!">
<param name=TxPointSize            value=30>
<param name=TxFont                value=TimesRoman>
<param name=TxDelayBetweenImages  value=130>
<param name=TxDelayBetweenRuns    value=130>
<param name=TxColor               value=white>
<param name=TxHorizCenter         value=true>
<param name=TxVertCenter          value=true>
<param name=TxFilter1    value="depthshade -20 -20|waveimage 20 14  0">
<param name=TxFilter2    value="depthshade -20 -20|waveimage 18 14  5">
<param name=TxFilter3    value="depthshade -20 -20|waveimage 16 14 10">
<param name=TxFilter4    value="depthshade -20 -20|waveimage 14 14 15">
<param name=TxFilter5    value="depthshade -20 -20|waveimage 12 14 20">
<param name=TxFilter6    value="depthshade -20 -20|waveimage 10 14 25">
<param name=TxFilter7    value="depthshade -20 -20|waveimage  8 14 30">
<param name=TxFilter8    value="depthshade -20 -20|waveimage  6 14 35">
<param name=TxFilter9    value="depthshade -20 -20|waveimage  4 14 40">
<param name=TxFilter10   value="depthshade -20 -20|waveimage  2 14 45">
<param name=TxFilter11   value="depthshade -20 -20|waveimage  0 14 50">
</applet>
```

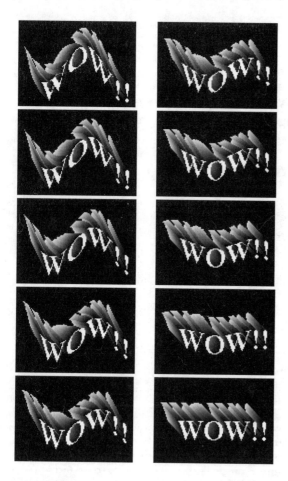

Animation Display for Example Nineteen

See Also

Related applets: **AnimateTwoWay** on page 191
                      DepthShade on page 77
                      WaveImage on page 128

URL for **Nineteen**:   http://www.vivids.com/ij2/bonus/Nineteen.html

Twenty

Continuously Waving Depthshade

Description

Example **Twenty** uses the **AnimateContinuous** applet. The string *Awesome!* is displayed using the **DepthShade** applet on page 77 and the **WaveImage** applet on page 128. The **XTranslate** parameter of the **WaveImage** applet is altered to create the continuous wavy text.

The HTML Code for Example **Twenty**

```
<applet
    archive  = Twenty.zip
    codebase = Twenty
    code     = AnimateContinuous.class
    width    = 160
    height   = 80>

<param name=AppBGColor             value=black>
<param name=TxNumImages            value=18>
<param name=Text                   value="Awesome!">
<param name=TxPointSize             value=30>
<param name=TxFont                  value=TimesRoman>
<param name=TxDelayBetweenImages   value=130>
<param name=TxDelayBetweenRuns     value=130>
<param name=TxColor                value=white>
<param name=TxHorizCenter          value=true>
<param name=TxVertCenter           value=true>
<param name=TxInitialImage         value=2>
<param name=TxFilter1              value="depthshade -12 -12">
<param name=TxFilter2              value="$1|waveimage 16 14 0">
<param name=TxFilter3              value="$1|waveimage 16 14 5">
<param name=TxFilter4              value="$1|waveimage 16 14 10">
<param name=TxFilter5              value="$1|waveimage 16 14 15">
<param name=TxFilter6              value="$1|waveimage 16 14 20">
<param name=TxFilter7              value="$1|waveimage 16 14 25">
<param name=TxFilter8              value="$1|waveimage 16 14 30">
<param name=TxFilter9              value="$1|waveimage 16 14 35">
<param name=TxFilter10             value="$1|waveimage 16 14 40">
<param name=TxFilter11             value="$1|waveimage 16 14 45">
<param name=TxFilter12             value="$1|waveimage 16 14 50">
<param name=TxFilter13             value="$1|waveimage 16 14 55">
<param name=TxFilter14             value="$1|waveimage 16 14 60">
<param name=TxFilter15             value="$1|waveimage 16 14 65">
<param name=TxFilter16             value="$1|waveimage 16 14 70">
```

```
<param name=TxFilter17        value="$1|waveimage 16 14 75">
<param name=TxFilter18        value="$1|waveimage 16 14 80">
</applet>
```

Animation Display for Example **Twenty**

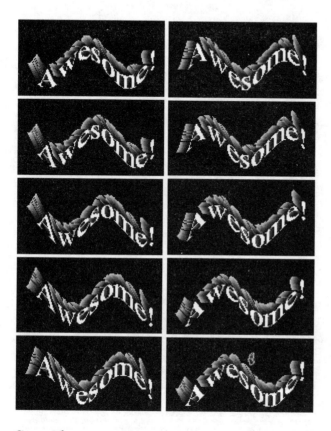

See Also

Related applets:

AnimateContinuous on page 189
DepthShade on page 77
WaveImage on page 128

URL for **Twenty**:

http://www.vivids.com/ij2/bonus/Twenty.html

TwentyOne

Moving Embossed Text Over Image

Description

Example **TwentyOne** uses the **AnimateTwoWay** applet. The string *Cruise, Anyone?* appears embossed against the sailboat background. The text is displayed using the **Emboss** applet on page 79 and moves across the screen.

The HTML Code for Example TwentyOne

```
<applet
    archive  = TwentyOne.zip
    codebase = TwentyOne
    code     = AnimateTwoWay.class
    width    = 340
    height   = 228>

<param name=AppBGImage          value=TwentyOne/sailboat.gif>
<param name=AppFrameThickness   value=4>
<param name=AppFrameType        value=ShadowEtchedOut>
<param name=AppBGColor          value=white>
<param name=WaitForEverything   value=true>
<param name=TxNumImages         value=40>
<param name=Text                value="Cruise, Anyone?">
<param name=TxPointSize          value=24>
<param name=TxStyle             value=bold>
<param name=TxDelayBetweenImages value=50>
<param name=TxDelayBetweenRuns   value=800>
<param name=TxFilter1           value="emboss 1 75">
<param name=TxFilter2           value="$1">
<param name=TxFilter3           value="$1">
<param name=TxFilter4           value="$1">
<param name=TxFilter5           value="$1">
<param name=TxFilter6           value="$1">
<param name=TxFilter7           value="$1">
<param name=TxFilter8           value="$1">
<param name=TxFilter9           value="$1">
<param name=TxFilter10          value="$1">
<param name=TxFilter11          value="$1">
<param name=TxFilter12          value="$1">
<param name=TxFilter13          value="$1">
<param name=TxFilter14          value="$1">
<param name=TxFilter15          value="$1">
<param name=TxFilter16          value="$1">
<param name=TxFilter17          value="$1">
```

```
<param name=TxFilter18          value="$1">
<param name=TxFilter19          value="$1">
<param name=TxFilter20          value="$1">
<param name=TxFilter21          value="$1">
<param name=TxFilter22          value="$1">
<param name=TxFilter23          value="$1">
<param name=TxFilter24          value="$1">
<param name=TxFilter25          value="$1">
<param name=TxFilter26          value="$1">
<param name=TxFilter27          value="$1">
<param name=TxFilter28          value="$1">
<param name=TxFilter29          value="$1">
<param name=TxFilter30          value="$1">
<param name=TxFilter31          value="$1">
<param name=TxFilter32          value="$1">
<param name=TxFilter33          value="$1">
<param name=TxFilter34          value="$1">
<param name=TxFilter35          value="$1">
<param name=TxFilter36          value="$1">
<param name=TxFilter37          value="$1">
<param name=TxFilter38          value="$1">
<param name=TxFilter39          value="$1">
<param name=TxFilter40          value="$1">

<param name=TxAutoMove          value=true>
<param name=TxXOffset1          value=0>
<param name=TxXOffset40         value=195>

<param name=TxYOffset1          value=0>
<param name=TxYOffset40         value=195>
</applet>
```

Animation Display for Example TwentyOne

See Also

Related applets: **AnimateTwoWay** on page 191
                     Emboss on page 79

URL for **TwentyOne**:   `http://www.vivids.com/ij2/bonus/TwentyOne.html`

TwentyTwo

Flashing Image

Description

Example **TwentyTwo** uses the **AnimateContinuous** applet. The eyeball image is displayed. At one second intervals the image alternates between full intensity and 60% faded black. The **Fade** applet on page 138 is used to created the faded effect.

The HTML Code for Example **TwentyTwo**

```
<applet
    archive  = TwentyTwo.zip
    codebase = TwentyTwo
    code     = AnimateContinuous.class
    width    = 80
    height   = 80>

<param name=AppBGColor            value=#000000>
<param name=ImgNumImages          value=2>
<param name=Image1                value=TwentyTwo/eyball.jpg>
<param name=ImgFilter1            value="noop">
<param name=ImgFilter2            value="fade 60 #000000">
<param name=ImgDelayBetweenImages value=1000>
<param name=ImgDelayBetweenRuns   value=1000>
<param name=ImgVertCenter         value=true>
<param name=ImgHorizCenter        value=true>
</applet>
Animation Display for Example TwentyTwo
```

See Also

Related applets:

AnimateContinuous on page 189
Fade on page 138

URL for **TwentyTwo**:

http://www.vivids.com/ij2/bonus/TwentyTwo.html

TwentyThree

Replace Each Color In Image With White

Description
Example **TwentyThree** uses the **AnimateContinuous** applet. The money image used in this example contains 16 unique colors (shades of gray). Each color in the image is replaced with white creating an unusual color flashing effect. The **ReplaceColor** applet on page 140 is used to replace the colors in the image.

The HTML Code for Example TwentyThree

```
<applet
    archive  = TwentyThree.zip
    codebase = TwentyThree
    code     = AnimateContinuous.class
    width    = 231
    height   = 146>

<param name=AppBGColor              value=#ffffff>
<param name=ImgNumImages            value=16>
<param name=Image1                  value=TwentyThree/money.gif>
<param name=ImgDelayBetweenRuns     value=80>
<param name=ImgDelayBetweenImages   value=80>
<param name=ImgFilter1              value="noop">
<param name=ImgFilter2              value="replacecolor #080818=#ffffff">
<param name=ImgFilter3              value="replacecolor #31294a=#ffffff">
<param name=ImgFilter4              value="replacecolor #635a7b=#ffffff">
<param name=ImgFilter5              value="replacecolor #423952=#ffffff">
<param name=ImgFilter6              value="replacecolor #000000=#ffffff">
<param name=ImgFilter7              value="replacecolor #181829=#ffffff">
<param name=ImgFilter8              value="replacecolor #212139=#ffffff">
<param name=ImgFilter9              value="replacecolor #c6d6d6=#ffffff">
<param name=ImgFilter10             value="replacecolor #d6dee7=#ffffff">
<param name=ImgFilter11             value="replacecolor #a5adbd=#ffffff">
<param name=ImgFilter12             value="replacecolor #8c94a5=#ffffff">
<param name=ImgFilter13             value="replacecolor #6b738c=#ffffff">
<param name=ImgFilter14             value="replacecolor #4a526b=#ffffff">
<param name=ImgFilter15             value="replacecolor #7b7b94=#ffffff">
<param name=ImgFilter16             value="replacecolor #8484a5=#ffffff">
</applet>
```

Animation Display for Example **TwentyThree**

See Also

Related applets: **AnimateContinuous** on page 189
ReplaceColor on page 140

URL for **TwentyThree**: http://www.vivids.com/ij2/bonus/TwentyThree.html

TwentyFour

Replace All Colors In Image With White

Description

Example **TwentyFour** uses the **AnimateOnEntryTwoWay** applet. The string *Move pointer here to make money* appears initially against a white background. When the pointer enters the image area, the money image gradually begins to appear. The money image used in this example contains 16 unique colors (shades of gray). Initially, each color in the image has been replaced with white. When the pointer enters the area the original colors begin replacing the white. The **ReplaceColor** applet on page 140 is used to replace the colors in the image.

The HTML Code for Example TwentyFour

```
<applet
    archive  = TwentyFour.zip
    codebase = TwentyFour
    code     = AnimateOnEntryTwoWay.class
    width    = 231
    height   = 146>

<param name=AppBGColor              value=#ffffff>
<param name=WaitForEverything       value=true>
<param name=ImgNumImages            value=31>
<param name=Image1                  value=TwentyFour/money.gif>
<param name=ImgDelayBetweenRuns     value=80>
<param name=ImgDelayBetweenImages   value=80>
<param name=ImgInitialImage         value=17>
<param name=ImgFilter1     value="noop">
<param name=ImgFilter2     value="$1|replacecolor #000000=#ffffff">
<param name=ImgFilter3     value="$2|replacecolor #d6dee7=#ffffff">
<param name=ImgFilter4     value="$3|replacecolor #c6d6d6=#ffffff">
<param name=ImgFilter5     value="$4|replacecolor #a5adbd=#ffffff">
<param name=ImgFilter6     value="$5|replacecolor #8c94a5=#ffffff">
<param name=ImgFilter7     value="$6|replacecolor #6b738c=#ffffff">
<param name=ImgFilter8     value="$7|replacecolor #4a526b=#ffffff">
<param name=ImgFilter9     value="$8|replacecolor #7b7b94=#ffffff">
<param name=ImgFilter10    value="$9|replacecolor #8484a5=#ffffff">
<param name=ImgFilter11    value="$10|replacecolor #181829=#ffffff">
<param name=ImgFilter12    value="$11|replacecolor #212139=#ffffff">
<param name=ImgFilter13    value="$12|replacecolor #080818=#ffffff">
<param name=ImgFilter14    value="$13|replacecolor #31294a=#ffffff">
<param name=ImgFilter15    value="$14|replacecolor #635a7b=#ffffff">
<param name=ImgFilter16    value="$15|replacecolor #423952=#ffffff">
```

```
<param name=ImgFilter17        value="$16">
<param name=ImgFilter18        value="$15">
<param name=ImgFilter19        value="$14">
<param name=ImgFilter20        value="$13">
<param name=ImgFilter21        value="$12">
<param name=ImgFilter22        value="$11">
<param name=ImgFilter23        value="$10">
<param name=ImgFilter24        value="$9">
<param name=ImgFilter25        value="$8">
<param name=ImgFilter26        value="$7">
<param name=ImgFilter27        value="$6">
<param name=ImgFilter28        value="$5">
<param name=ImgFilter29        value="$4">
<param name=ImgFilter30        value="$3">
<param name=ImgFilter31        value="$2">

<param name=Text               value="Move pointer here to make money">
<param name=TxNumImages        value=2>
<param name=TxFont             value=TimesRoman>
<param name=TxStyle            value=Bold>
<param name=TxPointSize        value=14>
<param name=TxVertCenter       value=true>
<param name=TxHorizCenter      value=true>

</applet>
```

Animation Display for Example **TwentyFour**

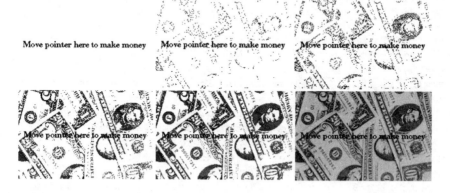

See Also

Related applets: **AnimateOnEntryTwoWay** on page 203
      ReplaceColor on page 140

URL for **TwentyFour**:   `http://www.vivids.com/ij2/bonus/TwentyFour.html`

TwentyFive

Fade An Image In And Out

Description

Example **TwentyFive** uses the **AnimateTwoWay** applet. The bouquet image is initially displayed at full intensity. It then fades in and out using the **Fade** applet on page 138.

The HTML Code for Example TwentyFive

```
<applet
    archive  = TwentyFive.zip
    codebase = TwentyFive
    code     = AnimateTwoWay.class
    width    = 108
    height   = 90>

<param name=AppBGColor           value=#ffffff>
<param name=ImgNumImages         value=16>
<param name=Image1               value=TwentyFive/bouquet.gif>
<param name=ImgFilter1           value="scale 40 40">
<param name=ImgFilter2           value="$1|fade 10 #ffffff">
<param name=ImgFilter3           value="$1|fade 20 #ffffff">
<param name=ImgFilter4           value="$1|fade 30 #ffffff">
<param name=ImgFilter5           value="$1|fade 40 #ffffff">
<param name=ImgFilter6           value="$1|fade 50 #ffffff">
<param name=ImgFilter7           value="$1|fade 70 #ffffff">
<param name=ImgFilter8           value="$1|fade 90 #ffffff">
<param name=ImgFilter9           value="$1|fade 100 #ffffff">
<param name=ImgFilter10          value="$8">
<param name=ImgFilter11          value="$7">
<param name=ImgFilter12          value="$6">
<param name=ImgFilter13          value="$5">
<param name=ImgFilter14          value="$4">
<param name=ImgFilter15          value="$3">
<param name=ImgFilter16          value="$2">
<param name=ImgDelayBetweenImages value=100>
<param name=ImgDelayBetweenRuns  value=1000>
<param name=ImgVertCenter        value=true>
<param name=ImgHorizCenter       value=true>
</applet>
```

Animation Display for Example **TwentyFive**

See Also

Related applets: **AnimateContinuous** on page 189
                                       Scale on page 135
                                       Fade on page 138

URL for **TwentyFive**:   `http://www.vivids.com/ij2/bonus/TwentyFive.html`

TwentySix

Negative An Image In And Out

Description

Example **TwentySix** uses the **AnimateTwoWay** applet. The eyeball image is initially displayed at full intensity. The image gradually changes to negative colors using **Negative** applet on page 137.

The HTML Code for Example **TwentySix**

```
<applet
    archive  = TwentySix.zip
    codebase = TwentySix
    code     = AnimateTwoWay.class
    width    = 100
    height   = 100>

<param name=ImgDelayBetweenRuns    value=250>
<param name=ImgDelayBetweenImages  value=50>
<param name=AppBGColor             value=black>

<param name=ImgNumImages           value=10>
<param name=ImgHorizCenter         value=true>
<param name=ImgVertCenter          value=true>
<param name=Image1                 value=TwentySix/eyball.jpg>
<param name=ImgFilter2             value="negative 10">
<param name=ImgFilter3             value="negative 40">
<param name=ImgFilter4             value="negative 70">
<param name=ImgFilter5             value="negative 100">
<param name=ImgFilter6             value="negative 130">
<param name=ImgFilter7             value="negative 160">
<param name=ImgFilter8             value="negative 190">
<param name=ImgFilter9             value="negative 220">
<param name=ImgFilter10            value="negative 255">
</applet>
```

Animation Display for Example **TwentySix**

See Also

Related applets: **AnimateContinuous** on page 189
                    Negative on page 137

URL for **TwentySix**:   `http://www.vivids.com/ij2/bonus/TwentySix.html`

TwentySeven

Flashing Colors

Description

Example **TwentySeven** uses the **AnimateContinuous** applet. The Emperor Limousine image fades in and out in yellow and cyan. The **Fade** applet on page 138 is used to create the fading effect.

The HTML Code for Example **TwentySeven**

```
<applet
    archive  = TwentySeven.zip
    codebase = TwentySeven
    code     = AnimateContinuous.class
    width    = 172
    height   = 69>

<param name=ImgDelayBetweenRuns   value=200>
<param name=ImgDelayBetweenImages value=200>

<param name=ImgNumImages          value=17>
<param name=ImgInitialImage       value=2>
<param name=ImgHorizCenter        value=true>
<param name=ImgVertCenter         value=true>
<param name=Image1                value=TwentySeven/emperor.gif>
<param name=ImgFilter1            value="scale 40 40">
<param name=ImgFilter2            value="$1|fade 5 yellow">
<param name=ImgFilter3            value="$1|fade 25 yellow">
<param name=ImgFilter4            value="$1|fade 50 yellow">
<param name=ImgFilter5            value="$1|fade 75 yellow">
<param name=ImgFilter6            value="$5">
<param name=ImgFilter7            value="$4">
<param name=ImgFilter8            value="$3">
<param name=ImgFilter9            value="$2">
<param name=ImgFilter10           value="$1|fade 5 cyan">
<param name=ImgFilter11           value="$1|fade 25 cyan">
<param name=ImgFilter12           value="$1|fade 50 cyan">
<param name=ImgFilter13           value="$1|fade 75 cyan">
<param name=ImgFilter14           value="$13">
<param name=ImgFilter15           value="$12">
<param name=ImgFilter16           value="$11">
<param name=ImgFilter17           value="$10">
</applet>
```

Animation Display for Example **TwentySeven**

See Also

Related applets: **AnimateContinuous** on page 189
Scale on page 135
Fade on page 138

URL for **TwentySeven**:   http://www.vivids.com/ij2/bonus/TwentySeven.html

TwentyEight

Fading Shadow

Description

Example **TwentyEight** uses the **AnimateTwoWay** applet. The string *Altered Shadow* appears with a faint shadow. The intensity of the shadow increases with each frame in the animation sequence.

The HTML Code for Example **TwentyEight**

```
<applet
    archive   = TwentyEight.zip
    codebase  = TwentyEight
    code      = AnimateTwoWay.class
    width     = 260
    height    = 45>

<param name=TxDelayBetweenRuns    value=1000>
<param name=TxDelayBetweenImages  value=150>
<param name=WaitForEverything     value=true>
<param name=AppBGColor            value=white>

<param name=TxNumImages           value=11>
<param name=TxPointSize           value=36>
<param name=TxFont                value=TimesRoman>
<param name=TxStyle               value=Bold>
<param name=TxHorizCenter         value=true>
<param name=TxVertCenter          value=true>
<param name=Text                  value="Altered Shadow">
<param name=TxFilter1             value="shadow 3 3 #eeeeee">
<param name=TxFilter2             value="shadow 3 3 #dddddd">
<param name=TxFilter3             value="shadow 3 3 #cccccc">
<param name=TxFilter4             value="shadow 3 3 #bbbbbb">
<param name=TxFilter5             value="shadow 3 3 #aaaaaa">
<param name=TxFilter6             value="shadow 3 3 #999999">
<param name=TxFilter7             value="$5">
<param name=TxFilter8             value="$4">
<param name=TxFilter9             value="$3">
<param name=TxFilter10            value="$2">
<param name=TxFilter11            value="$1">
</applet>
```

Animation Display for Example **TwentyEight**

Altered Shadow
Altered Shadow
Altered Shadow
Altered Shadow
Altered Shadow
Altered Shadow
Altered Shadow
Altered Shadow
Altered Shadow

See Also

Related applets: **AnimateTwoWay** on page 191
                       Shadow on page 64

URL for **TwentyEight**:   `http://www.vivids.com/ij2/bonus/TwentyEight.html`

TwentyNine

Rotating Shadow

Description

Example **TwentyNine** uses the **AnimateContinuous** applet. The string *Rotating Shadow* is displayed with a shadow. The X and Y offset of the shadow continuously changes, making it appear as though the light source is changing position. The shadow is created using the **Shadow** applet on page 64.

The HTML Code for Example **TwentyNine**

```
<applet
    archive  = TwentyNine.zip
    codebase = TwentyNine
    code     = AnimateContinuous.class
    width    = 300
    height   = 85>

<param name=TxDelayBetweenRuns    value=40>
<param name=TxDelayBetweenImages  value=40>
<param name=WaitForEverything     value=true>
<param name=AppBGColor            value=white>


<param name=Text                  value="Rotating Shadow">

<param name=TxNumImages           value=24>
<param name=TxPointSize           value=24>
<param name=TxFont                value=Timesroman>
<param name=TxStyle               value=Bold>
<param name=TxColor               value=salmon>
<param name=TxXOffset1            value=30>
<param name=TxYOffset1            value=30>

<param name=TxYOffset8            value=28>
<param name=TxYOffset9            value=26>
<param name=TxYOffset10           value=25>
<param name=TxYOffset11           value=25>
<param name=TxYOffset12           value=24>
<param name=TxYOffset13           value=24>

<param name=TxYOffset14           value=24>
<param name=TxYOffset15           value=24>
<param name=TxYOffset16           value=25>
<param name=TxYOffset17           value=25>
<param name=TxYOffset18           value=26>
```

```
<param name=TxYOffset19          value=28>
<param name=TxYOffset20          value=30>

<param name=TxXOffset14          value=28>
<param name=TxXOffset15          value=26>
<param name=TxXOffset16          value=25>
<param name=TxXOffset17          value=25>
<param name=TxXOffset18          value=24>
<param name=TxXOffset19          value=24>

<param name=TxXOffset20          value=24>
<param name=TxXOffset21          value=25>
<param name=TxXOffset22          value=25>
<param name=TxXOffset23          value=26>
<param name=TxXOffset24          value=28>
<param name=TxXOffset25          value=30>

<param name=TxFilter1            value="shadow 0 6 #bbbbbb">
<param name=TxFilter2            value="shadow 2 6 #bbbbbb">
<param name=TxFilter3            value="shadow 4 5 #bbbbbb">
<param name=TxFilter4            value="shadow 5 5 #bbbbbb">
<param name=TxFilter5            value="shadow 5 4 #bbbbbb">
<param name=TxFilter6            value="shadow 6 2 #bbbbbb">
<param name=TxFilter7            value="shadow 6 0 #bbbbbb">

<param name=TxFilter8            value="shadow 6 -2 #bbbbbb">
<param name=TxFilter9            value="shadow 5 -4 #bbbbbb">
<param name=TxFilter10           value="shadow 5 -5 #bbbbbb">
<param name=TxFilter11           value="shadow 4 -5 #bbbbbb">
<param name=TxFilter12           value="shadow 2 -6 #bbbbbb">
<param name=TxFilter13           value="shadow 0 -6 #bbbbbb">

<param name=TxFilter14           value="shadow -2 -6 #bbbbbb">
<param name=TxFilter15           value="shadow -4 -6 #bbbbbb">
<param name=TxFilter16           value="shadow -5 -5 #bbbbbb">
<param name=TxFilter17           value="shadow -5 -5 #bbbbbb">
<param name=TxFilter18           value="shadow -6 -4 #bbbbbb">
<param name=TxFilter19           value="shadow -6 -2 #bbbbbb">

<param name=TxFilter20           value="shadow -6 0 #bbbbbb">
<param name=TxFilter21           value="shadow -5 2 #bbbbbb">
<param name=TxFilter22           value="shadow -5 4 #bbbbbb">
<param name=TxFilter23           value="shadow -4 5 #bbbbbb">
<param name=TxFilter24           value="shadow -2 5 #bbbbbb">
<param name=TxFilter25           value="shadow  0 6 #bbbbbb">

</applet>
```

Animation Display for Example TwentyNine

Retating Shadew

Rotatiing Shadow

Retating Shadew

Rotatiing Shadow

See Also

Related applets: **AnimateContinuous** on page 189
                           Shadow on page 64

URL for **TwentyNine**:   `http://www.vivids.com/ij2/bonus/TwentyNine.html`

Thirty

Slanting Image

Description

Example **Thirty** uses the **AnimateTwoWay** applet. The company logo is displayed using the **SlantLeft** applet on page 115. The angle of the slant is continuously changing by altering the **Angle** parameter.

The HTML Code for Example Thirty

```
<applet
    archive  = Thirty.zip
    codebase = Thirty
    code     = AnimateTwoWay.class
    width    = 350
    height   = 159>

<param name=AppBGColor            value=#00849c>
<param name=ImgNumImages          value=27>
<param name=ImgDelayBetweenImages value=75>
<param name=ImgDelayBetweenRuns   value=75>
<param name=Image1                value=Thirty/vivid.gif>
<param name=ImgHorizCenter        value=true>
<param name=ImgVertCenter         value=true>
<param name=ImgFilter1            value="noop">
<param name=ImgFilter2            value="slantleft 2">
<param name=ImgFilter3            value="slantleft 4">
<param name=ImgFilter4            value="slantleft 6">
<param name=ImgFilter5            value="slantleft 8">
<param name=ImgFilter6            value="slantleft 10">
<param name=ImgFilter7            value="slantleft 12">
<param name=ImgFilter8            value="slantleft 14">
<param name=ImgFilter9            value="slantleft 16">
<param name=ImgFilter10           value="slantleft 18">
<param name=ImgFilter11           value="slantleft 20">
<param name=ImgFilter12           value="slantleft 22">
<param name=ImgFilter13           value="slantleft 24">
<param name=ImgFilter14           value="slantleft 26">
<param name=ImgFilter15           value="slantleft 28">
<param name=ImgFilter16           value="slantleft 30">
<param name=ImgFilter17           value="slantleft 32">
<param name=ImgFilter18           value="slantleft 34">
<param name=ImgFilter19           value="slantleft 36">
<param name=ImgFilter20           value="slantleft 38">
<param name=ImgFilter21           value="slantleft 40">
```

```
<param name=ImgFilter22          value="slantleft 42">
<param name=ImgFilter23          value="slantleft 44">
<param name=ImgFilter24          value="slantleft 46">
<param name=ImgFilter25          value="slantleft 48">
<param name=ImgFilter26          value="slantleft 50">
<param name=ImgFilter27          value="slantleft 52">
</applet>
```

Animation Display for Example Thirty

See Also

Related applets: **AnimateContinuous** on page 189

                                        SlantLeft on page 115

URL for **Thirty**:   `http://www.vivids.com/ij2/bonus/Thirty.html`

ThirtyOne

Raise Image With Shadow

Description

Example **ThirtyOne** uses the **AnimateTwoWay** applet. The bouquet image is displayed with a shadow whose X and Y offset vary. This creates the illusion that the image is coming out of the screen. The **ImageShadow** applet on page 110 is used to produce the shadow effect.

The HTML Code for Example **ThirtyOne**

```
<applet
    archive  = ThirtyOne.zip
    codebase = ThirtyOne
    code     = AnimateTwoWay.class
    width    = 230
    height   = 190>

<param name=ImgNumImages value=10>
<param name=AppBGColor    value=white>
<param name=Image1        value=ThirtyOne/bouquet.gif>
<param name=ImgFilter1    value="noop">
<param name=ImgFilter2    value="imageshadow 1 1 #888888">
<param name=ImgFilter3    value="imageshadow 2 2 #999999">
<param name=ImgFilter4    value="imageshadow 3 3 #aaaaaa">
<param name=ImgFilter5    value="imageshadow 4 4 #b8b8b8">
<param name=ImgFilter6    value="imageshadow 5 5 #bbbbbb">
<param name=ImgFilter7    value="imageshadow 6 6 #cccccc">
<param name=ImgFilter8    value="imageshadow 7 7 #d8d8d8">
<param name=ImgFilter9    value="imageshadow 8 8 #dddddd">
<param name=ImgFilter10   value="imageshadow 9 9 #dddddd">
<param name=ImgXoffset1   value=9>
<param name=ImgXoffset2   value=8>
<param name=ImgXoffset3   value=7>
<param name=ImgXoffset4   value=6>
<param name=ImgXoffset5   value=5>
<param name=ImgXoffset6   value=4>
<param name=ImgXoffset7   value=3>
<param name=ImgXoffset8   value=2>
<param name=ImgXoffset9   value=1>
<param name=ImgXoffset10  value=0>
<param name=ImgYoffset1   value=9>
<param name=ImgYoffset2   value=8>
<param name=ImgYoffset3   value=7>
<param name=ImgYoffset4   value=6>
```

```
<param name=ImgYoffset5   value=5>
<param name=ImgYoffset6   value=4>
<param name=ImgYoffset7   value=3>
<param name=ImgYoffset8   value=2>
<param name=ImgYoffset9   value=1>
<param name=ImgYoffset10  value=0>
</applet>
Animation Display for Example ThirtyOne
```

See Also

Related applets: **AnimateTwoWay** on page 191
                                      ImageShadow on page 110

URL for **ThirtyOne**:   `http://www.vivids.com/ij2/bonus/ThirtyOne.html`

ThirtyTwo

Raise And Rotate Image With Shadow

Description

Example **ThirtyTwo** uses the **AnimateTwoWay** applet. The bouquet image is displayed with a shadow whose X and Y offset vary. In addition, the image is rotated with each offset. This creates the illusion that the image is rotating and coming out of the screen. The **Image-Shadow** applet on page 110 is used to produce the shadow effect.

The HTML Code for Example **ThirtyTwo**

```
<applet
    archive  = ThirtyTwo.zip
    codebase = ThirtyTwo
    code     = AnimateTwoWay.class
    width    = 250
    height   = 250>

<param name=ImgNumImages    value=10>
<param name=AppBGColor      value=white>
<param name=Image1          value=ThirtyTwo/bouquet.gif>
<param name=ImgHorizCenter  value=true>
<param name=ImgVertCenter   value=true>
<param name=ImgFilter1      value="rotate 20">
<param name=ImgFilter2      value="rotate 10|imageshadow 1 1 #888888">
<param name=ImgFilter3      value="rotate 0|imageshadow 2 2 #999999">
<param name=ImgFilter4      value="rotate -10|imageshadow 3 3 #aaaaaa">
<param name=ImgFilter5      value="rotate -20|imageshadow 4 4 #b8b8b8">
<param name=ImgFilter6      value="rotate -30|imageshadow 5 5 #bbbbbb">
<param name=ImgFilter7      value="rotate -40|imageshadow 6 6 #c8c8c8">
<param name=ImgFilter8      value="rotate -50|imageshadow 7 7 #cccccc">
<param name=ImgFilter9      value="rotate -60|imageshadow 8 8 #d8d8d8">
<param name=ImgFilter10     value="rotate -70|imageshadow 9 9 #dddddd">
</applet>
```

Animation Display for Example ThirtyTwo

See Also

Related applets:	**AnimateTwoWay** on page 191
	ImageShadow on page 110
	Rotate on page 112
URL for **ThirtyTwo**:	`http://www.vivids.com/ij2/bonus/ThirtyTwo.html`

ThirtyThree

Smooth Wavy Text

Description

Example **ThirtyThree** uses the **AnimateTwoWay** applet. The string *Smooth wavy text keeps going* appears smoothed and wavy. The **XTranslate** parameter of the **WaveImage** applet on page 128 is varied as well as the **TxXoffset***N* to create the effect.

The HTML Code for Example **ThirtyThree**

```
<applet
    archive  = ThirtyThree.zip
    codebase = ThirtyThree
    code     = AnimateTwoWay.class
    width    = 480
    height   = 100>

<param name=AppBGColor              value=white>
<param name=TxNumImages             value=12>
<param name=Text                    value="Smooth wavy text keeps going">
<param name=TxPointSize             value=24>
<param name=TxFont                  value=TimesRoman>
<param name=TxStyle                 value=Bold>
<param name=TxDelayBetweenImages    value=80>
<param name=TxDelayBetweenRuns      value=80>
<param name=TxColor                 value=black>
<param name=TxInitialImage          value=2>
<param name=TxYOffset1              value=20>
<param name=TxXOffset1              value=120>
<param name=TxXOffset2              value=110>
<param name=TxXOffset3              value=100>
<param name=TxXOffset4              value=90>
<param name=TxXOffset5              value=80>
<param name=TxXOffset6              value=70>
<param name=TxXOffset7              value=60>
<param name=TxXOffset8              value=50>
<param name=TxXOffset9              value=40>
<param name=TxXOffset10             value=30>
<param name=TxXOffset11             value=20>
<param name=TxXOffset12             value=10>
<param name=TxFilter1               value="smoothtext">
<param name=TxFilter2               value="$1|waveimage 10 20 0">
<param name=TxFilter3               value="$1|waveimage 10 20 10 ">
<param name=TxFilter4               value="$1|waveimage 10 20 20">
<param name=TxFilter5               value="$1|waveimage 10 20 30">
```

```
<param name=TxFilter6        value="$1|waveimage 10 20 40">
<param name=TxFilter7        value="$1|waveimage 10 20 50">
<param name=TxFilter8        value="$1|waveimage 10 20 60">
<param name=TxFilter9        value="$1|waveimage 10 20 70">
<param name=TxFilter10       value="$1|waveimage 10 20 80">
<param name=TxFilter11       value="$1|waveimage 10 20 90">
<param name=TxFilter12       value="$1|waveimage 10 20 100">
</applet>
Animation Display for Example ThirtyThree
```

Smooth wavey text keeps going

Smooth wavey text keeps going

Smooth wavey text keeps going

Smooth wavey text keeps going

Smooth wavey text keeps going

See Also

Related applets:

AnimateTwoWay on page 191
WaveImage on page 128
SmoothText on page 68

URL for **ThirtyThree**:

`http://www.vivids.com/ij2/bonus/ThirtyThree.html`

ThirtyFour

Increasing Font Size

Description

Example **ThirtyFour** uses the **AnimateTwoWay** applet. The string *Don't Delay* is displayed in varying pointsizes.

The HTML Code for Example **ThirtyFour**

```
<applet
     archive  = ThirtyFour.zip
     codebase = ThirtyFour
     code     = AnimateTwoWay.class
     width    = 300
     height   = 80>
<param name=AppTile              value=true>
<param name=AppBgImage           value=ThirtyFour/pattern.gif>
<param name=AppFrameThickness    value=4>
<param name=AppFrameType         value=ShadowEtchedIn>

<param name=Text1                value="Don't Delay">
<param name=TxDelayBetweenImages value=50>
<param name=TxDelayBetweenRuns   value=50>
<param name=TxAnimationType      value=TwoWay>
<param name=TxYOffset1           value=50>
<param name=TxNumImages          value=10>
<param name=TxFilter1            value="text">
<param name=TxFont1              value=Helvetica>
<param name=TxStyle1             value=BoldItalic>
<param name=TxPointSize1         value=20>
<param name=TxPointSize2         value=22>
<param name=TxPointSize3         value=24>
<param name=TxPointSize4         value=26>
<param name=TxPointSize5         value=28>
<param name=TxPointSize6         value=30>
<param name=TxPointSize7         value=32>
<param name=TxPointSize8         value=34>
<param name=TxPointSize9         value=36>
<param name=TxPointSize10        value=38>
<param name=TxHorizCenter        value=true>
<param name=TxVertCenter         value=true>

</applet>
Animation Display for Example ThirtyFour
```

Don't Delay

Don't Delay

Don't Delay

Don't Delay

Don't Delay

Don't Delay

Don't Delay

Don't Delay

Don't Delay

See Also

Related applets: **AnimateTwoWay** on page 191

URL for **ThirtyFour**:   `http://www.vivids.com/ij2/bonus/ThirtyFour.html`

ThirtyFive

Fluctuating Depth

Description

Example **ThirtyFive** uses the **AnimateTwoWay** applet. The string *Don't Delay* is displayed using the **Depth** applet on page 72. The X and Y depth offsets are varied with each image in the animation sequence.

The HTML Code for Example ThirtyFive

```
<applet
    archive  = ThirtyFive.zip
    codebase = ThirtyFive
    code     = AnimateTwoWay.class
    width    = 300
    height   = 80>
<param name=AppBGColor              value=black>

<param name=Text1                   value="Don't Delay">
<param name=TxDelayBetweenImages    value=50>
<param name=TxDelayBetweenRuns      value=50>
<param name=TxAnimationType         value=TwoWay>
<param name=TxNumImages             value=10>
<param name=TxFilter1               value="text">
<param name=TxFilter2               value="depth -2 -2 yellow">
<param name=TxFilter3               value="depth -4 -4 yellow">
<param name=TxFilter4               value="depth -6 -6 yellow">
<param name=TxFilter5               value="depth -8 -8 yellow">
<param name=TxFilter6               value="depth -10 -10 yellow">
<param name=TxFilter7               value="depth -12 -12 yellow">
<param name=TxFilter8               value="depth -14 -14 yellow">
<param name=TxFilter9               value="depth -16 -16 yellow">
<param name=TxFilter10              value="depth -18 -18 yellow">
<param name=TxColor                 value=blue>
<param name=TxFont1                 value=Helvetica>
<param name=TxStyle1                value=BoldItalic>
<param name=TxPointSize1            value=38>
<param name=TxHorizCenter           value=true>
<param name=TxVertCenter            value=true>

</applet>
```

Animation Display for Example ThirtyFive

See Also

Related applets: **AnimateContinuous** on page 189
Depth on page 72

URL for **ThirtyFive**: `http://www.vivids.com/ij2/bonus/ThirtyFive.html`

ThirtySix

Fluctuating Depth Two Ways

Description

Example **ThirtySix** uses the **AnimateContinuous** applet. The string *Don't Delay* is displayed using the **Depth** applet on page 72. The X and Y depth offsets are varied with each image in the animation sequence.

The HTML Code for Example **ThirtySix**

```
<applet
    archive   = ThirtySix.zip
    codebase  = ThirtySix
    code      = AnimateContinuous.class
    width     = 300
    height    = 80>
<param name=AppBGColor          value=black>

<param name=Text1               value="Don't Delay">
<param name=TxDelayBetweenImages value=50>
<param name=TxDelayBetweenRuns  value=50>
<param name=TxNumImages         value=39>
<param name=TxFilter1           value="text">
<param name=TxFilter2           value="depth -2 -2 yellow">
<param name=TxFilter3           value="depth -4 -4 yellow">
<param name=TxFilter4           value="depth -6 -6 yellow">
<param name=TxFilter5           value="depth -8 -8 yellow">
<param name=TxFilter6           value="depth -10 -10 yellow">
<param name=TxFilter7           value="depth -12 -12 yellow">
<param name=TxFilter8           value="depth -14 -14 yellow">
<param name=TxFilter9           value="depth -16 -16 yellow">
<param name=TxFilter10          value="depth -18 -18 yellow">
<param name=TxFilter11          value="$9">
<param name=TxFilter12          value="$8">
<param name=TxFilter13          value="$7">
<param name=TxFilter14          value="$6">
<param name=TxFilter15          value="$5">
<param name=TxFilter16          value="$4">
<param name=TxFilter17          value="$3">
<param name=TxFilter18          value="$2">
<param name=TxFilter19          value="$1">
<param name=TxFilter20          value="text">
<param name=TxFilter21          value="depth 2 -2 blue">
<param name=TxFilter22          value="depth 4 -4 blue">
<param name=TxFilter23          value="depth 6 -6 blue">
```

```
<param name=TxFilter24              value="depth 8 -8 blue">
<param name=TxFilter25              value="depth 10 -10 blue">
<param name=TxFilter26              value="depth 12 -12 blue">
<param name=TxFilter27              value="depth 14 -14 blue">
<param name=TxFilter28              value="depth 16 -16 blue">
<param name=TxFilter29              value="depth 18 -18 blue">
<param name=TxFilter30              value="$29">
<param name=TxFilter31              value="$28">
<param name=TxFilter32              value="$27">
<param name=TxFilter33              value="$26">
<param name=TxFilter34              value="$25">
<param name=TxFilter35              value="$24">
<param name=TxFilter36              value="$23">
<param name=TxFilter37              value="$22">
<param name=TxFilter38              value="$21">
<param name=TxFilter39              value="$20">
<param name=TxColor1                value=blue>
<param name=TxColor20               value=yellow>
<param name=TxFont1                 value=Helvetica>
<param name=TxStyle1                value=BoldItalic>
<param name=TxPointSize1            value=38>
<param name=TxHorizCenter           value=true>
<param name=TxVertCenter            value=true>

</applet>
```

Animation Display for Example ThirtySix

Don't Delay
Don't Delay
Don't Delay
Don't Delay
Don't Delay
Don't Delay
Don't Delay
Don't Delay
Don't Delay

Don't Delay
Don't Delay
Don't Delay
Don't Delay
Don't Delay
Don't Delay
Don't Delay
Don't Delay
Don't Delay

See Also

Related applets:

AnimateContinuous on page 189
Depth on page 72

URL for **ThirtySix**:

http://www.vivids.com/ij2/bonus/ThirtySix.html

ThirtySeven

Fluctuating Depthshade Two Ways

Description

Example **ThirtySeven** uses the **AnimateContinuous** applet. The string *Check it out!* is displayed using the **DepthFade** applet on page 74. The X and Y depth offsets are varied with each image in the animation sequence. This example is identical to example **ThirtySix** except that it uses **DepthFade** rather than **Depth**.

The HTML Code for Example **ThirtySeven**

```
<applet
    archive  = ThirtySeven.zip
    codebase = ThirtySeven
    code     = AnimateContinuous.class
    width    = 300
    height   = 80>
<param name=AppBGColor          value=black>

<param name=Text1               value="Check it out!">
<param name=TxDelayBetweenImages value=50>
<param name=TxDelayBetweenRuns  value=50>
<param name=TxAnimationType     value=TwoWay>
<param name=TxNumImages         value=39>
<param name=TxFilter1           value="text">
<param name=TxFilter2           value="depthfade -2 -2 yellow">
<param name=TxFilter3           value="depthfade -4 -4 yellow">
<param name=TxFilter4           value="depthfade -6 -6 yellow">
<param name=TxFilter5           value="depthfade -8 -8 yellow">
<param name=TxFilter6           value="depthfade -10 -10 yellow">
<param name=TxFilter7           value="depthfade -12 -12 yellow">
<param name=TxFilter8           value="depthfade -14 -14 yellow">
<param name=TxFilter9           value="depthfade -16 -16 yellow">
<param name=TxFilter10          value="depthfade -18 -18 yellow">
<param name=TxFilter11          value="$9">
<param name=TxFilter12          value="$8">
<param name=TxFilter13          value="$7">
<param name=TxFilter14          value="$6">
<param name=TxFilter15          value="$5">
<param name=TxFilter16          value="$4">
<param name=TxFilter17          value="$3">
<param name=TxFilter18          value="$2">
<param name=TxFilter19          value="$1">
<param name=TxFilter20          value="text">
<param name=TxFilter21          value="depthfade 2 -2 blue">
```

```
<param name=TxFilter22        value="depthfade 4 -4 blue">
<param name=TxFilter23        value="depthfade 6 -6 blue">
<param name=TxFilter24        value="depthfade 8 -8 blue">
<param name=TxFilter25        value="depthfade 10 -10 blue">
<param name=TxFilter26        value="depthfade 12 -12 blue">
<param name=TxFilter27        value="depthfade 14 -14 blue">
<param name=TxFilter28        value="depthfade 16 -16 blue">
<param name=TxFilter29        value="depthfade 18 -18 blue">
<param name=TxFilter30        value="$29">
<param name=TxFilter31        value="$28">
<param name=TxFilter32        value="$27">
<param name=TxFilter33        value="$26">
<param name=TxFilter34        value="$25">
<param name=TxFilter35        value="$24">
<param name=TxFilter36        value="$23">
<param name=TxFilter37        value="$22">
<param name=TxFilter38        value="$21">
<param name=TxFilter39        value="$20">
<param name=TxColor1          value=blue>
<param name=TxColor20         value=yellow>
<param name=TxFont1           value=Helvetica>
<param name=TxStyle1          value=BoldItalic>
<param name=TxPointSize1      value=38>
<param name=TxHorizCenter     value=true>
<param name=TxVertCenter      value=true>

</applet>
```

Animation Display for Example ThirtySeven

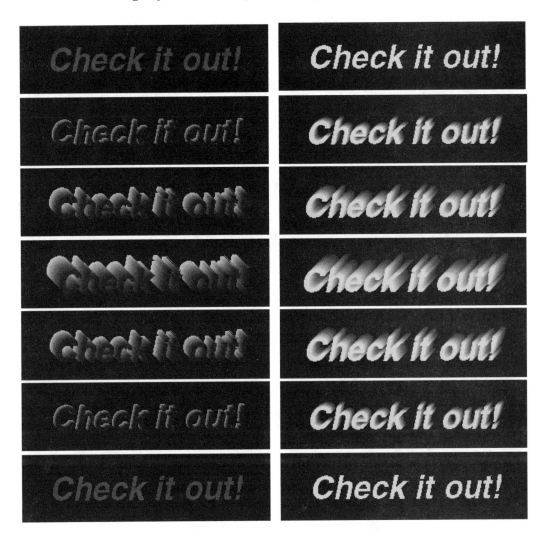

See Also

Related applets: **AnimateContinuous** on page 189
                                 DepthFade on page 74

URL for **ThirtySeven**:   `http://www.vivids.com/ij2/bonus/ThirtySeven.html`

ThirtyEight

Multiple Text Fluctuating Depthshade Two Ways

Description

Example **ThirtyEight** uses the **AnimateContinuous** applet. The strings *Welcome to* and *Acme Tools!* are displayed using the **DepthShade** applet on page 77. The X and Y depth offsets are varied with each image in the animation sequence. This example is similar to example **ThirtySeven** except that it uses **DepthShade** rather than **DepthFade** and two text strings are displayed rather than one.

The HTML Code for Example **ThirtyEight**

```
<applet
    archive  = ThirtyEight.zip
    codebase = ThirtyEight
    code     = AnimateContinuous.class
    width    = 250
    height   = 80>
<param name=AppBGColor           value=black>

<param name=Text1                value="Welcome to">
<param name=Text20               value="Acme Tools!">
<param name=TxDelayBetweenImages value=50>
<param name=TxDelayBetweenRuns   value=50>
<param name=TxAnimationType       value=TwoWay>
<param name=TxNumImages          value=39>
<param name=TxFilter1            value="text">
<param name=TxFilter2            value="depthshade -2 2 yellow">
<param name=TxFilter3            value="depthshade -6 6 yellow">
<param name=TxFilter4            value="depthshade -10 10 yellow">
<param name=TxFilter5            value="depthshade -14 14 yellow">
<param name=TxFilter6            value="depthshade -18 18 yellow">
<param name=TxFilter7            value="depthshade -22 22 yellow">
<param name=TxFilter8            value="depthshade -26 26 yellow">
<param name=TxFilter9            value="depthshade -30 30 yellow">
<param name=TxFilter10           value="depthshade -34 34 yellow">
<param name=TxFilter11           value="$9">
<param name=TxFilter12           value="$8">
<param name=TxFilter13           value="$7">
<param name=TxFilter14           value="$6">
<param name=TxFilter15           value="$5">
<param name=TxFilter16           value="$4">
<param name=TxFilter17           value="$3">
<param name=TxFilter18           value="$2">
<param name=TxFilter19           value="$1">
```

```
<param name=TxFilter20          value="text">
<param name=TxFilter21          value="depthshade 2 2 blue">
<param name=TxFilter22          value="depthshade 6 6 blue">
<param name=TxFilter23          value="depthshade 10 10 blue">
<param name=TxFilter24          value="depthshade 14 14 blue">
<param name=TxFilter25          value="depthshade 18 18 blue">
<param name=TxFilter26          value="depthshade 22 22 blue">
<param name=TxFilter27          value="depthshade 26 26 blue">
<param name=TxFilter28          value="depthshade 30 30 blue">
<param name=TxFilter29          value="depthshade 34 34 blue">
<param name=TxFilter30          value="$29">
<param name=TxFilter31          value="$28">
<param name=TxFilter32          value="$27">
<param name=TxFilter33          value="$26">
<param name=TxFilter34          value="$25">
<param name=TxFilter35          value="$24">
<param name=TxFilter36          value="$23">
<param name=TxFilter37          value="$22">
<param name=TxFilter38          value="$21">
<param name=TxFilter39          value="$20">
<param name=TxColor1            value=blue>
<param name=TxColor20           value=yellow>
<param name=TxFont1             value=TimesRoman>
<param name=TxStyle1            value=BoldItalic>
<param name=TxPointSize1        value=38>
<param name=TxHorizCenter       value=true>
<param name=TxVertCenter        value=true>

</applet>
```

Animation Display for Example ThirtyEight

![Animation frames showing "Welcome to" and "Acme Tools!" with depth-shaded 3D text effects]

See Also

Related applets: **AnimateContinuous** on page 189
DepthShade on page 77

URL for **ThirtyEight**:   http://www.vivids.com/ij2/bonus/ThirtyEight.html

ThirtyNine

Increasing Emboss Contrast

Description

Example **ThirtyNine** uses the **AnimateTwoWay** applet. The string *No Trespassing!* is displayed in embossed text using the **Emboss** applet on page 79. The size of the text and the intensity of the **Contrast** parameter vary with each image in the animation sequence.

The HTML Code for Example **ThirtyNine**

```
<applet
    archive  = ThirtyNine.zip
    codebase = ThirtyNine
    code     = AnimateTwoWay.class
    width    = 450
    height   = 75>

<param name=TxNumImages          value=10>
<param name=Text                 value="No Trespassing!">
<param name=TxPointSize1         value=24>
<param name=TxPointSize2         value=28>
<param name=TxPointSize3         value=32>
<param name=TxPointSize4         value=36>
<param name=TxPointSize5         value=40>
<param name=TxPointSize6         value=44>
<param name=TxPointSize7         value=48>
<param name=TxPointSize8         value=52>
<param name=TxPointSize9         value=56>
<param name=TxPointSize10        value=60>
<param name=TxStyle              value=bold>
<param name=TxFont               value=TimesRoman>
<param name=TxVertCenter         value=true>
<param name=TxHorizCenter        value=true>
<param name=TxDelayBetweenImages value=50>
<param name=TxDelayBetweenRuns   value=800>
<param name=TxFilter1            value="emboss 1 5">
<param name=TxFilter2            value="emboss 1 10">
<param name=TxFilter3            value="emboss 1 15">
<param name=TxFilter4            value="emboss 1 20">
<param name=TxFilter5            value="emboss 1 25">
<param name=TxFilter6            value="emboss 1 30">
<param name=TxFilter7            value="emboss 1 35">
<param name=TxFilter8            value="emboss 1 40">
<param name=TxFilter9            value="emboss 1 45">
<param name=TxFilter10           value="emboss 1 50">
```

```
</applet>
```

Animation Display for Example ThirtyNine

See Also

Related applets: **AnimateTwoWay** on page 191
                              Emboss on page 79

URL for **ThirtyNine**:   http://www.vivids.com/ij2/bonus/ThirtyNine.html

Forty

Spell It Out

Description

Example **Forty** uses the **AnimateContinuous** applet. The string *No Trespassing!* appears one character at a time. When the entire string is written, an audio message is played.

The HTML Code for Example Forty

```
<applet
    archive  = Forty.zip
    codebase = Forty
    code     = AnimateContinuous.class
    width    = 260
    height   = 50>

<param name=TxNumImages              value=16>
<param name=AppBGColor               value=white>

<param name=TxColor1                 value=white>
<param name=TxColor2                 value=black>
<param name=Text1                    value=".">
<param name=Text2                    value="N">
<param name=Text3                    value="No">
<param name=Text4                    value="No T">
<param name=Text5                    value="No Tr">
<param name=Text6                    value="No Tre">
<param name=Text7                    value="No Tres">
<param name=Text8                    value="No Tresp">
<param name=Text9                    value="No Trespa">
<param name=Text10                   value="No Trespas">
<param name=Text11                   value="No Trespas">
<param name=Text12                   value="No Trespass">
<param name=Text13                   value="No Trespassi">
<param name=Text14                   value="No Trespassin">
<param name=Text15                   value="No Trespassing">
<param name=Text16                   value="No Trespassing!">
<param name=TxPointSize              value=36>
<param name=TxStyle                  value=bold>
<param name=TxFont                   value=TimesRoman>
<param name=TxVertCenter             value=true>
<param name=TxHorizCenter            value=true>
<param name=TxDelayBetweenImages value=50>
<param name=TxDelayBetweenRuns   value=4000>
<param name=TxAudio16                value=Forty/notrespassing.au>
```

```
</applet>
```

Animation Display for Example Forty

N

No

No Tr

No Tres

No Trespa

No Trespas

No Trespassi

No Trespassing!

See Also

Related applets: **AnimateContinuous** on page 189

URL for **Forty**:   `http://www.vivids.com/ij2/bonus/Forty.html`

FortyOne

Type It Out

Description

Example **FortyOne** uses the **AnimateContinuous** applet. The string *Watch Your Step* is displayed one character at a time. As each character appears, the sound of a typewriter key is played.

The HTML Code for Example **FortyOne**

```
<applet
     archive  = FortyOne.zip
     codebase = FortyOne
     code     = AnimateContinuous.class
     width    = 290
     height   = 50>

<param name=TxNumImages        value=16>
<param name=AppBGColor         value=white>

<param name=TxColor1           value=white>
<param name=TxColor2           value=black>
<param name=Text1              value=".">
<param name=Text2              value="W">
<param name=Text3              value="Wa">
<param name=Text4              value="Wat">
<param name=Text5              value="Watc">
<param name=Text6              value="Watch">
<param name=Text7              value="Watch ">
<param name=Text8              value="Watch Y">
<param name=Text9              value="Watch Yo">
<param name=Text10             value="Watch You">
<param name=Text11             value="Watch Your">
<param name=Text12             value="Watch Your ">
<param name=Text13             value="Watch Your S">
<param name=Text14             value="Watch Your St">
<param name=Text15             value="Watch Your Ste">
<param name=Text16             value="Watch Your Step">
<param name=TxPointSize        value=36>
<param name=TxStyle            value=bold>
<param name=TxFont             value=TimesRoman>
<param name=TxXOffset1         value=10>
<param name=TxVertCenter       value=true>
<param name=TxDelayBetweenImages value=300>
<param name=TxDelayBetweenRuns   value=4000>
```

```
<param name=TxAudio2            value=FortyOne/keystroke.au>
<param name=TxAudio3            value=FortyOne/keystroke.au>
<param name=TxAudio4            value=FortyOne/keystroke.au>
<param name=TxAudio5            value=FortyOne/keystroke.au>
<param name=TxAudio6            value=FortyOne/keystroke.au>
<param name=TxAudio7            value=FortyOne/spacebar.au>
<param name=TxAudio8            value=FortyOne/keystroke.au>
<param name=TxAudio9            value=FortyOne/keystroke.au>
<param name=TxAudio10           value=FortyOne/keystroke.au>
<param name=TxAudio11           value=FortyOne/keystroke.au>
<param name=TxAudio12           value=FortyOne/spacebar.au>
<param name=TxAudio13           value=FortyOne/keystroke.au>
<param name=TxAudio14           value=FortyOne/keystroke.au>
<param name=TxAudio15           value=FortyOne/keystroke.au>
<param name=TxAudio16           value=FortyOne/keystroke.au>
</applet>
```

Animation Display for Example **FortyOne**

W

Wat

Watch

Watch Y

Watch Your

Watch Your St

Watch Your Step

See Also

Related applets: **AnimateContinuous** on page 189

URL for **FortyOne**: `http://www.vivids.com/ij2/bonus/FortyOne.html`

FortyTwo

Engrave With Hammer

Description

Example **FortyTwo** uses the **AnimateContinuous** applet. The string *Private!* is displayed one character at a time. Each character is displayed using the **Emboss** applet on page 79. As each character appears the sound of a hammer is played.

The HTML Code for Example **FortyTwo**

```
<applet
    archive  = FortyTwo.zip
    codebase = FortyTwo
    code     = AnimateContinuous.class
    width    = 140
    height   = 60>

<param name=AppBGColor              value=#cccccc>
<param name=TxColor                 value=#cccccc>
<param name=TxNumImages             value=9>
<param name=Text1                   value=".">
<param name=Text2                   value="P">
<param name=Text3                   value="Pr">
<param name=Text4                   value="Pri">
<param name=Text5                   value="Priv">
<param name=Text6                   value="Priva">
<param name=Text7                   value="Privat">
<param name=Text8                   value="Private">
<param name=Text9                   value="Private!">
<param name=TxPointSize             value=36>
<param name=TxStyle                 value=bold>
<param name=TxFont                  value=TimesRoman>
<param name=TxXOffset1              value=10>
<param name=TxYOffset1              value=10>
<param name=TxDelayBetweenImages    value=500>
<param name=TxDelayBetweenRuns      value=4000>
<param name=TxFilter1               value="text">
<param name=TxFilter2               value="engrave 1 50">
<param name=TxFilter3               value="engrave 1 50">
<param name=TxFilter4               value="engrave 1 50">
<param name=TxFilter5               value="engrave 1 50">
<param name=TxFilter6               value="engrave 1 50">
<param name=TxFilter7               value="engrave 1 50">
<param name=TxFilter8               value="engrave 1 50">
<param name=TxFilter9               value="engrave 1 50">
```

```
<param name=TxAudio2              value=FortyTwo/hammer.au>
<param name=TxAudio3              value=FortyTwo/hammer.au>
<param name=TxAudio4              value=FortyTwo/hammer.au>
<param name=TxAudio5              value=FortyTwo/hammer.au>
<param name=TxAudio6              value=FortyTwo/hammer.au>
<param name=TxAudio7              value=FortyTwo/hammer.au>
<param name=TxAudio8              value=FortyTwo/hammer.au>
<param name=TxAudio9              value=FortyTwo/hammer.au>
</applet>
```

Animation Display for Example **FortyTwo**

See Also

Related applets:

AnimateContinuous on page 189
Engrave on page 82

URL for **FortyTwo**:

http://www.vivids.com/ij2/bonus/FortyTwo.html

FortyThree

Type It Out With Corrected Mistakes

Description

Example **FortyThree** uses the **AnimateContinuous** applet. The string *Common typos.* is displayed one character at a time. As each character appears the sound of a typewriter key is played. A typing error is made and corrected during which time the backspace sound is played.

The HTML Code for Example FortyThree

```
<applet
    archive  = FortyThree.zip
    codebase = FortyThree
    code     = AnimateContinuous.class
    width    = 300
    height   = 60>

<param name=TxNumImages         value=22>
<param name=AppBGColor          value=white>

<param name=TxColor1            value=white>
<param name=TxColor2            value=black>
<param name=Text1               value="."> 
<param name=Text2               value="C">
<param name=Text3               value="Co">
<param name=Text4               value="Com">
<param name=Text5               value="Comm">
<param name=Text6               value="Commo">
<param name=Text7               value="Common">
<param name=Text8               value="Common ">
<param name=Text9               value="Common t">
<param name=Text10              value="Common ty">
<param name=Text11              value="Common tyo">
<param name=Text12              value="Common tyop">
<param name=Text13              value="Common tyo">
<param name=Text16              value="Common ty">
<param name=Text19              value="Common typ">
<param name=Text20              value="Common typo">
<param name=Text21              value="Common typos">
<param name=Text22              value="Common typos.">
<param name=TxPointSize          value=36>
<param name=TxStyle              value=bold>
<param name=TxFont               value=DialogInput>
<param name=TxXOffset1           value=10>
```

```
<param name=TxVertCenter           value=true>
<param name=TxDelayBetweenImages value=320>
<param name=TxDelayBetweenRuns   value=4000>
<param name=TxAudio2               value=FortyThree/keystroke.au>
<param name=TxAudio3               value=FortyThree/keystroke.au>
<param name=TxAudio4               value=FortyThree/keystroke.au>
<param name=TxAudio5               value=FortyThree/keystroke.au>
<param name=TxAudio6               value=FortyThree/keystroke.au>
<param name=TxAudio7               value=FortyThree/keystroke.au>
<param name=TxAudio8               value=FortyThree/spacebar.au>
<param name=TxAudio9               value=FortyThree/keystroke.au>
<param name=TxAudio10              value=FortyThree/keystroke.au>
<param name=TxAudio11              value=FortyThree/keystroke.au>
<param name=TxAudio12              value=FortyThree/keystroke.au>
<param name=TxAudio13              value=FortyThree/backspace.au>
<param name=TxAudio16              value=FortyThree/backspace.au>
<param name=TxAudio19              value=FortyThree/keystroke.au>
<param name=TxAudio20              value=FortyThree/keystroke.au>
<param name=TxAudio21              value=FortyThree/keystroke.au>
<param name=TxAudio22              value=FortyThree/keystroke.au>
</applet>
```

Animation Display for Example **FortyThree**

C	Common tyo
Com	Common ty
Commo	Common typ
Common t	Common typo
Common tyo	Common typos
Common tyop	Common typos.

See Also

Related applets: **AnimateContinuous** on page 189

URL for **FortyThree**:   http://www.vivids.com/ij2/bonus/FortyThree.html

FortyFour

Negative Eyeball

Description

Example **FortyFour** uses the **AnimateOnPressRelease** applet. The eyeball image is displayed with a string indicating a URL. When the pointer is over the image and the mouse button is pressed, the eyeball image displays with negative colors. When the pointer is over the string and the mouse button is pressed the string changes. If the button is pressed and released while over the image or text, the specified URL is loaded.

The HTML Code for Example FortyFour

```
<applet
    archive  = FortyFour.zip
    codebase = FortyFour
    code     = AnimateOnPressRelease.class
    width    = 300
    height   = 100>

<param name=AppBGColor      value=black>

<param name=ImgNumImages    value=2>
<param name=Image1          value=FortyFour/eyball.jpg>
<param name=ImgHorizCenter  value=true>
<param name=ImgVertCenter   value=true>
<param name=ImgFilter1      value="noop">
<param name=ImgFilter2      value="negative">
<param name=ImgURL          value="http://www.eyeball.com">

<param name=TxNumImages     value=2>
<param name=Text1           value="http://www.eyeball.com">
<param name=Text2           value="loading http://www.eyeball.com">
<param name=HorizCenter     value=true>
<param name=VertCenter      value=true>
<param name=TxHorizCenter   value=true>
<param name=TxVertCenter    value=true>
<param name=TxColor         value=white>
<param name=TxURL           value="http://www.eyeball.com">
</applet>
```

Animation Display for Example **FortyFour**

Initial Display

Button Press

> http://...

See Also

Related applets: **AnimateOnPressRelease** on page 206
Negative on page 137

URL for **FortyFour**:   `http://www.vivids.com/ij2/bonus/FortyFour.html`

FortyFive

Reverse Text

Description

Example **FortyFive** uses the **AnimateMultiple** applet. Two strings are displayed: *To Read...* and *Hold Mirror to Screen*. Each text string alternates between the regular text and mirrored, rotated text. This example uses the **Rotate** applet on page 112 and the **Mirror** applet on page 113 to create these effects.

The HTML Code for Example **FortyFive**

```
<applet
    archive  = FortyFive.zip
    codebase = FortyFive
    code     = AnimateMultiple.class
    width    = 400
    height   = 100>

<param name=AppBGColor            value=white>
<param name=TxCount               value=2>

<param name=Text1                 value="To Read...">
<param name=Tx1DelayBetweenImages value=1000>
<param name=Tx1DelayBetweenRuns   value=1000>
<param name=Tx1NumImages          value=2>
<param name=Tx1Filter1            value="text">
<param name=Tx1Filter2            value="text|rotate 180|mirror">
<param name=Tx1HorizCenter        value=true>
<param name=Tx1PointSize          value=36>
<param name=Tx1Font               value=TimesRoman>

<param name=Text2                 value="Hold Mirror to Screen">
<param name=Tx2DelayBetweenImages value=1000>
<param name=Tx2DelayBetweenRuns   value=1000>
<param name=Tx2NumImages          value=2>
<param name=Tx2Filter1            value="text">
<param name=Tx2Filter2            value="text|mirror">
<param name=Tx2YOffset1           value=60>
<param name=Tx2HorizCenter        value=true>
<param name=Tx2PointSize          value=36>
<param name=Tx2Font               value=TimesRoman>
</applet>
```

Animation Display for Example FortyFive

To Read...

Hold Mirror to Screen

...bɒɘЯ oT

nɘɘɿɔƧ oɟ ɿoɿɿiM bloH

See Also

Related applets: **AnimateMultiple** on page 209
                                             Mirror on page 113
                                             Rotate on page 112

URL for **FortyFive**:   `http://www.vivids.com/ij2/bonus/FortyFive.html`

FortySix

Split Personality

Description

Example **FortySix** uses the **AnimateMultiple** applet. The string *Split Personality* is displayed with a tiled background image. Alternate characters move vertically in opposite directions. This is accomplished by creating two identical strings with characters at even positions displayed transparently for one string, and characters at odd positions displayed transparently for the other string. Each string is displayed at exactly the same coordinates, then each character string is moved in opposite directions.

The HTML Code for Example FortySix

```
<applet
    archive  = FortySix.zip
    codebase = FortySix
    code     = AnimateMultiple.class
    width    = 380
    height   = 200>
<param name=AppTile                 value=true>
<param name=AppBgImage              value=FortySix/pattern2.gif>
<param name=AppFrameThickness       value=4>
<param name=AppFrameType            value=ShadowEtchedIn>

<param name=TxCount                 value=2>
<param name=TxSynchronous           value=true>

<param name=Text1                   value="Split Personality">
<param name=Tx1DelayBetweenImages value=100>
<param name=Tx1DelayBetweenRuns     value=1000>
<param name=Tx1AnimationType        value=TwoWay>
<param name=Tx1NumImages            value=6>
<param name=Tx1Filter1        value="multicolor black white|transcolor
black">
<param name=Tx1Filter2              value="$1">
<param name=Tx1Filter3              value="$1">
<param name=Tx1Filter4              value="$1">
<param name=Tx1Filter5              value="$1">
<param name=Tx1Filter6              value="$1">
<param name=Tx1HorizCenter          value=true>
<param name=Tx1YOffset1             value=80>
<param name=Tx1YOffset2             value=70>
<param name=Tx1YOffset3             value=60>
<param name=Tx1YOffset4             value=50>
```

```
<param name=Tx1YOffset5            value=40>
<param name=Tx1YOffset6            value=30>
<param name=Tx1Font1               value=TimesRoman>
<param name=Tx1Style1              value=Bold>
<param name=Tx1PointSize1          value=38>

<param name=Text2                  value="Split Personality">
<param name=Tx2DelayBetweenImages  value=100>
<param name=Tx2DelayBetweenRuns    value=1000>
<param name=Tx2AnimationType       value=TwoWay>
<param name=Tx2NumImages           value=6>
<param name=Tx2Filter1        value="multicolor white black|transcolor
black">
<param name=Tx2Filter2             value="$1">
<param name=Tx2Filter3             value="$1">
<param name=Tx2Filter4             value="$1">
<param name=Tx2Filter5             value="$1">
<param name=Tx2Filter6             value="$1">
<param name=Tx2HorizCenter         value=true>
<param name=Tx2YOffset1            value=80>
<param name=Tx2YOffset2            value=90>
<param name=Tx2YOffset3            value=100>
<param name=Tx2YOffset4            value=110>
<param name=Tx2YOffset5            value=120>
<param name=Tx2YOffset6            value=130>
<param name=Tx2Font1               value=TimesRoman>
<param name=Tx2Style1              value=Bold>
<param name=Tx2PointSize1          value=38>

</applet>
```

Animation Display for Example FortySix

Split Personality

> p i e s n l t
> S l t P r o a i y

S^pl_it P^er_soⁿa_il_yt

> p i e s n l t
> S l t P r o a i y

> p i e s n l t
> S l t P r o a i y

S^pl_it P^er_soⁿa_il_yt

> p i e s n l t
> S l t P r o a i y

Split Personality

See Also

Related applets: **AnimateMultiple** on page 209

URL for **FortySix**:   `http://www.vivids.com/ij2/bonus/FortySix.html`

FortySeven

Rotating Text

Description

Example **FortySeven** uses the **AnimateMultiple** applet. The string *Click to rotate* is displayed. Alternate characters rotate in opposite directions when the user clicks the mouse button with the pointer over the string. This is accomplished by creating two identical strings with characters at even positions displayed transparently for one string, and characters at odd positions displayed transparently for the other string. Each string is displayed at exactly the same coordinates, then each character string is rotated in opposite directions.

The HTML Code for Example FortySeven

```
<applet
    archive  = FortySeven.zip
    codebase = FortySeven
    code     = AnimateMultiple.class
    width    = 160
    height   = 160>
<param name=AppFrameThickness      value=4>
<param name=AppFrameType           value=ShadowEtchedIn>

<param name=TxCount                value=2>
<param name=TxSynchronous          value=true>

<param name=Text1                  value="Click to rotate">
<param name=Tx1DelayBetweenImages  value=80>
<param name=Tx1AnimationType       value=OnButtonTwoWay>
<param name=Tx1NumImages           value=37>
<param name=Tx1Filter1             value="multicolor black white|transcolor
white">
<param name=Tx1Filter2             value="$1|rotate 10">
<param name=Tx1Filter3             value="$1|rotate 20">
<param name=Tx1Filter4             value="$1|rotate 30">
<param name=Tx1Filter5             value="$1|rotate 40">
<param name=Tx1Filter6             value="$1|rotate 50">
<param name=Tx1Filter7             value="$1|rotate 60">
<param name=Tx1Filter8             value="$1|rotate 70">
<param name=Tx1Filter9             value="$1|rotate 80">
<param name=Tx1Filter10            value="$1|rotate 90">
<param name=Tx1Filter11            value="$1|rotate 100">
<param name=Tx1Filter12            value="$1|rotate 110">
<param name=Tx1Filter13            value="$1|rotate 120">
<param name=Tx1Filter14            value="$1|rotate 130">
```

```
<param name=Tx1Filter15          value="$1|rotate 140">
<param name=Tx1Filter16          value="$1|rotate 150">
<param name=Tx1Filter17          value="$1|rotate 160">
<param name=Tx1Filter18          value="$1|rotate 170">
<param name=Tx1Filter19          value="$1|rotate 180">
<param name=Tx1Filter20          value="$1|rotate 190">
<param name=Tx1Filter21          value="$1|rotate 200">
<param name=Tx1Filter22          value="$1|rotate 210">
<param name=Tx1Filter23          value="$1|rotate 220">
<param name=Tx1Filter24          value="$1|rotate 230">
<param name=Tx1Filter25          value="$1|rotate 240">
<param name=Tx1Filter26          value="$1|rotate 250">
<param name=Tx1Filter27          value="$1|rotate 260">
<param name=Tx1Filter28          value="$1|rotate 270">
<param name=Tx1Filter29          value="$1|rotate 280">
<param name=Tx1Filter30          value="$1|rotate 290">
<param name=Tx1Filter31          value="$1|rotate 300">
<param name=Tx1Filter32          value="$1|rotate 310">
<param name=Tx1Filter33          value="$1|rotate 320">
<param name=Tx1Filter34          value="$1|rotate 330">
<param name=Tx1Filter35          value="$1|rotate 340">
<param name=Tx1Filter36          value="$1|rotate 350">
<param name=Tx1Filter37          value="$1">
<param name=Tx1XCenter           value=80>
<param name=Tx1YCenter           value=80>
<param name=Tx1Font1             value=TimesRoman>
<param name=Tx1Style1            value=Bold>
<param name=Tx1PointSize1        value=20>

<param name=Text2                value="Click to rotate">
<param name=Tx2DelayBetweenImages value=80>
<param name=Tx2AnimationType     value=OnButtonTwoWay>
<param name=Tx2NumImages         value=37>
<param name=Tx2Filter1           value="multicolor white black|transcolor
white">
<param name=Tx2Filter2           value="$1|rotate 350">
<param name=Tx2Filter3           value="$1|rotate 340">
<param name=Tx2Filter4           value="$1|rotate 330">
<param name=Tx2Filter5           value="$1|rotate 320">
<param name=Tx2Filter6           value="$1|rotate 310">
<param name=Tx2Filter7           value="$1|rotate 300">
<param name=Tx2Filter8           value="$1|rotate 290">
<param name=Tx2Filter9           value="$1|rotate 280">
<param name=Tx2Filter10          value="$1|rotate 270">
<param name=Tx2Filter11          value="$1|rotate 260">
<param name=Tx2Filter12          value="$1|rotate 250">
<param name=Tx2Filter13          value="$1|rotate 240">
<param name=Tx2Filter14          value="$1|rotate 230">
```

```
<param name=Tx2Filter15          value="$1|rotate 220">
<param name=Tx2Filter16          value="$1|rotate 210">
<param name=Tx2Filter17          value="$1|rotate 200">
<param name=Tx2Filter18          value="$1|rotate 190">
<param name=Tx2Filter19          value="$1|rotate 180">
<param name=Tx2Filter20          value="$1|rotate 170">
<param name=Tx2Filter21          value="$1|rotate 160">
<param name=Tx2Filter22          value="$1|rotate 150">
<param name=Tx2Filter23          value="$1|rotate 140">
<param name=Tx2Filter24          value="$1|rotate 130">
<param name=Tx2Filter25          value="$1|rotate 120">
<param name=Tx2Filter26          value="$1|rotate 110">
<param name=Tx2Filter27          value="$1|rotate 100">
<param name=Tx2Filter28          value="$1|rotate 90">
<param name=Tx2Filter29          value="$1|rotate 80">
<param name=Tx2Filter30          value="$1|rotate 70">
<param name=Tx2Filter31          value="$1|rotate 60">
<param name=Tx2Filter32          value="$1|rotate 50">
<param name=Tx2Filter33          value="$1|rotate 40">
<param name=Tx2Filter34          value="$1|rotate 30">
<param name=Tx2Filter35          value="$1|rotate 20">
<param name=Tx2Filter36          value="$1|rotate 10">
<param name=Tx2Filter37          value="$1">
<param name=Tx2XCenter           value=80>
<param name=Tx2YCenter           value=80>
<param name=Tx2Font1             value=TimesRoman>
<param name=Tx2Style1            value=Bold>
<param name=Tx2PointSize1        value=20>

</applet>
```

Animation Display for Example **FortySeven**

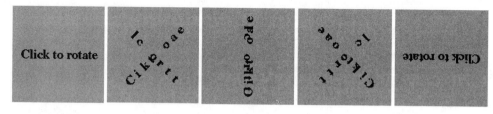

See Also

Related applets: **AnimateContinuous** on page 189
                          Rotate on page 112

URL for **FortySeven**:   `http://www.vivids.com/ij2/bonus/FortySeven.html`

FortyEight

Dos-A-Dos

Description

Example **FortyEight** uses the **AnimateMultiple** applet. The string *dos-a-dos* is displayed. Alternate characters move together vertically and horizontally and eventually back to their original positions. This is accomplished by creating two identical strings with characters at even positions displayed transparently for one string, and characters at odd positions displayed transparently for the other string. Each string is displayed at exactly the same coordinates, then each character string is moved is opposite corresponding directions.

The HTML Code for Example FortyEight

```
<applet
    archive   = FortyEight.zip
    codebase  = FortyEight
    code      = AnimateMultiple.class
    width     = 158
    height    = 70>
<param name=AppTile                   value=true>
<param name=AppBgImage                value=FortyEight/pattern2.gif>
<param name=AppBorderWidth            value=4>
<param name=AppBorderColor            value=white>

<param name=TxCount                   value=2>
<param name=TxSynchronous             value=true>

<param name=Text1                     value="dos-a-dos">
<param name=Tx1DelayBetweenImages value=100>
<param name=Tx1DelayBetweenRuns       value=1000>
<param name=Tx1AnimationType          value=TwoWay>
<param name=Tx1NumImages              value=13>
<param name=Tx1Filter1            value="multicolor black white|transcolor
black">
<param name=Tx1Filter2                value="$1">
<param name=Tx1Filter3                value="$1">
<param name=Tx1Filter4                value="$1">
<param name=Tx1Filter5                value="$1">
<param name=Tx1Filter6                value="$1">
<param name=Tx1Filter7                value="$1">
<param name=Tx1Filter8                value="$1">
<param name=Tx1Filter9                value="$1">
<param name=Tx1Filter10               value="$1">
<param name=Tx1Filter11               value="$1">
```

```
<param name=Tx1Filter12            value="$1">
<param name=Tx1Filter13            value="$1">

<param name=Tx1YOffset1            value=20>
<param name=Tx1XOffset1            value=20>
<param name=Tx1YOffset2            value=10>
<param name=Tx1YOffset3            value=0>
<param name=Tx1XOffset4            value=10>
<param name=Tx1XOffset5            value=0>

<param name=Tx1YOffset6            value=10>
<param name=Tx1YOffset7            value=20>
<param name=Tx1YOffset8            value=30>
<param name=Tx1YOffset9            value=40>

<param name=Tx1XOffset10           value=10>
<param name=Tx1XOffset11           value=20>

<param name=Tx1YOffset12           value=30>
<param name=Tx1YOffset13           value=20>

<param name=Tx1Font1               value=TimesRoman>
<param name=Tx1Style1              value=Bold>
<param name=Tx1PointSize1          value=24>

<param name=Text2                  value="dos-a-dos">
<param name=Tx2DelayBetweenImages value=100>
<param name=Tx2DelayBetweenRuns   value=1000>
<param name=Tx2AnimationType       value=TwoWay>
<param name=Tx2NumImages           value=13>
<param name=Tx2Filter1         value="multicolor white black|transcolor
black">
<param name=Tx2Filter2             value="$1">
<param name=Tx2Filter3             value="$1">
<param name=Tx2Filter4             value="$1">
<param name=Tx2Filter5             value="$1">
<param name=Tx2Filter6             value="$1">
<param name=Tx2Filter7             value="$1">
<param name=Tx2Filter8             value="$1">
<param name=Tx2Filter9             value="$1">
<param name=Tx2Filter10            value="$1">
<param name=Tx2Filter11            value="$1">
<param name=Tx2Filter12            value="$1">
<param name=Tx2Filter13            value="$1">

<param name=Tx2YOffset1            value=20>
<param name=Tx2XOffset1            value=20>
<param name=Tx2YOffset2            value=30>
```

```
<param name=Tx2YOffset3          value=40>

<param name=Tx2XOffset4          value=30>
<param name=Tx2XOffset5          value=40>

<param name=Tx2YOffset6          value=30>
<param name=Tx2YOffset7          value=20>
<param name=Tx2YOffset8          value=10>
<param name=Tx2YOffset9          value=0>

<param name=Tx2XOffset10         value=30>
<param name=Tx2XOffset11         value=20>

<param name=Tx2YOffset12         value=10>
<param name=Tx2YOffset13         value=20>

<param name=Tx2Font1             value=TimesRoman>
<param name=Tx2Style1            value=Bold>
<param name=Tx2PointSize1        value=24>

</applet>
```
Animation Display for Example **FortyEight**

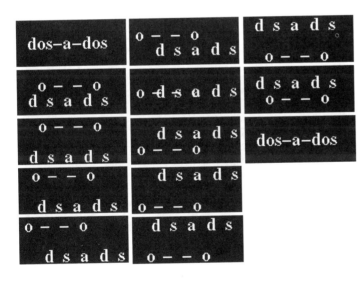

See Also

Related applets: **AnimateMultiple** on page 209

URL for **FortyEight**:   `http://www.vivids.com/ij2/bonus/FortyEight.html`

FortyNine

Moving Background Viewed Through Transparent Text

Description

Example **FortyNine** uses the **AnimateMultiple** applet. Two images are displayed. One is a scene of a forest, the other image contains the text string ALASKA in transparent characters against a white background. The image of the word ALASKA is displayed directly on top of the forest image. The forest image then moves creating an interesting effect.

The HTML Code for Example FortyNine

```
<applet
    archive   = FortyNine.zip
    codebase  = FortyNine
    code      = AnimateMultiple.class
    width     = 312
    height    = 179>
<param name=AppBGColor            value=white>
<param name=AppFrameThickness     value=4>
<param name=AppFrameType          value=ShadowEtchedIn>
<param name=WaitForEverything     value=true>

<param name=ImgCount              value=2>

<param name=Img1Image1            value=FortyNine/forest.gif>
<param name=Img1DelayBetweenImages value=100>
<param name=Img1DelayBetweenRuns  value=100>
<param name=Img1AnimationType     value=TwoWay>
<param name=Img1NumImages         value=27>
<param name=Img1Filter1           value="noop">
<param name=Img1YOffset1          value=0>
<param name=Img1YOffset2          value=5>
<param name=Img1YOffset3          value=10>
<param name=Img1YOffset4          value=15>
<param name=Img1YOffset5          value=20>
<param name=Img1YOffset6          value=25>
<param name=Img1YOffset7          value=30>
<param name=Img1YOffset8          value=35>
<param name=Img1YOffset9          value=40>
<param name=Img1YOffset10         value=45>
<param name=Img1XOffset1          value=0>
<param name=Img1XOffset11         value=5>
<param name=Img1XOffset12         value=10>
<param name=Img1XOffset13         value=15>
<param name=Img1XOffset14         value=20>
```

```
<param name=Img1YOffset15          value=40>
<param name=Img1YOffset16          value=35>
<param name=Img1YOffset17          value=30>
<param name=Img1YOffset18          value=25>
<param name=Img1YOffset19          value=20>
<param name=Img1YOffset20          value=15>
<param name=Img1YOffset21          value=10>
<param name=Img1YOffset22          value=5>
<param name=Img1YOffset23          value=0>
<param name=Img1XOffset24          value=15>
<param name=Img1XOffset25          value=10>
<param name=Img1XOffset26          value=5>
<param name=Img1XOffset27          value=0>

<param name=Img2Image1             value=FortyNine/alaska_trans.gif>
<param name=Img2NumImages          value=1>

</applet>
Animation Display for Example FortyNine
```

See Also

Related applets: **AnimateMultiple** on page 209

URL for **FortyNine**:   `http://www.vivids.com/ij2/bonus/FortyNine.html`

Fifty

Flashing Text And Image

Description

Example **Fifty** uses the **AnimateMultiple** applet. An image of a forest is displayed as a background with the word ALASKA displayed on top of the forest image. Two images, each containing ALASKA are used: one has transparent text against a white background, the other image has a transparent background with white characters.

The HTML Code for Example **Fifty**

```
<applet
    archive  = Fifty.zip
    codebase = Fifty
    code     = AnimateMultiple.class
    width    = 314
    height   = 181>
<param name=AppFrameThickness        value=4>
<param name=AppFrameType             value=ShadowEtchedOut>

<param name=ImgCount                 value=2>
<param name=WaitForEverything        value=true>

<param name=Img1Image1               value=Fifty/forest.gif>
<param name=Img1AnimationType        value=Continuous>
<param name=Img1NumImages            value=2>

<param name=Img2Image1               value=Fifty/alaska_trans.gif>
<param name=Img2Image2               value=Fifty/alaska_trans2.gif>
<param name=Img2NumImages            value=2>
<param name=Img2DelayBetweenImages value=600>
<param name=Img2DelayBetweenRuns   value=600>

</applet>
```

Animation Display for Example Fifty

See Also

Related applets: **AnimateMultiple** on page 209

URL for **Fifty**: `http://www.vivids.com/ij2/bonus/Fifty.html`

FiftyOne

Squeeze Away

Description

Example **FiftyOne** uses the **AnimateContinuous** applet. The string *Squeeze Away* is displayed. The **SqueezeLeft** applet on page 122 is used to squeeze the characters to the left.

The HTML Code for Example FiftyOne

```
<applet
    archive   = FiftyOne.zip
    codebase  = FiftyOne
    code      = AnimateContinuous.class
    width     = 225
    height    = 50>

<param name=Text1                   value="Squeeze Away">
<param name=Text12                  value="queeze Away">
<param name=Text13                  value="ueeze Away">
<param name=Text14                  value="eeze Away">
<param name=Text15                  value="eze Away">
<param name=Text16                  value="ze Away">
<param name=Text17                  value="e Away">
<param name=Text18                  value=" Away">
<param name=Text19                  value="Away">
<param name=Text20                  value="way">
<param name=Text21                  value="ay">
<param name=Text22                  value="y">
<param name=TxPointSize             value=36>
<param name=TxFont                  value=TimesRoman>
<param name=TxStyle                 value=Bold>
<param name=TxDelayBetweenImages value=100>
<param name=TxDelayBetweenRuns    value=1000>
<param name=TxNumImages             value=23>
<param name=TxFilter1               value="text">
<param name=TxFilter2               value="text|squeezeleft 5 down">
<param name=TxFilter3               value="text|squeezeleft 10 down">
<param name=TxFilter4               value="text|squeezeleft 15 down">
<param name=TxFilter5               value="text|squeezeleft 20 down">
<param name=TxFilter6               value="text|squeezeleft 25 down">
<param name=TxFilter7               value="text|squeezeleft 30 down">
<param name=TxFilter8               value="text|squeezeleft 45 down">
<param name=TxFilter9               value="text|squeezeleft 50 down">
<param name=TxFilter10              value="text|squeezeleft 60 down">
<param name=TxFilter11              value="text|squeezeleft 70 down">
```

```
<param name=TxFilter12          value="text|squeezeleft 80 down">
<param name=TxFilter13          value="text|squeezeleft 90 down">
<param name=TxFilter14          value="text|squeezeleft 90 down">
<param name=TxFilter15          value="text|squeezeleft 90 down">
<param name=TxFilter16          value="text|squeezeleft 90 down">
<param name=TxFilter17          value="text|squeezeleft 90 down">
<param name=TxFilter18          value="text|squeezeleft 90 down">
<param name=TxFilter19          value="text|squeezeleft 90 down">
<param name=TxFilter20          value="text|squeezeleft 90 down">
<param name=TxFilter21          value="text|squeezeleft 90 down">
<param name=TxFilter22          value="text|squeezeleft 90 down">

<param name=TxXoffset23         value=-100>

</applet>
```

Animation Display for Example **FiftyOne**

See Also

Related applets: **AnimateContinuous** on page 189
                     SqueezeLeft on page 122

URL for **FiftyOne**:   `http://www.vivids.com/ij2/bonus/FiftyOne.html`

FiftyTwo

Changing Wavelength

Description

Example **FiftyTwo** uses the **AnimateTwoWay** applet. The image is displayed using the **WaveImage** applet on page 128. The **WaveLength** parameter is altered with each image in the animation sequence.

The HTML Code for Example FiftyTwo

```
<applet
    archive  = FiftyTwo.zip
    codebase = FiftyTwo
    code     = AnimateTwoWay.class
    width    = 144
    height   = 250>

<param name=ImgNumImages           value=14>
<param name=ImgDelayBetweenImages value=130>
<param name=ImgDelayBetweenRuns   value=130>
<param name=ImgHorizCenter         value=true>
<param name=Image1                 value=FiftyTwo/brian.jpg>
<param name=ImgFilter1             value="waveimage 16 100">
<param name=ImgFilter2             value="waveimage 16  90">
<param name=ImgFilter3             value="waveimage 16  80">
<param name=ImgFilter4             value="waveimage 16  70">
<param name=ImgFilter5             value="waveimage 16  60">
<param name=ImgFilter6             value="waveimage 16  50">
<param name=ImgFilter7             value="waveimage 16  40">
<param name=ImgFilter8             value="waveimage 16  30">
<param name=ImgFilter9             value="waveimage 16  20">
<param name=ImgFilter10            value="waveimage 16  18">
<param name=ImgFilter11            value="waveimage 16  16">
<param name=ImgFilter12            value="waveimage 16  14">
<param name=ImgFilter13            value="waveimage 16  12">
<param name=ImgFilter14            value="waveimage 16  10">
</applet>
```

Animation Display for Example **FiftyTwo**

See Also

Related applets: **AnimateTwoWay** on page 191
                         WaveImage on page 128

URL for **FiftyTwo**:   http://www.vivids.com/ij2/bonus/FiftyTwo.html

FiftyThree

Squeeze Down

Description

Example **FiftyThree** uses the **AnimateTwoWay** applet. The image is squeezed down and to the right from 0 to 100 percent. The effect is created using the **SqueezeRight** applet on page 120.

The HTML Code for Example FiftyThree

```
<applet
    archive  = FiftyThree.zip
    codebase = FiftyThree
    code     = AnimateTwoWay.class
    width    = 144
    height   = 196>

<param name=ImgNumImages           value=11>
<param name=ImgDelayBetweenImages  value=130>
<param name=ImgDelayBetweenRuns    value=130>
<param name=ImgHorizCenter         value=true>
<param name=Image1                 value=FiftyThree/doug.jpg>
<param name=ImgFilter2             value="squeezeright 10 DOWN ">
<param name=ImgFilter3             value="squeezeright 20 DOWN">
<param name=ImgFilter4             value="squeezeright 30 DOWN">
<param name=ImgFilter5             value="squeezeright 40 DOWN">
<param name=ImgFilter6             value="squeezeright 50 DOWN">
<param name=ImgFilter7             value="squeezeright 60 DOWN">
<param name=ImgFilter8             value="squeezeright 70 DOWN">
<param name=ImgFilter9             value="squeezeright 80 DOWN">
<param name=ImgFilter10            value="squeezeright 90 DOWN">
<param name=ImgFilter11            value="squeezeright 100 DOWN">
</applet>
```

Animation Display for Example FiftyThree

See Also

Related applets: **AnimateTwoWay** on page 191
SqueezeRight on page 120

URL for **FiftyThree**: http://www.vivids.com/ij2/bonus/FiftyThree.html

FiftyFour

Multiple Squeezes

Description

Example **FiftyFour** uses the **AnimateTwoWay** applet. The image is squeezed right and left from 0 to 50 percent. The effect is created using the **SqueezeRight** applet on page 120 and the **SqueezeLeft** applet on page 122.

The HTML Code for Example FiftyFour

```
<applet
    archive  = FiftyFour.zip
    codebase = FiftyFour
    code     = AnimateTwoWay.class
    width    = 144
    height   = 204>

<param name=ImgNumImages        value=21>
<param name=ImgDelayBetweenImages value=130>
<param name=ImgDelayBetweenRuns  value=130>
<param name=ImgHorizCenter      value=true>
<param name=Image1              value=FiftyFour/brad.jpg>
<param name=ImgFilter2          value="squeezeright 10 DOWN">
<param name=ImgFilter3          value="squeezeright 20 DOWN">
<param name=ImgFilter4          value="squeezeright 30 DOWN">
<param name=ImgFilter5          value="squeezeright 40 DOWN">
<param name=ImgFilter6          value="squeezeright 50 DOWN">
<param name=ImgFilter7          value="$5|squeezeleft 10 DOWN">
<param name=ImgFilter8          value="$5|squeezeleft 20 DOWN">
<param name=ImgFilter9          value="$5|squeezeleft 30 DOWN">
<param name=ImgFilter10         value="$5|squeezeleft 40 DOWN">
<param name=ImgFilter11         value="$5|squeezeleft 50 DOWN">
<param name=ImgFilter12         value="$10|squeezeleft 10 UP">
<param name=ImgFilter13         value="$10|squeezeleft 20 UP">
<param name=ImgFilter14         value="$10|squeezeleft 30 UP">
<param name=ImgFilter15         value="$10|squeezeleft 40 UP">
<param name=ImgFilter16         value="$10|squeezeleft 50 UP">
<param name=ImgFilter17         value="$15|squeezeright 10 UP">
<param name=ImgFilter18         value="$15|squeezeright 20 UP">
<param name=ImgFilter19         value="$15|squeezeright 30 UP">
<param name=ImgFilter20         value="$15|squeezeright 40 UP">
<param name=ImgFilter21         value="$15|squeezeright 50 UP">
</applet>
```

Animation Display for Example FiftyFour

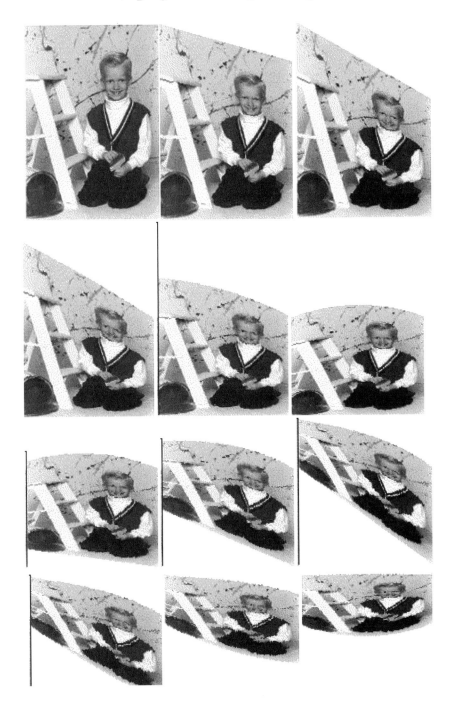

See Also

Related applets:

AnimateTwoWay on page 191
SqueezeRight on page 120
SqueezeLeft on page 122

URL for **FiftyFour**:

`http://www.vivids.com/ij2/bonus/FiftyFour.html`

FiftyFive

Squeeze All Directions

Description

Example **FiftyFive** uses the **AnimateTwoWay** applet. The image is squeezed right, left, up, and down, from 0 to 80 percent. The effect is created using the **SqueezeRight** applet on page 120, the **SqueezeLeft** applet on page 122, the **SqueezeUp** applet on page 124, and the **SqueezeDown** applet on page 126.

The HTML Code for Example FiftyFive

```
<applet
    archive  = FiftyFive.zip
    codebase = FiftyFive
    code     = AnimateTwoWay.class
    width    = 144
    height   = 144>

<param name=ImgNumImages              value=17>
<param name=ImgDelayBetweenImages value=130>
<param name=ImgDelayBetweenRuns    value=130>
<param name=ImgHorizCenter           value=true>
<param name=Image1                    value=FiftyFive/mary.jpg>

<param name=ImgFilter1    value="noop">
<param name=ImgFilter2    value="squeezeright 20 CENTER">
<param name=ImgFilter3    value="squeezeright 40 CENTER">
<param name=ImgFilter4    value="squeezeright 60 CENTER">
<param name=ImgFilter5    value="squeezeright 80 CENTER">

<param name=ImgFilter6    value="$5|squeezeleft 20 CENTER">
<param name=ImgFilter7    value="$5|squeezeleft 40 CENTER">
<param name=ImgFilter8    value="$5|squeezeleft 60 CENTER">
<param name=ImgFilter9    value="$5|squeezeleft 80 CENTER">

<param name=ImgFilter10   value="$9|squeezeup 40 CENTER">
<param name=ImgFilter11   value="$9|squeezeup 60 CENTER">
<param name=ImgFilter12   value="$9|squeezeup 80 CENTER">
<param name=ImgFilter13   value="$9|squeezeup 100 CENTER">

<param name=ImgFilter14   value="$13|squeezedown 40 CENTER">
<param name=ImgFilter15   value="$13|squeezedown 60 CENTER">
<param name=ImgFilter16   value="$13|squeezedown 80 CENTER">
<param name=ImgFilter17   value="$13|squeezedown 100 CENTER">
</applet>
```

Animation Display for Example **FiftyFive**

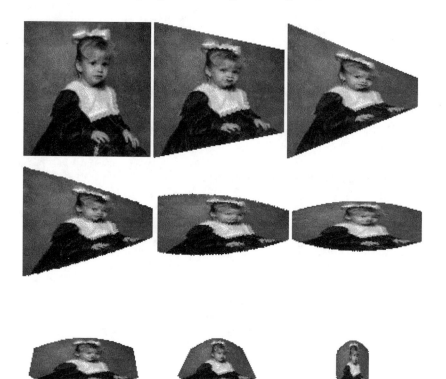

See Also

Related applets:

AnimateTwoWay on page 191
SqueezeRight on page 120
SqueezeLeft on page 122
SqueezeUp on page 124
SqueezeUp on page 124

URL for **FiftyFive**: http://www.vivids.com/ij2/bonus/FiftyFive.html

FiftySix

Expanding Circular View

Description

Example **FiftySix** uses the **AnimateTwoWay** applet. The image of the company logo is displayed using the **CropOval** applet on page 147. The size of the cropped oval begins small and increases in size until the image is displayed as a circle whose radius equals the width of the image. The **CropRoundRect** applet on page 151 is used extend the image to full size.

The HTML Code for Example FiftySix

```
<applet
    archive  = FiftySix.zip
    codebase = FiftySix
    code     = AnimateTwoWay.class
    width    = 159
    height   = 159>

<param name=ImgNumImages            value=24>
<param name=ImgDelayBetweenImages value=130>
<param name=ImgDelayBetweenRuns   value=130>
<param name=Image1                  value=FiftySix/vivid.gif>

<param name=ImgFilter1   value="cropoval 75 75 10  10">
<param name=ImgFilter2   value="cropoval 70 70 20  20">
<param name=ImgFilter3   value="cropoval 65 65 30  30">
<param name=ImgFilter4   value="cropoval 60 60 40  40">
<param name=ImgFilter5   value="cropoval 55 55 50  50">
<param name=ImgFilter6   value="cropoval 50 50 60  60">
<param name=ImgFilter7   value="cropoval 45 45 70  70">
<param name=ImgFilter8   value="cropoval 40 40 80  80">
<param name=ImgFilter9   value="cropoval 35 35 90  90">
<param name=ImgFilter10  value="cropoval 30 30 100 100">
<param name=ImgFilter11  value="cropoval 25 25 110 110">
<param name=ImgFilter12  value="cropoval 20 20 120 120">
<param name=ImgFilter13  value="cropoval 15 15 130 130">
<param name=ImgFilter14  value="cropoval 10 10 140 140">
<param name=ImgFilter15  value="cropoval  5  5 150 150">
<param name=ImgFilter16  value="cropoval  0  0 159 159">
<param name=ImgFilter17  value="croproundrect  0  0 159 159 140 140">
<param name=ImgFilter18  value="croproundrect  0  0 159 159 120 120">
<param name=ImgFilter19  value="croproundrect  0  0 159 159 100 100">
<param name=ImgFilter20  value="croproundrect  0  0 159 159  80  80">
<param name=ImgFilter21  value="croproundrect  0  0 159 159  60  60">
<param name=ImgFilter22  value="croproundrect  0  0 159 159  40  40">
```

```
<param name=ImgFilter23  value="croproundrect  0  0 159 159  20  20">
<param name=ImgFilter24  value="croproundrect  0  0 159 159   0   0">

</applet>
```

Animation Display for Example FiftySix

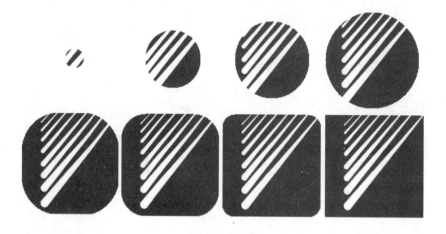

See Also

Related applets: **AnimateTwoWay** on page 191
CropOval on page 147
CropRoundRect on page 151

URL for **FiftySix**: http://www.vivids.com/ij2/bonus/FiftySix.html

FiftySeven

Replace Alternate Colors

Description

Example **FiftySeven** uses the **AnimateContinuous** applet. The Caledonai Railroad image is displayed with alternating colors. The effect is created by using the **ReplaceColor** applet on page 140.

The HTML Code for Example FiftySeven

```
<applet
    archive  = FiftySeven.zip
    codebase = FiftySeven
    code     = AnimateContinuous.class
    width    = 192
    height   = 336>

<param name=ImgNumImages          value=5>
<param name=ImgDelayBetweenImages value=1500>
<param name=ImgDelayBetweenRuns   value=1500>
<param name=Image1                value=FiftySeven/donia2.gif>

<param name=ImgFilter1            value="replacecolor green=yellow">
<param name=ImgFilter2            value="replacecolor green=cyan">
<param name=ImgFilter3          value="replacecolor green=cornsilk">
<param name=ImgFilter4            value="replacecolor green=white">
<param name=ImgFilter5            value="replacecolor green=pink">

</applet>
```

Animation Display for Example **FiftySeven**

Caledonia Railroad

Martin Canter
Vice President

1138 Bespin Drive
Suite 94
San Rafael, CA 94912

415/555-5555
415/555-4444 FAX

Caledonia Railroad

Martin Canter
Vice President

1138 Bespin Drive
Suite 94
San Rafael, CA 94912

415/555-5555
415/555-4444 FAX

Caledonia Railroad

Martin Canter
Vice President

1138 Bespin Drive
Suite 94
San Rafael, CA 94912

415/555-5555
415/555-4444 FAX

Caledonia Railroad

Martin Canter
Vice President

1138 Bespin Drive
Suite 94
San Rafael, CA 94912

415/555-5555
415/555-4444 FAX

See Also

Related applets:

AnimateContinuous on page 189
ReplaceColor on page 140

URL for **FiftySeven**:

`http://www.vivids.com/ij2/bonus/FiftySeven.html`

FiftyEight

Fluctuating Color Intensity

Description

Example **FiftyEight** uses the **AnimateTwoWay** applet. The image is displayed initially in full color. The image then fades to black and white. The **BlackAndWhite** applet on page 142 is used to create this effect.

The HTML Code for Example FiftyEight

```
<applet
    archive  = FiftyEight.zip
    codebase = FiftyEight
    code     = AnimateTwoWay.class
    width    = 144
    height   = 204>

<param name=ImgNumImages          value=11>
<param name=ImgDelayBetweenImages value=150>
<param name=ImgDelayBetweenRuns   value=1500>
<param name=Image1                value=FiftyEight/brad.jpg>

<param name=ImgFilter2            value="blackandwhite 10">
<param name=ImgFilter3            value="blackandwhite 20">
<param name=ImgFilter4            value="blackandwhite 30">
<param name=ImgFilter5            value="blackandwhite 40">
<param name=ImgFilter6            value="blackandwhite 50">
<param name=ImgFilter7            value="blackandwhite 60">
<param name=ImgFilter8            value="blackandwhite 70">
<param name=ImgFilter9            value="blackandwhite 80">
<param name=ImgFilter10           value="blackandwhite 90">
<param name=ImgFilter11           value="blackandwhite 100">

</applet>
```

Animation Display for Example **FiftyEight**

| Full Color | Decreasing Color | No Color |

See Also

Related applets: **AnimateTwoWay** on page 191
      BlackAndWhite on page 142

URL for **FiftyEight**:   `http://www.vivids.com/ij2/bonus/FiftyEight.html`

FiftyNine

Color On Button Press

Description

Example **FiftyNine** uses the **AnimateOnPressRelease** applet. The image is displayed without color. When the user presses a mouse button with the pointer over the image, the image displays in full color. The **BlackAndWhite** applet on page 142 is used to create this effect.

The HTML Code for Example FiftyNine

```
<applet
    archive  = FiftyNine.zip
    codebase = FiftyNine
    code     = AnimateOnPressRelease.class
    width    = 141
    height   = 141>

<param name=ImgNumImages        value=2>
<param name=Image1              value=FiftyNine/mary.jpg>

<param name=ImgFilter1          value="blackandwhite 100">
<param name=ImgFilter2          value="noop">

<param name=TxNumImages         value=2>
<param name=Text                value="Press for color">
<param name=TxColor1            value=white>
<param name=TxColor2            value=yellow>
<param name=TxHorizCenter       value=true>
<param name=TxYOffset1          value=120>
<param name=TxFilter1           value=text>
<param name=TxFilter2           value=text>

</applet>
```

Animation Display for Example **FiftyNine**

| Initial Display | Button Press |
| Black And White | Full Color |

See Also

Related applets:

AnimateOnPressRelease on page 206
BlackAndWhite on page 142

URL for **FiftyNine**:

`http://www.vivids.com/ij2/bonus/FiftyNine.html`

See Also

Related applets:

AnimateContinuous on page 189

URL for **See Also**:

`http://www.vivids.com/ij2/bonus/FiftyNine.html`

Sixty

Welcome Home

Description

Example **Sixty** uses the **AnimateContinuous** applet. The strings *Welcome* and *Home* are displayed using the **Text** applet on page 63 and altered using the **CropRectangle** applet on page 143. The size of the cropped rectangle increases to create the effect that the text is being erased from the screen. Then new text appears.

The HTML Code for Example Sixty

```
<applet
    archive  = Sixty.zip
    codebase = Sixty
    code     = AnimateContinuous.class
    width    = 300
    height   = 50>

<param name=TxNumImages            value=28>
<param name=TxDelayBetweenImages value=200>
<param name=TxDelayBetweenRuns   value=200>
<param name=Text1                  value=Welcome>
<param name=Text12                 value=Home>
<param name=TxPointSize            value=48>
<param name=TxVertCenter          value=true>
<param name=TxHorizCenter          value=true>

<param name=TxFilter1    value="text|croprectangle 0 0 300 00">
<param name=TxFilter2    value="text|croprectangle 0 0 300 10">
<param name=TxFilter3    value="text|croprectangle 0 0 300 20">
<param name=TxFilter4    value="text|croprectangle 0 0 300 30">
<param name=TxFilter5    value="text|croprectangle 0 0 300 40">
<param name=TxFilter6    value="text|croprectangle 0 0 300 50">
<param name=TxFilter7    value=$6>
<param name=TxFilter8    value=$6>
<param name=TxFilter9    value=$6>
<param name=TxFilter10   value=$5>
<param name=TxFilter11   value=$4>
<param name=TxFilter12   value=$3>
<param name=TxFilter13   value=$2>
<param name=TxFilter14   value=$1>
<param name=TxFilter15   value="text|croprectangle 0 0 300 00">
<param name=TxFilter16   value="text|croprectangle 0 0 300 10">
<param name=TxFilter17   value="text|croprectangle 0 0 300 20">
<param name=TxFilter18   value="text|croprectangle 0 0 300 30">
```

```
<param name=TxFilter19    value="text|croprectangle 0 0 300 40">
<param name=TxFilter20    value="text|croprectangle 0 0 300 50">
<param name=TxFilter21    value=$20>
<param name=TxFilter22    value=$20>
<param name=TxFilter23    value=$20>
<param name=TxFilter24    value=$19>
<param name=TxFilter25    value=$18>
<param name=TxFilter26    value=$17>
<param name=TxFilter27    value=$16>
<param name=TxFilter28    value=$15>

</applet>
```

Animation Display for Example Sixty

See Also

Related applets: **AnimateContinuous** on page 189
                     CropRectangle on page 143

URL for **Sixty**:   `http://www.vivids.com/ij2/bonus/Sixty.html`

APPENDIX A

Supported Applet Colors

Color	Value
aliceblue	f0f8ff
antiquewhite	faebd7
aquamarine	7fffd4
azure	f0ffff
beige	f5f5dc
bisque	ffe4c4
black	000000
blanchedalmond	ffebcd
blue	0000ff
blueviolet	8a2be2
brown	a52a2a
burlywood	deb887
cadetblue	5f9ea0
chartreuse	7fff00

Color	Value
chocolate	d2691e
coral	ff7f50
cornflowerblue	6495ed
cornsilk	fff8dc
cyan	00ffff
darkgoldenrod	b8860b
darkgreen	006400
darkkhaki	bdb76b
darkolivegreen	556b2f
darkorange	ff8c00
darkorchid	9932cc
darksalmon	e9967a
darkseagreen	8fbc8f
darkslateblue	483d8b

Color	Value
darkslategray	2f4f4f
darkslategrey	2f4f4f
darkturquoise	00ced1
darkviolet	9400d3
deeppink	ff1493
deepskyblue	00bfff
dimgray	696969
dimgrey	696969
dodgerblue	1e90ff
firebrick	b22222
floralwhite	fffaf0
forestgreen	228b22
green	00ff00
gainsboro	dcdcdc
ghostwhite	f8f8ff
gold	ffd700
goldenrod	daa520
gray	bebebe
honeydew	f0fff0
hotpink	ff69b4
indianred	cd5c5c
ivory	fffff0
khaki	f0e68c
lavender	e6e6fa
lavenderblush	fff0f5
lawngreen	7cfc00
lemonchiffon	fffacd

Color	Value
lightblue	add8e6
lightcoral	f08080
lightcyan	e0ffff
lightgoldenrod	eedd82
lightgray	d3d3d3
lightgrey	d3d3d3
lightpink	ffb6c1
lightsalmon	ffa07a
lightseagreen	20b2aa
lightskyblue	87cefa
lightslateblue	8470ff
lightslategray	778899
lightslategrey	778899
lightsteelblue	b0c4de
lightyellow	ffffe0
limegreen	32cd32
linen	faf0e6
magenta	ff00ff
maroon	b03060
mediumaquamarine	66cdaa
mediumblue	0000cd
mediumorchid	ba55d3
mediumpurple	9370db
mediumseagreen	3cb371
mediumslateblue	7b68ee
mediumspringgreen	00fa9a
mediumturquoise	48d1cc

Color	Value
mediumvioletred	c71585
midnightblue	191970
mintcream	f5fffa
mistyrose	ffe4e1
moccasin	ffe4b5
navajowhite	ffdead
navy	000080
navyblue	000080
oldlace	fdf5e6
olivedrab	6b8e23
orange	ffa500
orangered	ff4500
orchid	da70d6
palegoldenrod	eee8aa
palegreen	98fb98
paleturquoise	afeeee
palevioletred	db7093
papayawhip	ffefd5
peachpuff	ffdab9
peru	cd853f
pink	ffc0cb
plum	dda0dd
powderblue	b0e0e6
purple	a020f0
red	ff0000
rosybrown	bc8f8f

Color	Value
royalblue	4169e1
saddlebrown	8b4513
salmon	fa8072
sandybrown	f4a460
seagreen	2e8b57
seashell	fff5ee
sienna	a0522d
skyblue	87ceeb
slateblue	6a5acd
slategray	708090
slategrey	708090
snow	fffafa
springgreen	00ff7f
steelblue	4682b4
tan	d2b48c
thistle	d8bfd8
tomato	ff6347
turquoise	40e0d0
violet	ee82ee
violetred	d02090
wheat	f5deb3
white	ffffff
whitesmoke	f5f5f5
yellow	ffff00
yellowgreen	9acd32

Index

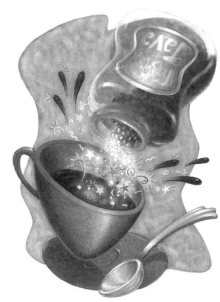

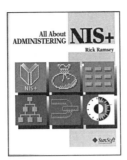

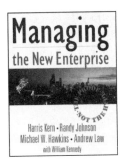

MANAGING THE NEW ENTERPRISE:
The Proof, Not The Hype

Harris Kern, Randy Johnson, Andrew Law, and Michael Hawkins with William Kennedy

In this follow-up to the best selling *Rightsizing the New Enterprise*, the authors discuss how to build and manage a heterogeneous client/ server environment. *Managing the New Enterprise* describes in detail the key technology support infrastructures, including networking, data centers, and system administration, as well as how Information Technology must change in order to manage the New Enterprise. This is an indispensable reference for anyone within Information Technology who is facing the challenges of building and managing client/server computing.

1996, 240 pp., Cloth, 0-13-231184-4 (23118-3)

NETWORKING THE NEW ENTERPRISE:
The Proof, Not The Hype

Harris Kern and Randy Johnson

The final volume in the New Enterprise Trilogy, this book focuses on planning network projects, developing architectures, and implementations of expanding distributed computing and client server technologies. A must for any business in today's growing marketplace.

Networking the New Enterprise includes in-depth ideas for developing network architectures; including, key methods, and strategies for network management, security and design; details on implementing Network Management Systems; Methods for enhancing, securing and optimizing Networks.

1997, 350 pages, paper, 0-13-263427-9 (26342-6)

INTERACTIVE UNIX OPERATING SYSTEM:
A Guide for System Administrators

Marty C. Stewart

Written for first-time system administrators and end users, this practical guide describes the common system administration menus and commands of the INTERACTIVE UNIX System V/386 Release 3.2, Version 4.0 and SVR 3.2 UNIX in general. Loaded with step-by-step instructions and examples, it discusses how to install and configure the INTERACTIVE UNIX system, including the hardware requirements. It describes the unique CUI menu interface, basic OS commands, administration of new user accounts, configuration of customized kernels, and working with the INTERACTIVE UNIX system as an end user.

1996, 320 pp., Paper, 0-13-161613-7 (16161-2)

PC HARDWARE CONFIGURATION GUIDE:
For DOS and Solaris

Ron Ledesma

This book eliminates trial-and-error methodology by presenting a simple, structured approach to PC hardware configuration. The author's time-tested approach is to configure your system in stages, verify and test at each stage, and troubleshoot and fix problems before going on to the next stage. Covers both standalone and networked machines. Discusses how to determine x86 hardware configuration requirements, how to configure hardware components (MCA, ISA, and EISA), partitioning hard disks for DOS and UNIX, and installing DOS and/or UNIX (Solaris x86). Includes configuration instructions, checklists, worksheets, diagrams of popular SCSI host bus, network, and video adapters, and basic installation troubleshooting.

1995, 352 pp., Paper,
0-13-124678-X (12467-7)

MULTIPROCESSOR SYSTEM ARCHITECTURES:
A Technical Survey of Multiprocessor / Multithreaded Systems Using SPARC, Multi-level Bus Architectures and Solaris (SunOS)
Ben Catanzaro

Written for engineers seeking to understand the problems and solutions of multi-processor system design, this hands-on guide is the first comprehensive description of the elements involved in the design and development of Sun's multiprocessor systems. Topics covered include SPARC processor design and its implementations, an introduction to multilevel bus architectures including MBus and XBus/XDBus, an overview of the Solaris/SunOS™ multithreaded architecture and programming, and an MBus Interface Specification and Design Guide. This book can serve as a reference text for design engineers as well as a hands-on design guide to MP systems for hardware/software engineers.

1994, 528 pp., Paper, 0-13-089137-1 (08913-6)

PANIC! UNIX System Crash Dump Analysis
Chris Drake and Kimberley Brown

PANIC! is the first book to discuss in detail UNIX system panics, crashes and hangs, their causes, what to do when they occur, how to collect information about them, how to analyze that information, and how to get the problem resolved. *PANIC!* presents this highly technical and intricate subject in a friendly, easy style which even the novice UNIX system administrator will find readable, educational and enjoyable. It is written for systems and network administrators and technical support engineers who are responsible for maintaining and supporting UNIX computer systems and networks. Includes a CD-ROM containing several useful analysis tools, such as adb macros and C tags output from the source trees of two different UNIX systems.

1995, 496 pp., Paper, 0-13-149386-8 (14938-5) Book/CD-ROM

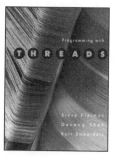

PROGRAMMING WITH THREADS
Steve Kleiman, Devang Shah, and Bart Smaalders

Written by senior threads engineers at Sun Microsystems, Inc., this book is the definitive guide to programming with threads. It is intended for both novice and more sophisticated threads programmers, and for developers multithreading existing programs as well as for those writing new multithreaded programs. The book provides structured techniques for mastering the complexity of threads programming with an emphasis on performance issues. Included are detailed examples using the new POSIX threads (Pthreads) standard interfaces. The book also covers the other UNIX threads interface defined by UNIX International.

1996, 250 pp., Paper, 0-13-172389-8 (17238-9)

RIGHTSIZING THE NEW ENTERPRISE:
The Proof, Not The Hype
Harris Kern and Randy Johnson

A detailed account of how Sun Micro-systems implemented its rightsizing strategy going from a mainframe data center to a heterogeneous client/server distributed environment. This book covers the key infrastructures of an IT organization (the network, data center, and system administration), the rightsizing/management tools, and the training/resource issues involved in transitioning from mainframe to UNIX support. The facts contained in this book provide you with the PROOF that 'right-sizing' can be done.and has been done.

1995, 352 pp., Cloth, 0-13-490384-6 (49038-3)

RIGHTSIZING FOR CORPORATE SURVIVAL:
An IS Manager's Guide
Robert Massoudi, Astrid Julienne, Bob Millradt, and Reed Hornberger

This book provides IS managers with "hands-on" guidance for developing a rightsizing strategy and plan. Based upon research conducted through customer visits with multinational corporations, it details the experiences and insights gained by IS professionals that have implemented systems in distributed, client-server environments. Topics covered include:

- Why rightsize?
- What business results can rightsizing produce?
- Key technologies critical to rightsizing
- Good starting points for rightsizing
- What is the process to rightsize an information system?
- Cost considerations and return on investment (ROI) analysis

• How to manage the transition

Throughout the book, case studies and "lessons learned" reinforce the discussion and document best practices associated with rightsizing.

1995, 272 pp., Paper,
0-13-123126-X (12312-5)

READ ME FIRST!
A Style Guide for the Computer Industry
Sun Technical Publications

A comprehensive look at documenting computer products, from style pointers to legal guidelines, from working with an editor to building a publications department—in both hard copy and electronic copy with an on line viewer, FrameMaker templates for instant page design, and a detailed guide to establishing a documentation department and its processes. Based on an internationally award-winning Sun Microsystems style guide (Award of Excellence in the STC International Technical Publications Competition, 1994)

1996, 300 pp., Paper,
0-13-455347-0 (45534-6)
Book/CD-ROM

SOLARIS IMPLEMENTATION:
A Guide for System Administrators
George Becker, Mary E. S. Morris and Kathy Slattery

Written by three expert Sun system administrators, this book discusses real world, day-to-day Solaris 2 system administration for both new installations and for those migrating an installed Solaris 1 base. It presents tested procedures to help system administrators to improve and customize their networks by eliminating trial-and-error methodologies. Also includes advice for managing heterogeneous Solaris environments and provides autoinstall sample scripts and disk partitioning schemes (with recommended sizes) used at Sun.

1995, 368 pp., Paper,
0-13-353350-6 (35335-9)

CREATING WORLD WIDE WEB SOFTWARE:
SOLARIS, Second Edtion
Bill Tuthill and David Smallberg

Written for software developers and business managers interested in creating global applications for the Solaris environment (SPARC and x86), this second edition expands on the first edition and has updated information on international markets, standards organizations, and writing international documents. New topics in the second edition include CDE/Motif, NEO (formerly project DOE)/ OpenStep, Universal codesets, global internet applications, code examples, and success stories.

1996, 250 pp., Paper,
0-13-494493-3 (49449-2)

SOLARIS PORTING GUIDE,
Second Edition
SunSoft Developer Engineering

Ideal for application programmers and software developers, the *Solaris Porting Guide, Second Edition*, provides a comprehensive technical overview of the Solaris 2.x operating environment and its related migration strategy. The second edition is current through Solaris 2.4 (both the SPARC and x86 platforms) and provides all the information necessary to migrate from Solaris 1 (SunOS 4.x) to Solaris 2 (SunOS 5.x). Other additions include a discussion of emerging technologies such as the Common Desktop Environment (CDE), hints for application performance tuning, and extensive pointers to further information, including Internet sources.

1995, 752 pp., Paper,
0-13-443672-5 (44367-1)

SUN PERFORMANCE AND TUNING:
SPARC and Solaris
Adrian Cockcroft

An indispensable reference for anyone working with Sun workstations running the Solaris environment, this book provides detailed performance and configuration information on all SPARC machines and peripherals, as well as on all operating system releases from SunOS 4.1 through Solaris 2.4. It includes hard-to-find tuning information and offers insights that cannot be found elsewhere. This book is written for developers who want to design for performance and for system administrators who have a system running applications on which they want to improve performance.

1995, 288 pp., Paper,
0-13-149642-5 (14964-1)

ALSO AVAILABLE FROM SUNSOFT PRESS...

THREADS PRIMER:
A Guide to Solaris Multithreaded Programming
Bil Lewis and Daniel J. Berg

Written for developers interested in MT programming, this primer overviews the concepts involved in multithreaded development. Based on the Solaris multithreaded architecture, the primer delivers threading concepts that can be applied to almost any multithreaded platform. The book covers the design and implementation of multithreaded programs as well as the business and technical benefits of threads. Both the Solaris and the POSIX threads API are used as the interface needed to develop applications. Extensive examples highlight the use of threads in real-world applications. This book is a must read for developers interested in MT technology!

*1996, 352 pp., Paper,
0-13-443698-9 (44369-7)*

WABI 2: Opening Windows
Scott Fordin and Susan Nolin

Wabi™ 2 is here and now you can run Microsoft and Windows 3.1 applications on UNIX-based computers! Written for both users and system administrators of Wabi software, this book covers everything you wanted to know about Wabi 2, including: Wabi technical history, how Wabi works, UNIX for Microsoft Windows users, Microsoft Windows for UNIX users, X Window terminology and interface objects, additional sources of information on Wabi, sample settings in which Wabi is used, and common questions asked by users.

*1996, 400 pp., Paper,
0-13-461617-0 (46161-6)*

NEW!

VERILOG HDL:
A Guide to Digital Design and Synthesis
Samir Palnitkar

Everything you always wanted to know about Verilog HDL, from fundamentals such as gate, RTL and behavioral modeling to advanced concepts such as timing simulation, switch level modeling, PLI and logic synthesis. This book approaches Verilog HDL from a practical design perspective rather than from a language standpoint. Includes over 300 illustrations, examples, and exercises, and a Verilog Internet reference resource list. Learning objectives and summaries are provided for each chapter. The CD-ROM contains a verilog simulator with a graphical user interface and the source code for the examples in the book. This book is of value to new and experienced Verilog HDL users, both in industry and at universities (logic design courses).

1996, 400 pp., Cloth, 0-13-451675-3 (45167-4) Book/CD-ROM

TOOLTALK AND OPEN PROTOCOLS:
Interapplication Communication
Astrid M. Julienne and Brian Holtz

This book discusses how to design, write, and implement open protocols and includes examples using the ToolTalk™ messaging service. Both procedural and object-oriented protocols are covered in detail. While the ToolTalk service is used as a point of reference throughout, the information provided conforms to the standardization efforts currently in progress for inter-application communication. A valuable resource for the developer writing applications for both the common desktop environment (CDE) and SunSoft's Project DOE system (now known as NEO™).

1994, 384 pp., Paper, 0-13-031055-7 (03105-4)

WEB PAGE DESIGN:
A Different Multimedia
Mary E. S. Morris and Randy J. Hinrichs

Everything you always wanted to know about practical Web page design from the best-selling author of *HTML for Fun and Profit*. Written for Web page authors, this hands on guide covers the key aspects of designing a successful web site including cognitive design, content design, audience consideration, interactivity, organization, navigational pathways, and graphical elements. Includes designing for VRML and Java sites as well as designing with templates, style sheets, and Netscape Frames. Also contains many examples of successful Web pages, including 16 color plates.

1996, 200 pp., Paper, 0-13-239880-X (23988-9)

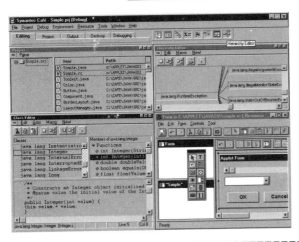

State Sales/Use Tax

In the following states, add sales/use tax: CO-3%; GA, LA, NY-4%; VA-4.5%; KS-4.9%; AZ, IA, IN, MA, MD, OH, SC, WI-5%; CT, FL, ME, MI, NC, NJ, PA, TN-6%; CA, IL, TX-6.25%; MN, WA-6.5%;DC-5.75%.

Please add local tax for AZ, CA, FL, GA, MO, NY, OH, SC, TN, TX, WA, WI.

Order Information:

- Please allow 2-4 weeks for processing your order.
- Please attach the order form with your payment.
- No P.O. boxes and no C.O.D.s accepted.
- Order form good in the U.S. only.
- If you are tax exempt, please include exemption certificate or letter with tax-exempt number.
- Resellers not eligible.
- Offer not valid with any other promotion.
- One copy per product, per order.

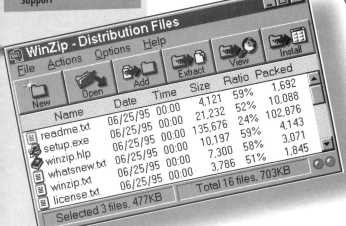

IMPORTANT—READ CAREFULLY BEFORE OPENING SEALED CD-ROM

This CD-ROM contains the Java Development Kit and sample code from Instant Java, as well as other copyrighted software.

SUN MICROSYSTEMS LICENSE AGREEMENT

This is a legal agreement between the purchaser of this book/CD-ROM package ("You") and Sun Microsystems, Inc. By opening the sealed CD-ROM you are agreeing to be bound by the terms of this agreement. If you do not agree to the terms of this agreement, promptly return the unopened book/CD-ROM package to the place you obtained it for a full refund.

SOFTWARE LICENSE FOR SAMPLE CODE

1. Grant of License. Sun Microsystems grants to you ("Licensee") a non-exclusive, non-transferable license to use the software programs (sample code) included on the CD-ROM without fee. The software is in "use" on a computer when it is loaded into the temporary memory (i.e. RAM) or installed into the permanent memory (e.g. hard disk, CD-ROM, or other storage device). You may network the software or otherwise use it on more than one computer or computer terminal at the same time.

2. Copyright. The CD-ROM is copyrighted by Sun Microsystems, Inc. and is protected by United States copyright laws and international treaty provisions. Therefore, you must treat the CD-ROM like any other copyrighted material. Individual software programs on the CD-ROM are copyrighted by their respective owners and may require separate licensing. The Java Development Kit is copyrighted by Sun Microsystems, Inc. and is covered by a separate license agreement provided on the CD-ROM and reprinted below.

3. Instant Java Sample Code and Applets. Sun Microsystems, Inc. grants you a royalty-free right to reproduce and distribute the sample code or applets provided that you: (a) distribute the sample code or applets only in conjunction with and as a part of your software application; (b) do not use Sun Microsystems, Inc. or its authors' names, logos, or trademarks to market your software product; and (c) agree to indemnify, hold harmless and defend Sun Microsystems, Inc. and its authors and suppliers from and against any claims or lawsuits, including attorneys fees, that arise or result from the use or distribution of your software product.

DISCLAIMER OF WARRANTY

The SOFTWARE (including instructions for its use) is provided "AS IS" WITHOUT WARRANTY OF ANY KIND. SUN MICROSYSTEMS and any distributor of the SOFTWARE FURTHER DISCLAIM ALL IMPLIED WARRANTIES INCLUDING WITHOUT LIMITATION ANY IMPLIED WARRANTIES OF MERCHANTABILITY OR OF FITNESS FOR A PARTICULAR PURPOSE. THE ENTIRE RISK ARISING OUT OF THE USE OR PERFORMANCE OF THE SOFTWARE OR DOCUMENTATION REMAINS WITH YOU.

IN NO EVENT SHALL SUN MICROSYSTEMS, ITS AUTHORS, OR ANY ONE ELSE INVOLVED IN THE CREATION, PRODUCTION, OR DELIVERY OF THE SOFTWARE BE LIABLE FOR ANY DAMAGES WHATSOEVER (INCLUDING, WITHOUT LIMITATION, DAMAGES FOR LOSS OF BUSINESS PROFITS, BUSINESS INTERRUPTION, LOSS OF BUSINESS INFORMATION, OR OTHER PECUNIARY LOSS) ARISING OUT OF THE USE OF OR INABILITY TO USE THE SOFTWARE OR DOCUMENTATION, EVEN IF SUN MICROSYSTEMS HAS BEEN ADVISED OF THE POSSIBILITY OF SUCH DAMAGES, BECAUSE SOME STATES/COUNTRIES DO NOT ALLOW THE EXCLUSION OF LIMITATION OF LIABILITY FOR CONSEQUENTIAL OR INCIDENTAL DAMAGES, THE ABOVE LIMITATION MAY NOT APPLY TO YOU.

U.S. GOVERNMENT RESTRICTED RIGHTS

The SOFTWARE and documentation are provided with RESTRICTED RIGHTS. Use, duplication, or disclosure is subject to restrictions as set forth in subparagraph (c)(1)(ii) of The Rights in Technical Data and Computer Software clause at DFARS 252.227-7013 or subparagraphs (c)(1) and (2) of the Commercial Computer Software—Restricted Rights 48 CFR 52.227-19.

Java Development Kit, Version 1.0.2, Binary Code License

This binary code license ("License") contains rights and restrictions associated with use of the accompanying software and documentation ("Software"). Read the License carefully before installing Software. By installing Software, you agree to the terms and conditions of this License.

1. Limited License Grant. Sun grants to you ("Licensee") a non-exclusive, non-transferable limited license to use Software without fee. Licensee may re-distribute complete and unmodified Software to third parties provided that this License conspicuously appear with all copies of the Software and that Licensee does not charge a fee for such re-distribution of Software.

2. Java Platform Interface. In the event that Licensee creates any Java-related API and distributes such API to others for applet or application development. Licensee must promptly publish an accurate specification for such API for free use by all developers of Java-based software. Licensee may not modify the Java Platform Interface ("JPI," identified as classes contained within the "java" package or any subpackages of the "java" package), by creating additional classes within the JPI or otherwise causing the addition to or modification of the classes in the JPI.

3. Restrictions. Software is confidential copyrighted information of Sun and title to all copies is retained by Sun and/or its licensors. Licensee shall not modify, decompile, disassemble, decrypt, extract, or otherwise reverse engineer Software. Software may not be leased, assigned, or sublicensed, in whole or in part. Software is not designed or intended for use in on-line control of aircraft, air traffic, aircraft navigation or aircraft communications; or in the design, construction, operation or maintenance of any nuclear facility. Licensee warrants that it will not use or redistribute the Software for such purposes.

4. Trademarks and Logos. Licensee acknowledges that Sun owns the Java trademark and all Java-related trademarks, logos, and icons including the Coffee Cup and Duke ("Java Marks") and agrees to: (i) comply with the Java Trademark Guidelines at http://java.com/trademarks.html; (ii) not do anything harmful to or inconsistent with Sun's rights in the Java Marks; and (iii) assist Sun in protecting those rights, including assigning to Sun any rights acquired by Licensee in any Java Mark.

5. Disclaimer of Warranty. Software is provided "AS IS," without a warranty of any kind. ALL EXPRESS OR IMPLIED REPRESENTATIONS AND WARRANTIES, INCLUDING ANY IMPLIED WARRANTY OF MERCHANT-ABILITY, FITNESS FOR A PARTICULAR PURPOSE OR NON-INFRINGEMENT, ARE HEREBY EXCLUDED.

6. Limitation of Liability. SUN AND ITS LICENSORS SHALL NOT BE LIABLE FOR ANY DAMAGES SUFFERED BY LICENSEE OR ANY THIRD PARTY AS A RESULT OF USING OR DISTRIBUTING SOFTWARE. IN NO EVENT WILL SUN OR ITS LICENSORS BE LIABLE FOR ANY LOST REVENUE, PROFIT OR DATA, OR FOR DIRECT, INDIRECT, SPECIAL, CONSEQUENTIAL, INCIDENTAL OR PUNITIVE DAMAGES, HOWEVER CAUSED AND REGARDLESS OF THE THEORY OF LIABILITY, ARISING OUT OF THE USE OF OR INABILITY TO USE SOFTWARE, EVEN IF SUN HAS BEEN ADVISED OF THE POSSIBILITY OF SUCH DAMAGES.

7. Termination. Licensee may terminate this License at any time by destroying all copies of Software. This License will terminate immediately without notice from Sun if Licensee fails to comply with any provisions of this License. Upon such termination, Licensee must destroy all copies of Software.

8. Export Regulations. Software, including technical data, is subject to U.S. export control laws, including the U.S. Export Administration Act and its associated regulations, and may be subject to export or import regulations in other countries. Licensee agrees to comply strictly with all such regulations and acknowledges that it has the responsibility to obtain licenses to export, re-export, or import Software. Software may not be downloaded, or otherwise exported or re-exported (i) into, or to a national or resident of, Cuba, Iraq, Iran, North Korea, Libya, Sudan, Syria or any country to which the U.S. has embargoed goods; or (ii) to anyone on the U.S. Treasury Department's list of Specially Designated Nations or the U.S. Commerce Department's Table of Denial Orders.

9. Restricted Rights. Use, duplication or disclosure by the United States government is subject to the restrictions as set forth in the Rights in Technical Data and Computer Software Clauses in DFARS 252.227-7013(c) (1) (ii) and FAR 52.227-19(c) (2) as applicable.

10. Governing Law. Any action related to this License will be governed by California law and controlling U.S. federal law. No choice of law rules of any jurisdiction will apply.

11. Severability. If any of the above provisions are held to be in violation of applicable law, void, or unenforceable in any jurisdiction, then such provisions are herewith waived to the extent necessary for the License to be otherwise enforceable in such jurisdiction. However, if in Sun's opinion deletion of any provisions of the License by operation of this paragraph unreasonably compromises the rights or increase the liabilities of Sun or its licensors, Sun reserves the right to terminate the License and refund the fee paid by License, if any, as Licensee's sole and exclusive remedy.